THE HOMOSEXUALITIES
AND THE
THERAPEUTIC PROCESS

THE
HOMOSEXUALITIES
AND THE
THERAPEUTIC PROCESS

Edited by

Charles W. Socarides, M.D.
Vamik D. Volkan, M.D.

INTERNATIONAL UNIVERSITIES PRESS, INC.
Madison   Connecticut

Library of Congress Cataloging in Publication Data

The Homosexualities and the therapeutic process / edited by Charles W. Socarides and Vamik D. Volkan.
p. cm.
Companion v. to: The Homosexualities : reality, fantasy, and the arts / edited by Charles W. Socarides, Vamik D. Volkan. 1990.
Includes bibliographical references and index.
ISBN 0-8236-2348-3
1. Gays—Mental health. 2. Psychotherapy. 3. Psychoanalysis.
4. Homosexuality. 5. Psychoanalysis. I. Socarides, Charles W.,
1922– . II. Volkan, Vamik D., 1932– . III. Title:
Homosexualities.
[DNLM: 1. Homosexuality—psychology. WM 615 H7663]
RC558.H63 1991
616.85′834—dc20
DNLM/DLC
for Library of Congress   91-20827
                                                                  CIP

Manufactured in the United States of America

This book is dedicated to
Claire Alford Socarides and Elizabeth Palonen Volkan

TABLE OF CONTENTS

viii

ACKNOWLEDGMENTS

We wish to express our thanks to the homosexual patients described within these pages, who with courage and endurance have furthered our comprehension of the various forms of homosexuality.

We also owe our gratitude to Ms. Liza Altman, our editorial consultant, whose ability as an editor and critic is surpassed only by her superb organizational skill and extraordinary efficiency in working with so many of us on such varied and often complex tasks.

CONTRIBUTORS

Jerome S. Blackman, M.D., F.A.P.A., is a Director of the Center for Psychoanalytic Studies and Associate Professor of Clinical Psychiatry and Behavioral Sciences, Medical College of Hampton Roads, Norfolk, VA; and in private practice as a psychoanalyst in Virginia Beach, VA.

Ira Brenner, M.D., is on the faculty of the Philadelphia Psychoanalytic Institute; Clinical Assistant Professor at the University of Pennsylvania School of Medicine; Attending Psychiatrist at the Institute of Pennsylvania Hospital.

Robert Dickes, M.D., is Professor Emeritus at the State University of New York, Health Science Center, Department of Psychiatry.

Abraham Freedman, M.D., is Honorary Clinical Professor of Psychiatry, Jefferson Medical College; he is on the faculty of the Institute of the Philadelphia Association for Psychoanalysis.

John Frosch, M.D., is Professor of Psychiatry, New York University School of Medicine; Editor Emeritus of the *Journal of the American Psychoanalytic Association;* Emeritus Director of Psychiatry, Brookdale Hospital Medical Center, New York.

William F. Greer, Jr., Ph.D., is Assistant Professor, Department of Psychiatry and Behavioral Sciences, Medical College of Hampton Roads, Norfolk, VA, and in private practice as a psychoanalytic psychotherapist in Hampton, VA.

Charles R. Keith, M.D., is Associate Professor of Psychiatry and Director of Training, Division of Child and Adolescent Psychiatry, Duke University Medical Center; Training analyst and Child Supervisor, UNC-Duke Psychoanalytic Training Program.

Howard B. Levine, M.D., is on the Faculty of the Boston Psychoanalytic Institute; and in private practice as a psychoanalyst.

Felix F. Loeb, Jr., M.D., is Clinical Professor of Psychiatry, Oregon Health Science University; and in private practice as a psychoanalyst.

William S. Meyer, M.S.W., is Director of Training and Assistant Clinical Professor, Department of Psychiatry, Division of Psychiatric Social Work at the Duke University Medical Center, Durham, NC.

Wayne A. Myers, M.D., is Clinical Professor of Psychiatry, Cornell Medical Center; Training and Supervising Psychoanalyst at the Columbia University Center for Psychoanalytic Training and Research, New York.

Harvey L. Rich, M.D., is Supervising and Training Analyst at Washington Psychoanalytic Institute, Washington, DC.

Elaine V. Siegel, Ph.D., is Supervising and Training Analyst at the New York Center for Psychoanalytic Training; she is in private practice.

Charles W. Socarides, M.D., is Clinical Professor of Psychiatry, Albert Einstein College of Medicine, New York City; and in private practice as a psychiatrist and psychoanalyst.

Robert D. Stolorow, Ph.D., is Clinical Professor of Psychiatry, UCLA School of Medicine; Founding Member, Institute of Contemporary Psychoanalysis, Los Angeles; and a Member of the Faculty of the Southern California Psychoanalytic Institute.

Jeffrey L. Trop, M.D., is Assistant Clinical Professor of Psychiatry, UCLA School of Medicine; and a Member of the Faculty of the Los Angeles Psychoanalytic Institute.

Vamik D. Volkan, M.D., is Director, Center for the Study of Mind and Human Interactions; Professor of Psychiatry, Medical Director, Blue Ridge Hospital, University of Virginia; Supervising and Training Analyst, Washington Psychoanalytic Institute, Washington, DC.

Introduction

CHARLES W. SOCARIDES AND VAMIK D. VOLKAN

Many homosexuals seek psychoanalytic treatment in the hope, which they may or may not acknowledge, of overcoming their developmental deficits and/or resolving the conflicts that account for their sexual problems.

As the use of the plural in our title indicates, the phenomenon called homosexuality appears on a spectrum at one end of which oedipal conflicts dominate, while at the other is evidence of an inability to differentiate the self-representation from the representation of the object. Homosexuals at the midpoint of the spectrum are those involved in preoedipal conflict.

Charles Socarides's (1978, 1988) classification shows the necessity of a multidimensional approach that will take into account the libidinal development, the ability to neutralize aggression, the developmental deficits of each individual under study, as well as his or her ego strength, and conflicts concerning psychic structuring and object relations. This volume, a companion to *The Homosexualities: Reality, Fantasy, and the Arts* (Socarides and Volkan, 1991), explores techniques for the psychoanalytic treatment of homosexuals.

Socarides has described the preoedipal origin of sexual deviations, including homosexuality, and most of the contributors to this volume give clinical evidence to support his views. We have found that all obligatory homosexuals suffer from preoedipal conflicts although emphasis on preoedipally influenced homosexuality does not justify neglect of oedipal considerations; some chapters herein give convincing case illustrations

1

of the vicissitudes of the Oedipus complex. Moreover, a homosexual whose symptoms are primarily determined by preoedipal conflicts will exhibit contamination with them, and will negotiate oedipal issues at some time during treatment.

In the analysis of a homosexual the analyst comes to understand the many causative factors such as ego deficits, the organization of experience, traumas, and pathogenic fantasies and their interactions accompanying the formation of homosexual symptoms that represent a compromise in dealing with many unconscious factors. The surface picture usually fails to disclose the degree of regression or specifics of a fixation or deficit, but it may supply useful clues. The man anxiously engaging in passive homosexual activity when forced to compete with a father figure may be seen as having an oedipal form of homosexuality if he has also a cohesive sense of self along with structural conflict.

One homosexual reported needing a homosexual partner from four to five hours every night for fellatio; he was compelled to engage in this activity because without eating another man's semen he was afraid of becoming nothing. His symptom echoed his infantile need to suck his mother's breast, and to fuse with his mental representation of her lest he lose his sense of self. He might be seen as suffering from a lower form of homosexuality as it would appear on the diagnostic spectrum of Socarides.

Another, who spoke of the great beauty of his body and the preeminent social position he enjoyed, bathed in expensive French champagne and required his male partners to lick the champagne from his body while paying it homage. Such behavior would seem to indicate narcissistic personality organization and the role played by it in maintaining the patient's grandiose self.

The discovery that most homosexuals have preoedipal conflicts obviously changed therapeutic considerations and maneuvers. Volkan's (1976, 1987) points dealing with borderline patients in general should be considered in treating homosexuals whose dominant conflicts are preoedipal. Oedipal and preoedipal conflicts, as well as those involving object relations and structural problems, may coexist, but when the dominant problem is preoedipal, object relations conflicts are dealt with first, and this may take several years before the real work on structural conflict is undertaken. It should be remembered that patients whose dominant "hot" conflicts are preoedipal may reactivate seemingly oedipal issues as resistance.

When the patient with preoedipal conflict can hear genetic interpretations but is unable to use them, an effort must be made to help him mend his sense of self before going further. Throughout the treatment the analyst should actively observe and maintain a therapeutic alliance, which is challenged at all times by the patient's dominant orientation to life that involves splitting good object representations from bad. Identification with the analyst's functions is crucial in filling in the gaps caused by early developmental defects; this can best be brought about when the analyst can regress in the service of the patient (Olinick, 1980), and meet him on a level of primitive functioning, although the patient may be exhibiting vestiges of transference psychosis and/or temporary psychotic transference. Once he achieves a cohesive sense of self and moves away from conflicts in object relations, a more typical transference neurosis will evolve (Boyer, 1983; Volkan, 1987).

Although Volkan's suggestions apply to all patients with preoedipal fixation, specific ways of modifying homosexuality are offered. Socarides's notion of making sexually deviant behavior unpleasurable—"spoiling" perverse gratification—is discussed within the framework of the psychoanalytic process. A need to engage in perverse activity is in the preoedipal homosexual a manifestation of at least a temporary developmental necessity rather than evidence of resistance. In such cases special techniques are needed to promote the maturation of arrested ego functions (Socarides, 1988). The contributors to this volume describe therapeutic processes in which, although interpretation remains the essential therapeutic tool, what accompanies it within the transference–countertransference interaction must be elucidated if we are to understand what reverses homosexual symptoms.

Robert Dickes reminds us of the importance of maternal transference. Well aware that all the usual transference manifestations can be expected, he nevertheless warns male therapists not to overlook the fact that their homosexual patients transfer not only old relationships with male objects onto them, but also those they have had with female objects. Although early maternal transference may be hidden, it must be brought to light and worked through. Dickes, among others, points to another critical issue in the treatment of homosexuals—recognition and management of aggression.

While Dickes deals with the analyzable homosexual, indicating who qualifies for analysis and what their treatment should be, the following chapters are arranged to illuminate the homosexual behavior that reflects deficits, arrests, and regressions from higher to lower levels of development, and the accompanying unconscious fantasies.

John Frosch focuses on the relationship between homosexuality and psychosis, and examines the clinical evidence that some overt homosexuals become psychotic. He gives examples from clinical experience of overt homosexuality's being a defense against an underlying incipient psychotic process, and points to the role unconscious homosexuality plays in the development in either sex of paranoia and other morbid constellations.

Elaine Siegel (1988), who analyzed twelve female homosexuals, reports on her systematic study. It is interesting that none of these women were initially interested in becoming heterosexual; all had a strong dislike of penetration. Siegel found that all had deficits of body image because of disturbed relationships with both of their parents, and had not specifically schematized the body and its inner representations. Her treatment technique included handling the projection of body image distortions onto the analyst, and took into account the countertransferentially difficult phases of treatment.

William Meyer and Charles Keith continue focusing on preoedipal issues. They describe the treatment of a 37-year-old woman fixated at the phallic narcissistic phase of development who identified herself as a female transsexual. They saw transsexualism in this case as evidence of a blocking of the homosexual developmental line, and suggest that progress in her treatment would bring, besides positive oedipal fantasies, homosexual ones reflecting a negative Oedipus complex.

Howard Levine also deals with narcissism, indicating that homosexual activity and fantasies, as regulators of self-esteem and modulators of affect, are narcissistic necessities for the patient who is resisting alteration of his sexual orientation. This type of resistance is usually seen in the opening phases of treatment in the case of many homosexual men, even those consciously desirous of changing their sexual orientation. The analyst must then address what Levine calls *the narcissistic imperative* in order to be analytically engaged with the patient.

William Greer and Vamik Volkan describe the latent homosexual, reporting on the psychoanalytic psychotherapy of such a patient, one inhibited from sexual activity. They raise questions about the similarities and dissimilarities of men who have homosexual fantasies but who do not engage regularly in sexual acts, and those who are actively homosexual. They tell how their patient activated transitional phenomena and used anal narcissism to control his inner relationship with the representations of his mother and father.

Jerome Blackman holds that in many homosexuals defects in the ego and object relations may be primary. He illustrates the assessment of defects in ego strength, ego functions, and object relations as well as formulating the preoedipal or oedipal psychodynamics that are involved. He warns that in the case of ego defects, the ego must be strengthened, and suggests maneuvers to use before transference interpretation can be effective without causing non-therapeutic ego regression.

With chapter 8, Abraham Freedman changes the focus, bringing into the foreground the vicissitudes of the Oedipus complex. He gives in detail two cases of oedipal homosexuality and their treatment, along with other clinical material. He maintains that radical changes in analytical technique are not necessary in the case of the oedipal homosexual, and notes that masculine-appearing and seemingly effeminate homosexuals are not a unique species. With his male patients their identification with him proved to be a crucial curative element.

Felix Loeb also deals with the oedipal male homosexual, focusing on unacceptable sexual impulses and the defenses used against them. His patient's castration anxiety undid his ability to integrate genital primacy. Loeb's clinical experience indicates that a patient suffering from the oedipal form of homosexuality can be treated successfully with psychoanalysis without radically changed technique.

Stolorow and Trop ponder the reasons why some people use "sexual enactments" in order to maintain preconscious structures of experience, and offer technical considerations. They refer to the need to maintain the organization of experience and the encapsulation of the structure of experience by concrete, sensorimotor symbols (concretization). Their ideas are echoed by other contributors. For example, Socarides describes "organizing experiences" that not only provide genital excitement but also supply a sense of self-cohesion due to the accompanying affective release. Frosch speaks of some "real experiences" having degrading and humiliating qualities that can cause paranoid constellations and affect unconscious homosexuality. Volkan and Greer emphasize the role of some actual trauma that has been superimposed on a specific family constellation, but the theoretical orientation of Stolorow and Trop focuses on Kohut's (1977) suggestion that oedipal dramas may be viewed as a pivotal phase in the structuralization of the self. They describe the successful seven-year treatment of a homosexual and the transference and its resolution in terms of Kohutian self psychology.

Harvey Rich returns in the eleventh chapter to the classical view of psychoanalysis and its process, and describes the cruising compulsion of a 35-year-old homosexual whose personality was organized on a neurotic level. He gives a telling account of the way he helped this patient work through his compulsion.

Wayne Myers also makes a clinical presentation, describing a patient who had difficulty in obtaining erection, but who clung to the fantasy that were he to attain erection he could have any man he fancied. He had an unusual exhibitionistic way of seeking sexual partners, displaying his photograph as if it were his American Express credit card. Myers points to the intense increment of aggression in these photoexhibitionistic acts, and tells how he dealt with it.

These discussions would be incomplete without reference to AIDS, which is *not* a homosexual disease, but one unfortunately suffered more often by some groups than others. We are not aware of any unusual increase in the number of homo-sexuals seeking treatment because of the threat of AIDS; in fact, many of the cases described in this volume suggest that the homosexuals cited were reporting behavior that took place before the advent of this disease. Ira Brenner's discussion of the unconscious wish to contract AIDS reflects the way masoch-ism and sadism find an echo in the malign activity of a virus. Obviously there is no cure for AIDS in any psychoanalytically oriented therapy. However, it is important to understand the psychodynamics and vicissitudes of human sexuality in AIDS research, and to take into account the role of libidinously and aggressively colored unconscious motivations and denials in the spread of the virus among homosexual and heterosexual popu-lations alike.

In the final chapter Charles Socarides summarizes the spe-cific tasks the analyst and the patient face in the psychoanalytic treatment of those for whom sexually deviant acts are usually the only means of obtaining sexual gratification. Socarides asks if, in the midst of this dreadful plague, the analyst should change his clinical stance vis-à-vis the homosexual patient. He questions the analyst's role in seeking to protect the patient from untimely death by efforts to modify his ego defects and work through his conflicts before his sexual activity puts him at grave risk. There is an urgent need to expand our under-standing of homosexuality in response to the challenge posed by AIDS. Socarides suggests a parameter that he feels should be used in treatment in a time of this dread disease.

With a few exceptions no psychoanalyst has the chance to study a series of homosexuals and their therapeutic course systematically. Accordingly, the sharing of experience among seventeen clinicians dealing with this phenomenon offers some-thing of considerable value to our attempt to understand it and to develop and update ever better therapeutic techniques for treatment.

As editors, we are aware that many of the papers within these pages concentrate on preoedipal and oedipal develop-mental factors, arising from separation anxieties and separation of self from object, and leading to new formulations of caus-ative processes in homosexuality which differ from those of the past. This should not be construed as a rejection of castration anxiety in favor of separation anxiety, but as a new focus for investigative research. We are in agreement with Rangell's (1991) affirmation of the importance of castration anxiety in the formation of all psychopathology, and especially conditions involving sexual functioning. He states: "Castration anxiety is not a metaphor within the array of psychoanalytic theories, but a pathological belief operative in the unconscious which originated during the period of childhood sexuality. Of the two major anxieties, separation and castration, castration anxiety is the most overlooked in clincal discourse and theoretical aware-ness. Castration conflicts have a developmental history and are composed of phases as much as separation–individuation. These extend from the preoedipal to the oedipal years and beyond and, as separation conflicts, persist throughout life" (p. 3).

CHAPTER 1

Observations on the Treatment of Homosexual Patients

ROBERT DICKES, M.D.

INTRODUCTION

The establishment of treatment procedures for homosexual men and women poses major problems, not only because of the inherent psychological complexities of the cases, but also because of the complex interplay between biological, developmental (innate as well as interactional), psychosocial, and cognitive factors. The latter includes ego functions both conscious and unconscious. Controversies of various types also becloud the issues involving etiologies, as well as treatment modalities. These differences concern even the most fundamental aspects of the behavioral patterns and include the definition of homosexuality itself. The suggestions that homosexual orientation should no more be subject to treatment than is heterosexual behavior, both being manifestations of normal attitudes, implies that heterosexual behavior is not subject to study and treatment. This is not the case. Heterosexual activities are the subject of investigation in every analytic situation and the results of analytic work do affect the behavior of people, usually for the better.

The Diagnostic and Statistical Manual of Mental Disorders, DSM III (American Psychiatric Association, 1980), and *DSM III-R*

(American Psychiatric Association, 1987) state: "Since homosexuality itself is not considered a mental disorder, the factors that predispose to homosexuality are not included in this section nor is the category discussed in any other section," a remark tending to produce closure rather than leave the matter open for future enlightenment.

DSM III next considers ego dystonic homosexuality: "The factors that predispose Ego-dystonic Homosexuality are those negative societal attitudes toward homosexuality that have been internalized." Unfortunately, this approach leads to the idea that it is not the individual who is to be helped; rather it is society which should be remodeled. This tends to stultify our approaches to treatment. The definition omits all consideration of the large body of evidence implicating the family structure and interactions beginning in the first year of life. *DSM III*'s approach would even discourage investigation of unconscious forces and the affects on children of the interactions between parents and offspring. Psychodynamic inquiry as to the family interactions would thus be disparaged. Nevertheless, the type of treatment I advocate here rests upon the theoretical framework of the psychoanalytic model and clinical observations reported upon and refined for almost a century.

TREATMENT

Among the first of the general considerations concerning treatment, two questions are raised by *DSM III*'s criteria, the writings of Friedman (1986, 1988), and those of others. The first question is: Why treat homosexuality at all? Second, if a homosexual person seeks treatment for emotional difficulties, should the homosexuality itself be subject to investigation and treatment or should the emphasis in the treatment focus mainly on the hostile sociocultural environment? Leavy (1986) and Friedman (1988) have written rather movingly about the plight of the homosexual in our society and point out the need for dealing with society's hostility.

The initial question, Why treat homosexuals at all, applies especially to the persons who feel well, have faced the world as it is, and have formed good, long-term intimate relationships.

Such people have made their "peace" with their sexual orienta-tion and society. In my experience, they do not seek treatment nor do they need it. People who have reached such an equilib-rium are entitled, I think, to be accepted as they are. No oppo-brium should be attached to them. The remaining question deserves further consideration.

There are people, homosexual in orientation, who do seek help for emotional problems, some directly related to homosex-uality and some not. In these cases, it is not always possible to tell, early in the treatment, which symptom complex is or is not related to sexual orientation. Some patients do not wish anything impinging on their homosexuality to be brought into the treatment process, especially in psychoanalysis. Such poten-tial patients must be made aware that no analyst can predict in advance what course the analysis will take. It must be made clear to them that their orientation might well be affected. Those who do not wish to take this risk will, of course, refuse psychoanalytic treatment, but they should not be denied treat-ment. There are other types of treatment available, including dynamically oriented psychotherapy which is based upon ana-lytic principles. Skilled psychotherapists exist and many analysts also practice psychotherapy, which relies upon modifications of the standard psychoanalytic techniques. Patients who fear that analysis might interfere with their sexual orientation still may be greatly helped by modified approaches. Some patients, once their fears and resistances are dealt with, may even face their sexual problems and then work on their same-sex orientation. Strict adherence to standard analytic techniques in all situations may be counterproductive to therapeutic goals. Even in stan-dard analysis, adherence to the strictest type of analytic tech-nique in very severe regression can defeat the therapeutic aim (Dickes, 1967). Contrary to Isay (Friedman, 1986), modifica-tions of technique are not necessarily based on countertrans-ference.

We must avoid the Procrustean approach: Procrustus ran an inn with a one-sized bed. If travelers were too short for the bed he stretched them, if they were too long, he shortened them by lopping off their limbs. Let us agree that this is not the best approach to all patients. One couch does not necessarily fit one and all and at all times. The "purity" of treatment is not compromised by appropriate modifications which can be analyzed later.

People who seek help for symptoms which may or may not be related to their sexual orientation can be and are treated in a variety of ways. Psychodynamic approaches are probably the most widely used. Focal approaches as advocated by Mann (1973) are also useful, but are usually short term and aimed at symptom alleviation and some character remodeling; they rarely approach the painstaking examination of the unconscious processes and the origins of symptoms and character. But they have proven their value and can be applied to the treatment of homosexuals without necessarily affecting their sexual preferences.

A man in his thirties came to see me. He had suffered greatly from the consequences of undue passivity in many aspects of his life. He informed me that he was exclusively homosexual, and that he was satisfied with his orientation and had no wish to change it. He also indicated that he had never been promiscuous and had tried to pick his partners with care. In spite of this, he said that "somehow or other," most of his partners victimized him in one way or another, usually financially.

It became apparent that his sexual partners had made all the advances, including the initial one. Though well off financially due to an inheritance, he had suffered business reverses and had failed in many ventures. In each instance, he had become the silent partner in a business and later bore the brunt of the failures without understanding how the business in question had failed. Some of the ventures did succeed, and he therefore thought he would profit from these successes, only to find that the contract allowed the other people to buy him out on their terms. Needless to say, he had not used his own lawyer. It was the last successful business venture, from which he had accrued much less than expected, that led him to admit to himself that he "didn't know why but that something must be wrong with my judgment." It was his repetitive pattern that led him to seek treatment. He had become aware that his behavior pattern was extremely damaging to his welfare. He was willing to deal with this problem in treatment but not his sexual orientation.

I told him that I could not promise that treatment would leave his sexual orientation unaffected, nor could I change his orientation without his cooperation. We agreed to focus on his professed difficulty, and treatment concentrated on his passive and masochistic behavior. He was psychologically minded, responding to interpretations with further useful material. He also grasped the nature of his characterological problem. In the course of the work, the behavior that regularly made him a victim became ego dystonic. He also saw that the unfavorable results in his life were not the faults of others but were due to his seeking out the role of victim. Little could be done with the underlying guilt and the need to suffer. The treatment ended with the patient well satisfied with his better understanding of himself and his ability to protect himself from arranging his own victimization; but many problems were left untouched. Some will regard this type of treatment as unacceptable, but the alleviation of the patient's suffering, I believe, should be our main goal. It is not our province to sit in judgment but to help.

Another treatment modality was described by Masters and Johnson (1979), reporting on a group of homosexual men treated at their Institute. The men involved all wished very strongly to change their orientation to heterosexual. The treatment program was a very brief procedure akin to the authors' well-known approach developed for sexual dysfunction in heterosexuals. Schwartz and Masters (1984) then reported on the outcome of the treatment: the original failure rate was 20.9 percent; five years later this rate rose to only 28.4 percent; and they stressed that the patients were not encouraged to consider changing their orientation unless they were strongly committed to exploring their heterosexual potential.

I quote the above not only to demonstrate that more than one modality has been used to change a person's sexual orientation but also that each method has its reported successes: the idea that homosexuality per se is innate and immutable cannot be true. Some homosexuals can and do change, while others cannot. The ability to change sexual orientation depends on the innate malleability of the newborn. Some are so genetically or biologically disposed as to be quite resistant to parental and environmental pressures. Development seems to proceed in its own way from internal causes to an eventual behavior pattern that may lead to same-sex orientation. There are others, however, who respond rather strongly to parenting and environment. Thus the influence of nurture on some is small and on others very large. It is those in the in-between group, shaped by environment, who may be helped and whose behavioral patterns can be changed by treatment.

Only further clinical observation and scientifically oriented study will determine what each method can accomplish and which treatment will achieve a better long-term result. Let us also remember that the mental health of a person encompasses more than sexual orientation.

SUITABILITY FOR TREATMENT

The remainder of this chapter will be devoted to a discussion of a few aspects of the psychological treatment of patients with a focus on psychoanalysis and psychoanalytically oriented psychotherapy. It is useful first to mention some characteristics that are important in assessing a person's suitability for the treatment of homosexuality by psychoanalysis. Along with some brief remarks on the assessment, some attention will be directed to facets of the treatment process. It should be understood that only a few of the many features involved in treatment can be discussed and these only sparingly. A much more complete consideration of therapy and its course can be found in Socarides (1978, 1988).

The characteristics to consider in terms of suitability for treatment of homosexuals are, in general, similar to those for other prospective patients. Primary to the selection is the person's own feelings of suffering, the wish to be rid of them, and an awareness of the need for help. A distinction between neurotic symptoms and homosexual activity must be pointed out. Symptoms in neurotics usually produce suffering; but homosexual activity provides intense gratification and relief that is for many ego syntonic. People in this group may seek treatment for other reasons which, unknown to them, may be offshoots of problems related to their sexual activity. Care must be taken to avoid any attempt to intervene and change their sexual orientation without the expressed wish of the patient. As the analysis unfolds, the patient may become aware that the suffering that brought him or her to therapy is in fact founded on their homosexuality.

Even then, the analyst should not intervene actively to discourage the homosexual behavior. Neither should the analyst extol heterosexual viewpoints. Such behavior might even be considered a countertransference reaction. Proper interpretive work will allow the patient to see and decide on his or her own. Attempts to encourage change may even produce a quite negative reaction. The therapist should maintain neutrality and objectivity.

There is also another group in which homosexual activity is, for whatever reason, dystonic. These people often seek treatment. Even in these patients, it should be remembered that any attempt to modify the behavior too early in treatment is apt to be doomed to failure. Here too, countertransference may be at work.

We must also assess the person's ability to grasp the meaning of the rather abstract concepts presented in the form of interpretations and confrontations. This may be illustrated by the remark of a bachelor patient who was a mathematician and researcher. Following an interpretation rather early in the treatment, he paused and said; "That's a rather remarkable hypothesis and rather strange at that. I must think a moment." Shortly thereafter, he said; "I must agree that the data [his associations] leaves no doubt in my mind." This man clearly had the capacity to grasp the meaning of an interpretation.

Patients must also possess a fair amount of psychological mindedness as well as intelligence. Psychological mindedness is at times absent or minimal in highly intelligent people. In addition, the person must also possess a reasonably mature ego, and the ability to form fairly stable object relationships as well as the ability to delay gratifications. The person must also be able to inhibit both the sexual and aggressive drives in a reasonable fashion, factors extremely important in the course of treatment of the somewhat paranoid men who engage in homosexual behavior.

A man, in treatment for some time, presented a rather strange mixture of homo- and heterosexual activity. When sober, his behavior was exclusively heterosexual. When under the influence of alcohol, he engaged in strictly homosexual activity (I avoid writing "drunk" because his behavior showed no evidence indicating that he had had a great deal to drink). At the beginning of treatment, he was unaware of the homosexuality. It was only with the greatest difficulty that he finally became aware of his dual behavior.

Some of his developing awareness was elucidated via dreams. One dream and his reaction to it illustrates the point about control of drives. He dreamed that he was in a library which he thought was his uncle's. His uncle began to move toward him menacingly. To his horror, he then noticed a large sharp knife in his uncle's hand. He became so frightened that he ran to the window and jumped out. He fell to the ground one floor below where he realized that he had broken his leg. No associations followed. Instead, he began to look around at my office which was also a library in that there were many books. He suddenly said in a most threatening way, "I don't like what's going on here." He got up, looked at me and said, "You're getting bigger and bigger. You're huge!" He then started toward me with clawed hands and a look of fury. I was more than slightly perturbed, especially since my only way out was through the door which he blocked, and he was much bigger than I am. Before extremis set in, however, I said loudly, "Your dream is about homosexuality and you know we have been talking about it. Your dream shows your fear of the subject." The word *subject* temporarily neutralized the situation by making it less personal to him and more intellectual. Supporting the ego and intellectual functions of this very bright man allowed him to regain control. He stopped, looked bewildered, and said "What happened?"

I will not go into the analysis of the dream and its relation to me (uncle) since my intent at this time is to emphasize the importance of a patient's ability to control drives. If this man had been unable to hear me, note the content of what I said, and stop the action, I might not be writing this chapter. I might add that although he had not entered treatment for homosexuality, he abandoned homosexual behavior during his analysis. Two or three years later, he called me to tell me he had married and was quite happy.

THE WORKING ALLIANCE

Let us now consider some of the aspects of the very complex relationship between patient and analyst. Important to the evaluation of the patient is the estimate of his or her ability to form a satisfactory relationship to the therapist, based upon the ability to form stable object interactions and the possession of a sufficiently mature ego so as to function in a "reasonable" way. The relationship of patient to therapist constitutes part of what has been termed the working alliance (Dickes, 1975; 1981), which is subsumed under the rubric of the therapeutic alliance. The therapeutic alliance includes all the elements that contribute to the progress of an analysis, including transference, a nonrational element, about which Freud (1940) wrote: "So long as it is positive it serves us admirably. . . . It alters the whole analytic situation. . . . There emerges the aim of pleasing the analyst. . . . It becomes the true motive force of the patient's collaboration" (p. 175). Actually, it is only one of the motives. Since the transference motive is not rational and furthers the general therapeutic alliance, it is distinct from the working alliance which is akin to what Freud called the analytic pact.

The understanding of these distinctions is of great importance in the treatment of many homosexual patients. Constant care must be taken to preserve the working alliance and avoid its disruption as much as possible. Severe regressions may result that require the introductions of parameters of which so many analysts disapprove. Parameters, however, are at times necessary in order to maintain the continuity of treatment. The following example may clarify my meaning concerning the alliances as well as some transference phenomena.

A woman I have previously described in another context (1967) had, in addition to a husband, a woman who had been her lover for many years. Such an affair is easily disguised in our culture and no hint of this liaison was known for some time. One day she recalled some of her mother's exhibitionistic seductions which continued into this patient's adolescence. The family lived in a suburban area, the house located on several acres. Her mother would lie down in the backyard and under the guise of getting some sunshine, exposed her genitalia to the patient. So repetitive and complete was the exposure that the patient's description of the genitalia included idiosyncratic features. As the patient was remembering this, she became sexually aroused and aware of my neutrality. She then bitterly accused me of being cruel and unresponsive. Interpretive work failed as deep regression set in.

The patient did not attend the next session. She had taken to her bed, was asthmatic and greatly regressed. Before further interpretation could take place, an undoing of the regression and a repair of the working alliance was required. I telephoned. At first she refused to answer, punishing me for my unresponsiveness, but finally she relented. She had gained her point. To her, my telephoning meant that she had made me respond. Further, the telephone unconsciously serves as a mouth to mouth contact. (None of this was pointed out at this time.) Gratification had been obtained. A lengthy session via telephone ensued that repaired the working alliance by concentrating on helping the patient to use the reasonable part of her ego.

She returned to treatment the next day. It was only later that I was able to show her that the libidinal wish was *not* only that I failed to respond as a man, but as a woman as well. Patients transfer both parents onto the analyst who must always be aware of the dual aspects of transference in dealing with homosexual patients. She also learned that the telephone is a complex instrument useful in several ways, some unconscious: does not the telephone company advertise, "Reach out and touch someone?" A final point about this woman is that she eventually gave up both her asthma and her homosexuality. Neither she nor the man with the library dream mentioned homosexuality when beginning treatment, yet both gave up their homosexual object choices: Their emotional problems were deeply involved with their same-sex choices. Even though people enter treatment without any intent to become exclusively heterosexual, sexual reorientation can occur.

These are but a few considerations involved in patient selection. Now I wish to discuss some key factors important in the actual treatment itself. I make no attempt to establish a special order of importance since each of the topics will vary in significance from patient to patient and from time to time.

GENDER IDENTITY CONSIDERATIONS

The development of a person's gender identity is important in the establishment of a final sexual orientation. Stoller (1968, 1975) has contributed much to the understanding of the sequential order that establishes an individual's final identity, which may or may not be appropriate to the person's body configuration. The biological substrate is the basic state that the infant brings into this world. All further influences must act upon this substrate. Freud (1923a) recognized this when he wrote that the outcome of the oedipal situation in an identification with either the father or the mother and is dependent on the relative strengths of the masculine and feminine disposition. This also refers to gender identity since both are interwoven into the person's final solution. Attention must also be called to the use of *relative*, a key word. In some, the initial disposition is such that upbringing will have very little influence not only on eventual masculine or feminine identification, but also on gender identity, which is distinct from anatomical identity. But there are many people in whom the relative strength of the masculine and feminine dispositions is such that both upbringing and treatment can have an influence on determining the outcome in the person's sexual orientation. It is this group with which we are concerned.

In each case of homosexuality I have treated, aberrant gender identity was present, aberrant because by far the great majority of individuals develop identity consistent with their anatomy. Those who have not developed gender and anatomical congruence have indeed deviated from the usual pattern. This may be due, in some, to a biochemical pattern established in fetal development. Others, and probably the majority, have their gender identity disturbed by a lack of the average expected environmental influences, the most important of which remains the parental responses and general behavior. Money and Ehrhardt's case (1972) of the identical twins clearly demonstrates the power of environmental and parental approaches. Those who are able to be influenced in these ways are more amenable to a reorientation of their same-sex choice.

A young man, seen by me some years ago, arrived with his mother. The latter entered the consultation room uninvited and told me that her son's first year at college had been a disaster. She didn't know what had happened to him but that she suspected he now had homosexual leanings. She felt that the college was at fault for permitting "undesirable elements" to enter the school. It was her belief that these "elements" were corrupting her son and that it was my task to "straighten him out."

I then saw the young man alone. He had always felt feminine and he remembered his mother treating him as a girl. He was the last of four children, all male. The parental disappointment of having another boy was considerable, so much so that his first name could be considered that of a girl. He also remembered being called "a sissy." He was indeed homosexual and college had nothing to do with it. His challenging approach dared me to try to change him. I explained that it was not my function to do his mother's bidding and that he was free to choose any orientation he wished. I asked if there were other problems for which he might want help. He admitted that there were and agreed to try analysis and see what happened. The conditions were hardly the best under which to begin therapy but I agreed to see how it went.

What eventually emerged, via recollections, shed some light on the development of his gender identity. His mother had dressed him in baby's dresses long past the time this should have stopped. A boy's haircut was denied him until friends and relatives pointed out how wrong this was. All terms of endearment were feminine in character. Girls' games were permitted while boys' activities were interdicted as too rough. The type of parental behavior here described tends to form a feminine gender identity in a young boy. Obtaining such information about the childhood of a patient is not too difficult. More marked parental aberrations are more powerfully repressed and become available with much less frequency. The following, I think, was important in helping fix this young man's feminine identity.

One day while lying on the analytic couch with his legs spread, he was reminded of a favorite pastime of his mother's. The television set was in his mother's room, facing her bed. She lay on the bed in various states of undress; he lay between her legs copying her position, his head pillowed on her crotch. He did not remember how early this "game" had begun but it continued into his latency, by which time his feminization was thoroughly fixed. The close physical contact and his mother's protracted exhibitionism, as well as his adopting his mother's position, all aided in the establishment of his feminine identity.

Dealing with gender identity problems is a particularly important aspect of therapy for homosexuals. If one is to be successful in producing a change in orientation, one should demonstrate the origins of the skewed pattern to the patient. For example, I pointed out how his own posture on the couch copied that of his mother: he behaved much as a woman (his mother) did. Further association clarified the fact that it was precisely the position he used as an adult in sexual activity. He then really became aware of how much he had taken on his mother's role via identification. As he worked with this concept, he became far less accepting of the general feminine characteristics his mother had inculcated in him.

When he first came for treatment, his walk and general movements were effeminate. As time went on, he developed an identity suitable to his male anatomy. This was extremely important for his developing interest in heterosexuality, an interest of his own and not one advocated by me. In such patients it is important not to take sides: to have advocated heterosexuality would have immediately provoked an attack on me and furthered the negative transference of his mother onto me.

TRANSFERENCE ISSUES

All the usual transference manifestations and their permutations occur, but in treating homosexuality, the underlying maternal transference is of major significance. Some male therapists tend to overlook the fact that their patients not only transfer males onto them but also females. As in all transference manifestations, recognition and interpretations are essential for progress. The earliest transference phenomena, preoedipal in type, are at least as significant as the oedipal. Not only must anal and oedipal transferential material be analyzed but oral phase material also must be clarified.

Gillespie (1964) early raised the key question confronting analysts as to whether or not homosexuality is due to a primary failure in the oedipal period. I wrote previously (1971) that it would be more fruitful to study the effects of all phases in an attempt to understand the contributions of each. I offered the proposition, based on my own data, that each developmental phase, oral, anal, oedipal, manifests specific problems and that the final outcome in homosexuality is dependent on these earlier phase-specific difficulties. They contribute to and narrow the options available to the child in the phallic phase. The emphasis placed on the prephallic material is to point out that the fateful events of these periods limit the child's options in the phallic period. Libido, aggression, identity, and methods of object choice are all involved. Today, most people accept the idea that the preoedipal phases are as significant as is the oedipal phase (Socarides, 1988) for gender identification and object choice.

While the transference manifestations to the father are more obvious, especially with a same-sex male therapist, the elucidation of aspects of the early maternal transference is critical. I refer not only to the oedipal love for the mother but to the much earlier preoedipal relationship. It is in these earlier times that the normal later fusion of eros and aggression have yet to take place. Object relationships have not matured: the mother is still viewed as a split object and the child's relationship to the world is, to say the least, confused. Transference of preoedipal attitudes onto the therapist is not clear-cut and can shift rapidly from hate to love and back again. In a single session one may see shifts from one parent to the other. These fleeting shifts require, at times, immediate interpretation. The following is an example of how rapidly preoedipal attitudes to the parent change.

One day I was walking down a street when I observed a little boy hitting his mother and crying at the same time. He was yelling and shouting, "I hate you, Mommy. I'll chop you to pieces. I'll eat you up. I'll run away," and more. His mother simply stood there and let him scream. As the boy's rage peaked and began to subside, she suddenly smiled at him and patted his head. The boy stopped crying and striking her, threw his arms around her knees (as high as he could reach) and said, "I love you, Mommy." The mother intuitively seemed to know enough to allow him to vent his rage. We must watch for these rapid shifts from rage to love in the analytic hour. These fluctuations do not occur in each session and are not so evident early in the treatment. It is the establishment of a good working alliance as well as the maintenance of a good therapeutic alliance that permits the emergence of the deeply repressed material of early childhood. The patient's early, only partially fused aggression requires careful management. If the regression is extensive enough and the drive separation complete enough, the object relationship may disappear. This causes a rupture of both alliances and may end the treatment if not dealt with as soon as possible; at times, reparation requires the use of parameters. The woman whom I had to telephone exemplifies this need.

The role of aggression and its management is an ever-present problem in our patients. The aggression observed at times is clearly phase related. The little boy, for example, chopped his mother up and ate her: his regression was back to the oral, cannibalistic stage. Some patients report that their parents actually tell their children that they are like wild animals. I have also heard such remarks as "You are tearing my heart out." I've even heard an adult, not a patient, talk about how children "eat your life up."

Usually, individuals traverse each developmental phase without undue stress. They experience an appropriate parental response which produces a good "fit" between parent and child. Unless something is innately wrong, such as hyperactivity, a learning disability or other substrate problem, the child's object relationships develop according to the expected norm as does the expression of eros and aggression. If either the endowment or the environment is sufficiently skewed, then the developmental process is also skewed. As indicated, this can begin in the earliest days.

There is a large body of experimental work already available showing how mothering affects the infant's behavior, confirming the effects of caretaker responses on the substrate. It also demonstrates that there are innate differences in the patterning of biological responses of boys and girls. Studies show that nurture can and does have an effect on the biological framework. Since this substrate in humans does not produce a precise, preordained and invariable behavior pattern, treatment can and does profoundly influence how a person restructures his or her life.

It is to be noted that the parental responses to the child may be set even before birth. Some parents have fixed wishes and expectations concerning the sex of the unborn child. The actual infant is then not fully accepted for what it is and unconsciously the parents attempt to mold it into their originally expressed wishes. Even the fact of giving a boy child a girl's name has a profound effect on the child's psychological growth. It also affects the other children's behavior: Playmates mock and call him "sissy" and "girlie." But not all children succumb to the parents' attempts to modify their gender identity and sexual orientation. Indeed some resist completely and revolt at any attempt, usually by the mother, to impose her will on the child: an indication that there is a spectrum ranging from the most compliant to the obdurate.

To illustrate the importance of the oral phase: A patient immediately demonstrated some of his oral fixations upon entering my office, when he said, "I had to ring three times. What took you so long?" He had rung three times but in rapid succession, reminding me of the "horn tooters" who cannot wait for the traffic light to turn green. Aggressive orality abounded in his behavior and speech. He had a history of profound disturbances in the oral phase. He had been bottle-fed and seemed unable to hold any of the feeding, vomiting shortly thereafter. This infuriated his mother who believed the infant was doing it on purpose. Later it was discovered that the child was allergic to cow's milk. During the whole time, however, his mother remained hostile to him. He heard reminiscences about how bad he had been as a child. She also described how she had to take him into bed to soothe him. Soothing included genital fondling, and kissing, behavior which was quite sexual. As he grew she considered him skinny, funny, and more like a girl than a boy.

Later, when he began to dress himself in her clothes, she was much amused. She frequently had him don her clothes and then delightedly presented him to her friends, telling him that he fooled all the women and then calling him her little girl. In time he accepted the "fact" that he was more girl than boy, his gender identity was distorted. The mother's general hostility to the child, begun in infancy, continued. He himself, using the defense of identification with the aggressor, became hostile to others and with feminine overtones. In spite of this, he was most uncomfortable with his homosexuality and tried at times to become heterosexual on his own. In his case, analysis led to a favorable conclusion.

In my cases of gender identity distortion, the role of the parents was crucial to inducing the changes. Usually the father's role was negative and passive. I have noted only one exception (1971): The patient's physical union with his mother was extensive, as in other cases. Even up to the age of nine or ten, his mother invited him into bed, presumably for a nap, but actually pulled him on top of her and behaved sexually. He even remembered stroking her pubic hair with her aid. What was unusual, however, was that his father had no objection to this. He remembered that at the age of fifteen he entered his parents' bedroom and found them engaged in intercourse. His father pulled him into bed where he was fondled much the same as was his mother. He also remembered that when he was little, his father stroked his penis. As a teenager, his father insisted on kissing him on the mouth.

Such events change the usual developmental course, affecting not only gender identity but object relationships, interfering with the gradual maturing of the infant. The insults of the oral period are continued into the anal period where again there is deviation from the usual expected environment. One factor concerns the use of enemas and the role they play in inducing passivity and pleasure in anal penetration. In the above-mentioned patient, the anal zone maintained high charges of libido and aggression due to the fierce battle waged over bowel control. Enemas were a way of life for him. They were given regardless of whether or not there had been a successful evacuation.

He recalled the many conflicts over his mother's insistence on giving him an enema. Many times he fought and suffered pain. He finally began to find the entry of the enema nozzle pleasurable. Did this contribute to his adult pleasure in male-to-male sexuality? Is this true for others? I can vouch for it in one other case.

This patient also suffered the indignity of repeated enemas. In his recollections, they became pleasurable and anticipated. He recalled the gush of pleasure when he evacuated the fluid. He called it his orgasm. In telling me about this, he developed rectal throbbing which he also experienced in anal intercourse. He eventually made a heterosexual adjustment. I suggest that enemas can play a role in creating a same-sex orientation, especially when gender identity manipulation has already caused a modification in the appropriate fit between identity and anatomy. Further study would help clarify this proposal.

I have not reported on homosexual people who have had normal parenting since I have not had such patients in treatment. There may indeed be such situations based on biological or other factors, matters awaiting clarification which may depend on other disciplines.

COUNTERTRANSFERENCE

Countertransference can function as an asset in therapy and need not be only an impediment. Careful attention to one's own reactions has become an essential part of a therapist's work. If one feels irritation or becomes bored, one should look for causes not only within but also note what in the patient's behavior and associations triggered the reaction. The information may then become useful therapeutically.

Many homosexual patients, who have long been frustrated and have suffered from societal attitudes, are rather skillful in arousing frustration in others and especially in therapists. Aggression in both therapist and patient must be monitored carefully at all times but it is especially important in the management of some homosexuals.

Central to my thesis is the fact that many therapists have reported success in helping homosexual people. A nihilistic viewpoint is unwarranted. I also stress the need to remain objective and scientific in our attitudes. Biological and psychological work continues to bring information from which new insights can then develop. The recent discoveries pointing to genetic factors in schizophrenia and major depressive disorders are very much to the point. Such new developments may eventually lead to organic methods of treatment, but not to the exclusion of analytic, dynamic approaches. The impact of nurture will still have to be considered.

SUMMARY

Analysis has contributed much to our understanding of the behavioral processes. Sufficient anecdotal material, gathered over many years, forms a very large data bank from which it has been possible to formulate appropriate hypotheses. Revalidation of the propositions can then be checked by the examination of fresh clinical data. This requires the use of appropriate technical methods. It should be clear that the failure to obtain similar results without applying the same technique is only to be expected. Duplication of methodology is essential to validation. The scientific method does apply.

CHAPTER 2

Homosexuality and Psychosis

JOHN FROSCH, M.D.

INTRODUCTION

Before entering into a discussion of the relationship between homosexuality and psychosis, let me differentiate among overt and latent homosexuality, and preconscious and unconscious homosexuality, before describing the nature of the paranoid constellation and the psychotic process and homosexuality.

In overt homosexuality there is a manifest sexual relationship between individuals of the same sex. Latent homosexuality has, although existing in a concealed or dormant form, the potential of achieving overt expression. A case in point is that of a twenty-three-year-old student social worker. During a course on psychoanalytic concepts, he became very tense and anxious when the concept of unconscious homosexuality was discussed. When I saw him he was panicked by recollections of incidents in his life that pointed in the direction of overt homosexuality. For instance, as an adolescent he had found himself fascinated by the genitals of the other boys while taking showers at the gym. On occasion he had had erotic feelings and begun to have an erection, and had rushed out of the shower in embarrassment. Other experiences also suggested a homosexual orientation which, while not overt, nonetheless had the potential of becoming so. The patient had not recognized the homosexual nature of his feelings until he took the course and the concept of unconscious homosexuality was discussed. Now

29

he began to wonder whether all these experiences implied that he was a homosexual. Shortly thereafter he began to accept this as his preference: his latent homosexuality became overt. In another instance, a doctor, while lecturing at school, suddenly had an erection when the thought of some of his male students in a sexual act occurred to him. His mind went blank, he became very anxious, and broke out into a sweat. He also eventually became an overt homosexual.

The type of conflict and anxiety such patients develop has been referred to as a *homosexual panic*. This term has been used in many senses, thus leading to confusion. I reserve the term for the type of patients I described above, who are thrown into a panic by a conscious awareness of homosexual feelings.

Homosexual panic may appear in other ways, and is most typically seen in alcoholic hallucinosis. In these cases it takes the form of auditory hallucinations characterized by the wish to castrate or mutilate the victim. In contrast to the cases of latent homosexuality described above, however, these patients do not manifest homosexual wishes.

In preconscious homosexuality we are dealing with unacceptable homosexual conflicts which break into consciousness, resulting in psychosis or psychoticlike manifestations. In both latent and overt homosexuality we are dealing with what I believe to be different psychic constellations, in which the genetic, dynamic, and therapeutic implications are different from those in preconscious and unconscious homosexuality. The latter may be encountered in the analysis of characterological disturbances, neuroses, dreams, and psychoses. Yet it is clear that these patients will not become overt homosexuals. In such instances perhaps the term *homosexual* should not be used but rather the *passive feminine position,* insofar as it appears in the male.

PRECONSCIOUS HOMOSEXUALITY

When unacceptable homosexual conflicts break into consciousness, resulting in psychosis or psychoticlike manifestations, there is a real struggle over and rejection of the homosexuality. In some cases one can see an actual breakthrough of direct homosexual material. A twenty-six-year-old seaman got along quite well until he married, when a psychiatric picture developed in which he was preoccupied with homosexuality. He looked at pictures of men and felt that he was developing feminine features. While lying in bed he felt that numbers of men were breaking in and he jumped out of the window.

I once observed the impact of homosexual conflict in a psychotic female over an extended period (Frosch, 1967). The role of preconscious homosexuality in precipitating flareups of her psychosis was quite clear. The patient, after an initial period of disturbance on admission, quieted down, and was transferred to another ward. On her third day there, however, she became withdrawn, untidy, and mute. She would not leave her bed, even urinating in it. When she did speak, she indicated that her life was in danger, that she would be killed. The patient subsequently revealed that another female patient had kissed her and suggested they live together. The patient had thought it would be all right to accept this offer, since it would present a means of getting out of the hospital. Yet it became obvious from what she said that she had toyed with homosexuality as a defense against heterosexuality, which she had begun to consider "bad." In a sense, she retreated from the heterosexual to the homosexual position, but she could not maintain it and distintegration ensued. This was followed by a period of religious conversion lasting about three weeks, during which she walked around with a markedly ecstatic and beatific expression. She renounced and denied all sexuality.

She was quite perturbed by a dream in which she was a prostitute, and after a brief period of remission, there was a flareup of psychotic behavior and she actually became a prostitute for two weeks. This behavior was clearly related to a delusion in which she believed that she was being tested to determine whether she was homosexual. She was convinced that the men with whom she was having intercourse were women in disguise, and their penises were not real; on occasion she attempted to tear them off. During her subsequent hospitalization, she displayed reactions to both the conscious and unconscious homosexual preoccupations against which she was defending herself. She viewed homosexuality as very degrading.

At one point, when the patient was especially attuned to the homosexual climate on the ward, she expressed overt sexual fantasies about me and had repeated orgasms (even when she was with me). She dreamed about a woman whom she clearly identified in her associations as her mother. Other associations established the provocative effect on her of a homosexual patient on the ward. Her intense preoccupation with me, to the point of erotomania, was an attempt to ward off her reaction to this homosexual patient.

Another patient, a psychotic character, also experienced intense fear of homosexual impulses mixed with marked aggression. These fears were precipitated by what she thought was an approach by a lesbian. She found this shattering and felt as though she would explode. She projected these feelings, resulting in a feeling of world destruction linked to a childhood experience in which she actually lived through an earthquake. She had always wondered whether her mother had homosexual tendencies, and even toyed with the idea that her mother had made sexual advances to her. She was devastated by these thoughts. The only time that her mother had actually sheltered and protected her was during the earthquake when the patient was three years old. During the analysis, the patient had fleeting, almost psychotic episodes. Even more manifest, however, was a general paranoid attitude.

In the case of a chronic paranoid, preconscious homosexuality played a definitive role in his psychosis. At the time he was first seen the patient was sixty-one years old. He came to the emergency room after having been beaten by some boys. The examining physician thought he seemed somewhat confused, and psychiatric consultation was asked for. What had appeared to be simply confused thinking turned out to be a highly complex delusional system.

He saw himself as destined for great things in life. He had a mission, but because of interference with certain "basic" physiological functions such as moving his bowels, his whole system had been upset and he could not fulfill this mission. Furthermore, he thought that inside him there was a "power" that controlled his behavior and feelings, both negatively and positively. He had not quite reached the stage of being God, but he definitely felt that he had some kind of mission and one didn't have to search far to find an underlying "Messiah" delusion. Many people were involved in the plot that prevented him from carrying out his mission, among them members of his family, including his dead parents. He reconstructed situations and events to integrate people from the past into his developing delusional system. Eventually, clear delusions of persecution and grandeur emerged.

Let us go back a little, however, and look at his idea that his biological functions were being interfered with, and his claim, "I could live forever provided I'm allowed to enjoy my physiological health." A key element was a memory from age six or seven. He had wanted to go to the bathroom and the teacher had not permitted him to do so.[1] He wove this insult into his delusional system; it was part of a plot to interfere with his "constitutional" right to enjoy his physical health. His fellow students had humiliated him, made fun of him, and also prevented him from exercising this right. Moreover, his parents were not sympathetic about his being so humiliated, and their indifference—"they looked away"—he found equally humiliating. "When people want to downtrod me and make me nothing," he commented, "they don't look at me."

In addition to his chronic bowel accumulations, he thought poison gas was formed, which befogged and prevented him from fulfilling the mission for which he had been born—to lead all humans to better life. Clinically, the evolution of his hypochondriacal complaints into somatic delusions, ideas of influence, persecution, and grandiose ideas were interwoven and given some semblance of rational appearance.

At one point the patient referred to an incident that "broke [him] down" and actually broke into tears. He said that, when he was about seven years old, his older brother and his friends had manipulated his genitals: "He had, like, homosexuality with

---

[1]Of interest is that Schreber (Freud, 1911) too had the delusion that people were interfering with his bowel activities. Whenever he wanted to go to the bathroom, someone deliberately occupied it or made a comment that prevented him from moving his bowels.

me." The patient remembered crying and escaping into his mother's bed, but he lived in constant dread that it would happen again. He felt both ashamed and degraded. He then likened his bowel troubles to masturbation: the accumulation of feces exerted pressure on his genitals, stimulating him, but "the genital organ must not be played with." In this way, he conceived of the various interferences with his bowel movements as part of a plot to arouse him sexually and force him to masturbate.

The humiliating quality of such real experiences has major significance for the paranoid constellation and the impact of unconscious homosexuality. In this patient there were indications of even earlier experiences of a similarly humiliating nature, the later ones appearing almost as screen memories for the earlier. Moreover, this man's subsequent life was hardly free from events in which he was a passive victim. At the age of eighteen, he claimed, he underwent a murderous assault that injured him so badly that his chance of recovering his "constitutional physiological rights" was almost totally thwarted. He alluded to terrible things of a humiliating nature done to him during a previous hospitalization. I do not know exactly what these things were or if they indeed took place, but what was important was his concept of his relation to his environment: he saw himself as the injured victim of a world that did not understand him, that tortured and tormented him externally and internally. "They are all able to persecute me and have a leeway and freedom with me because of the power that I have within me. He lets them do what they want. I'm a very nice character and a lovely human being and maybe they would like to fall in love with me."

Behind this man's "torturers" lurked the malevolent figure of his seducer—brother, who, he said, made the murderous attempt on his life, and not too far behind was the father. But there were mixed feelings toward these torturers, seen in his remarks about an all-good teacher and an all-bad teacher. The good teacher had loved him, praised him, made him feel very proud; the bad one had only criticized and humiliated him in front of others. He insisted that their attitudes toward him were "in direct opposition." "The first teacher always pointed me out to the parents of the other pupils as an exceptionally good student. The second teacher, in total contrast, made my life so miserable that I prayed to be dismissed [from school] but tragically for me [this] was never realized." Mixed feelings also appeared in his attitude toward the introjected object in his body, which he called "the power in me."

Central to being a victim was the "homosexuality" he had experienced at the hands of his brother, which he felt as degrading and humiliating, a recurrent theme in many of his experiences. In this regard we might ask: Were all his experiences of being the victim of assault fortuitous, truly accidental, or were they an integral part of an ongoing conflict and struggle, necessary perhaps for the preservation of the psyche? In many ways the assaults upon him seemed almost invited. He presented the appearance of a victim and almost deliberately exposed himself to these situations. He lent himself to being beaten. Ultimately, his end was tragic—he was found dead in his apartment, the victim of a burglary attempt during which he was murdered.

In all the above instances the homosexual conflict was preconscious and on becoming conscious was rejected by the patient and defended against, producing various clinical manifestations.

UNCONSCIOUS HOMOSEXUALITY

In unconscious homosexuality the individual has no awareness of any aspect of homosexuality, and it is not manifest. Unconscious homosexuality may operate as an organizing principle in diverse clinical pictures, and has particular revelance in the paranoid constellation.

To begin with, Freud's (1911) exposition on the unconscious proposition "I love him" discussed various clinical manifestations such as delusions of persecution, erotomania, delusions of jealousy, and megalomania. Might there not be a variant combining a denial with projection: "I do not love him (her)—he (she) loves him (her)"? In this variant, the homosexuality is projected and the other is accused of being homosexual. In the context of this projected homosexuality, I have in certain instances found a special kind of delusional idea and acting out. The special idea may not evolve into a full-blown delusional system; the patient may not make any overt accusations nor exhibit any behavior that suggests to others that he entertains the idea. Yet there may be a kind of acting out that hints at the underlying unconscious homosexuality.

As an example, a patient in analysis temporarily thought that his wife might be having homosexual relations with a masseuse who came to give her treatment at the house. He wondered when he left the house whether more was going on than he was aware of. The patient assiduously inquired about the specific hour of the massage, but he never voiced his suspicions. It became evident that this idea was an outward expression, and at the very edge of his own unconscious homosexual feelings.

This man had what appeared to be a rescue fantasy, reflected in his very choice of a wife. She had been exposed to cruel treatment by her father. Before their marriage, when the patient took her home he frequently on leaving heard her being chastised and abused by her father for being a "bum" and a "tramp." It was rumored that the father had sexually abused his children and in particular the patient's future wife. The patient decided to marry her and save her; at the same time he had a persistent curiosity about what had actually transpired, asking his wife for exact details about her father's actions from time to time. On occasion, when he was angry with her, he called his wife a "tramp," echoing her father. It emerged during his analysis that here too was a projection of an underlying unconscious homosexuality.

His sedulous inquiries about the details of his wife's experiences evolved into what I call a pimp fantasy: the man, either in fantasy or actuality, uses the female to effect contact with another male. Unaccompanied by delusions of jealousy, to the contrary, it is consciously gratifying. The woman is used both as a sacrificial object to ward off attack from the male and to make sexual contact with him. Although this fantasy does not necessarily produce specific delusions, it may be accompanied by hypersensitivity and paranoid trends. Most important, however, the wish to share a woman, and through her make contact with a man, reflects unconscious homosexuality as an organizing principle.[2]

The clinical impact of unconscious homosexuality was seen in wartime soldiers sent to the hospital by the army as psychotic and for commitment; but by the time they were seen they were apparently free of any psychotic manifestations and we were able to discharge them. They showed a fairly consistent picture of ideas of reference and persecutory ideas. They were even hallucinatory, but the content was not of a homosexual nature. Nor were we able to assess any major clinical psychiatric picture before their military induction. The symptoms apparently developed during their army service and lasted a short time, clearing up as soon as they were discharged. When these individuals, in whom the homosexuality was repressed and not acted out, were thrown into daily contact with a group of men, they apparently were unable to keep the homosexuality under control. From the revival of the homosexuality arose process formation, with an attempt to handle the problem by projection. Here we find a return of the repressed, not in the form of homosexuality as such but in disguise, where it is rejected and projected, frequently in the form of superego accusations.

Some men seem to have a peculiar fascination with the activities of lesbians. I treated a manic-depressive woman who during her manic phase had both hetero- and homosexual experiences. During her depressed phase she felt very guilty about them and confessed them to her husband. During subsequent sexual relations he made her recount, in great detail, the actual events of her extramarital relations, especially the homosexual ones. The recounting was very exciting for him, culminating in orgasm. His wife indicated that his potency difficulties were resolved by these narratives. One of the demands of some customers in houses of prostitution is to have two women engage in sexual intercourse; the customer watches avidly and urges them on with mounting excitement, ejaculating

---

[2]Bradley (1983) describes King Arthur as urging Guinevere to have relations with Lancelot in order to provide offspring, even urging them to have intercourse while in bed with him. Guinevere recognized the unconscious motivation in this by accusing Lancelot of wanting to make contact with Arthur through her. At one point Lancelot says, "I know not but what I love her only because I come close, thus to him" (p. 482).

at the end. The man's identification with the woman seems obvious.

As to the role of unconscious homosexuality in female paranoia, in one of the earliest cases reported by Freud (1896a), the patient was defending herself against unconscious homosexual ideas. In another case, Freud (1915), aware of some seeming inconsistency when a paranoid female's persecutor was male, was able to establish that the male persecutor represented a homosexual object, the patient's mother. Many of the patients whose treatment was used by Ferenczi (1911, 1912) to develop his concept of the importance of unconscious homosexuality in paranoid delusional systems were female.

Another example of the role of unconscious homosexuality in female paranoia is a special form of erotomania in women frequently described as the Clérambault syndrome (Arieti and Bemporad, 1974; Lehman, 1975) which deserves mention here. The Clérambault syndrome (erotomania) or the "psychose passionnelle" is generally seen in women who become attached to a prominent figure who hardly knows them, if at all. These women interpret everything as a manifestation of the person's love for them. The reported cases of the "psychose passionnelle" do not deal with unconscious features. Nonetheless, they fit in with the erotomania described by Freud (1911) in his famous proposition, "I do not love him, I love her," transposed by the female into "I do not love her, I love him." A case of psychose passionelle occurred in the wife of a patient I was treating who developed a marked attachment to me. Behind this attachment to me and incidental to it was her attachment to my wife, whom she had never met or seen, but about whom she had multiple dreams and fantasies.

THE PARANOID CONSTELLATION

The paranoid constellation underlies paranoid development (Frosch, 1981, 1983a). In the paranoid constellation unconscious homosexuality is denied, rejected, and projected onto a replica of a significant childhood object. The subject then becomes the unwilling, persecuted, passive victim. The "persecution" is seen as an anal-sadomasochistic attack, which is felt as

degrading and humiliating. Behind this view lie real humiliating experiences at the hands of significant same-sex objects
from the past, generally a father figure in the male and a
mother figure in the female. These events occur at crucial
stages in psychic development, before sexual identity has been
established. They are particularly traumatic because they are
out of phase with the child's existing level of ego and libidinal
development and are tied into the child's fantasies. These experiences, then, make passivity humiliating, degrading, and possibly catastrophic. Although there are contributions from many
levels of psychic development to the paranoid picture, it is unconscious homosexuality in this form that is the organizing
principle.

How, then, is the paranoid constellation structured in
women? For instance, where do the anal-sadomasochistic features fit it? Freud (1920) felt that, as with men, the essential
conflict in paranoid women was over unconscious homosexuality. However, at the time he wrote about paranoia in women
he did not mention the anal-sadomasochistic relation to the
object at any length. Klein (1946) circumvented the question by
asserting that the postulated infantile paranoid position formed
the basis for future paranoia in both men and women. In a
sense this denigrates the importance of unconscious homosexuality in paranoia and makes it unnecessary to differentiate between male and female paranoia. Since unconscious homosexuality in the male was relegated by many authors to a secondary
role, and in a sense was viewed as a pseudophenomenon, it was
also treated as an unimportant factor in the female paranoid.

I suggest that in males a particularly cruel and sadistic
father may augment the potential for the development of the
paranoid constellation. Such a father's sadism and cruelty is not
confined to an isolated event, but may be chronic. Yet his cruelty may become crystallized in the child's mind during a critical
phase of psychic development, when it lends a particular real-
ness to the child's fantasies. In males the phase is most likely to
be an anal-sadistic one, where the father is generally not an oral
provider or depriver. For the female child, it is the mother
who may be the menacing object, and particular humiliating
experiences with her may become the core of the paranoid

constellation. In the female paranoid the anal-sadistic component does not appear to be as central as in the male. In both
male and female, however, the trauma of actual humiliating
experiences in early psychic development is incorporated into
a dread of unconscious homosexuality. The unconscious homosexuality then becomes the organizing principle for the paranoid constellation.

We are not yet, however, dealing with paranoid psychosis.
The presence of the paranoid constellation per se does not
indicate psychosis, although it contains the ingredients for a
psychosis. The paranoid constellation provides the content but
does not determine the form in which the content is expressed.

While the paranoid constellation may lend many ingredients to the clinical picture, such as oversuspiciousness or acute
sensitivity to slights, none of these may in and of themselves
be psychotic and may even be, under certain circumstances,
sociosyntonic (Frosch, 1983b). In order for a paranoid psychosis to develop, other factors must supplement the paranoid
constellation—specifically the components of the psychotic
process.

THE PSYCHOTIC PROCESS

To clarify the concept of the psychotic process (Frosch, 1983a),
I want to make it clear that I am not referring to overt psychosis
as such. Rather, we are dealing with a continuous interplay of
factors and operations moving toward an end-product. Various
clinically observable phenomena grow out of these processes,
either in isolated manifestations or more organized clinical syndromes, be they characterological distortions or more defined
clinical syndromes.

There are factors within the psychotic process which can
occur in many clinical manifestations. These may result in clinical psychoses or character psychopathology such as the psychotic character, or other clinical phenomena having an impact
on producing unusual behavioral manifestations.

Characteristic of the psychotic process is the nature of the
danger and conflict to be dealt with: a basic anxiety evolving
as a response to the sensed possibility of disintegration and

dissolution of self, ultimately revolving around the issue of survival. The possibility of dedifferentiation and self–object fusion with a loss of identity is crucial to the formation of basic anxiety.

The defenses to deal with this anxiety are primitive: splitting, denial, introjection, and projective identification. The ego and its functions have specific impairments which characterize the psychotic process. There is an ego weakness or fragility related to (1) instability in the ego's capacity for defense; (2) a marked vulnerability to stress; (3) fragmentation of the ego; (4) poor resistance to aggression; (5) a tendency to dedifferentiation; (6) difficulty in reversing such dedifferentiation and reestablishing identity; and (7) disturbances in object relations.

Such defects produce many clinical manifestations reflecting regressed ego states. These include disordered states of consciousness such as hypnoid, twilight, or dream states; oceanic feelings, cosmic identity; feelings of unreality; depersonalization, estrangement; and Isakower phenomena, as well as feelings of dissolution. They may be accompanied by mild to severe disturbances in identity, such as identity diffusion or severe body-image disturbances.

Defects in ego functions are a key element in the psychotic process, especially with regard to impairment vis-à-vis reality; for example, the relationship with reality and the object, the sense of reality, but above all, the capacity to test reality. I view the loss of the capacity to test reality as crucial for the diagnosis of psychosis.

DISCUSSION

Turning to a consideration of the development of psychosis in overt homosexuality, an often-asked question is: Why do some overt homosexuals become psychotic? Freud (1922, 1923a) considered both sides of the picture: aggression as a defense against unconscious homosexuality and manifest overt homosexuality as a defense against unconscious aggression. He subsequently maintained and reaffirmed these views, which raises another interesting question: When we see psychosis developing in certain homosexuals, are we seeing the failure of a major defensive operation which has borrowed from strong instinctual inclinations, namely, the homosexuality?

Rosenfield (1949), taking Klein's (1946) primary paranoid stage of development as his frame of reference, says that increased paranoid anxieties encourage the development of strong "manifest" or "latent" homosexual tendencies as a defense. When the defensive function of the homosexuality fails, paranoia develops. In his opinion it is the fixation to the early narcissistic level of psychic development, where projective identification operates, that is responsible for the frequent combination of paranoia and homosexuality.

Katan (1950) suggests something similar when he indicates that in the paranoid the unconscious homosexuality represents a retreat from a weak oedipal position and is a valiant attempt to hold onto reality and objects. If this defense falls under the impact of anxiety and danger, there is further regression, possibly to the point of undifferentiation. This may have occurred in the hospitalized psychotic patient I described above, who developed fantasies around her own destruction after she was approached by a homosexual patient, and had transiently toyed with the idea of going along with the woman's proposal that they live together. Heterosexuality had apparently become dangerous and a source of anxiety to her. But my patient was not an overt homosexual, nor, to my knowledge, had she any overt homosexual experiences of any sort. On the contrary, she felt homosexuality to be the greatest degradation and humiliation. It should be emphasized that both Katan and I are referring here not to overt homosexuality but rather to defenses against unconscious homosexuality.

The paranoid constellation results in paranoid psychosis under the impact of the psychotic process on the constellation. Ira Miller (personal communication, 1963) described an overt homosexual in whom the homosexuality appeared to be a defense against the disintegration fears and self-dissolution characteristic of the psychotic anxiety described above. This patient revealed the type of reaction to change and uncertainty I have described for the psychotic character (Frosch, 1970). Once, for instance, when Miller shifted the furniture in his office, practically reversing the whole setup, the patient became panic-stricken and confused. He said he felt lost, sobbed, and was unable to lie down on the couch. During the course of the analysis a suggestion was made that the patient suspend his homosexual activities; he then had a series of dreams associated with an indescribable feeling of terror. While speaking of one of these dreams he again panicked, breaking into profuse and violent sobbing. He was terrified he would become insane and fall apart. Then he interrupted the analysis. Miller thought that the threatened loss of his homosexuality evoked the panic and disintegrative anxieties (psychotic in nature) and that the homosexuality enabled him to defend against an underlying psychosis.

In a case mentioned to me by Wolfe (personal communication, 1962), a homosexual was induced to give up his homosexual activities by a priest who convinced him of their sinfulness. He became very depressed, guilt-ridden, and eventually developed a florid paranoid psychosis, with ideas of reference, delusions of persecution, and hallucinations. At this point he came to see Wolfe, who felt that the overt homosexuality was a more welcome condition than the psychosis and made a return to homosexuality a goal of therapy. The psychosis did indeed subside with the patient's return to homosexual activities, and he felt less guilt-ridden than before. Years later Wolfe met him at a bar with his lover. He seemed relaxed and introduced his companion with equanimity. The issues involved in this case are more complex than such a brief description can suggest, but in his own way, Wolfe recognized the defensive nature of the overt homosexuality.

The above material suggests that in those instances in which overt homosexuals become psychotic and paranoid, the overt homosexuality may be a defense against an underlying, incipient psychotic process. One would expect in such instances to find clinical evidence of the underlying psychotic process, indicating that if the overt homosexuality were abandoned for some reason, a psychotic break might ensue.

Bak (1971) describes psychosis in perversions as due to alterations of the ego whereby the ego may resort to temporary abandonment of object representations. He feels that the perverse symptoms in such instances are frantic attempts to create and reestablish object relations. Gillespie (1956) suggests that in psychoses associated with perversions, marked castration anxiety leads such patients to a regression to pregenital levels, facilitated by a split in the ego.

Socarides (1988), discussing the association of homosexuality and psychosis, uses the term *schizohomosexuality*. He takes issue with Gillespie's (1956) formulation, feeling that:

> [It] is due neither to a fixation to the preoedipal phase of development nor to a failure of resolution of the Oedipus complex and a flight from castration fears leading to a regression in part to anal and oral conflicts. . . . Although unconsciously motivated and arising from anxiety, the perverse act in the schizophrenic does not serve the magical restorative function of the preoedipal form of perversion. Severe gender-identity disturbances, when preset, are part and parcel of an underlying schizophrenic process which has led to profound identity disturbances and a confusion with the object. The schizopervert shows a failure to invest the object successfully, and thus the object cannot be retained or cathected, even though there are fused body images and fused genital representations. This is in direct contrast to the nonpsychotic preoedipal perversion in which objects are retained, protected, and invested successfully despite some degree of fused body image or fused genital representation [pp. 55–56].

To sum up, Socarides states that "perverse symptoms in the psychotic are an attempt to create object relations in the face of severe regression, threatened or actual destruction of object relations in an individual severely damaged by a primary defect or deficiency in the autonomous functions of the ego, and an inability to maintain a protective stimulus barrier" (1988, pp. 57–58).

SUMMARY

Before entering the discussion of the relationship between homosexuality and psychosis I clarified certain concepts among which were those of unconscious, preconscious, and latent and overt homosexuality. I equally discussed the concept of the psychotic process which I felt was operative in those cases which eventuated in psychosis as well as psychotic characterological

disturbances. I then discussed in some detail the role of unconscious homosexuality in the development of the paranoid constellation and other psychotic developments in both male and
female. In another series of cases I described the role of preconscious homosexual conflicts which eventuated in overt psychosis. I finally turned to an extensive description of overt homosexuals who developed psychotic reactions. I presented
formulations to explain the above reactions.

CHAPTER 3

The Search for the Vagina in Homosexual Women

ELAINE V. SIEGEL, Ph.D.

INTRODUCTION

During the last fifteen years I have conducted the analysis of twelve women who were obligatory homosexuals. I also saw several others in psychoanalytic psychotherapy.

On presenting themselves for treatment, none of these women was interested in becoming heterosexual, being firmly convinced that homosexuality was more satisfying, ecstatic, and "evolved" than heterosexuality. However, they all complained of lack of personal fulfillment, inability to stay happily in any one relationship, and were beset by many overwhelming anxiety states that seemed to them to be caused by the environment. The imperative need for homosexual encounters was rationalized as being due to a strong sex drive. The women had been referred by a women's center which listed me as one of its therapists.

Reports about my clinical experience and investigations were published in 1984, 1986, and 1988. In my opinion, the most important clinical finding consisted of the fact that these women suffered a very specific type of developmental arrest. When schematization of the body and its inner representation was being laid down, the vagina and inner space per se were not included. This unhappy turn of events was traceable to

47

chronically disturbed relationships with both parents. Most often, the relationship to their mothers traumatized the little girls to such an extent that they could not identify with their mother's femininity and femaleness. The mothers were fragile women who needed mothering themselves. When the girls turned to their fathers, they didn't fare much better. Most of these parents had needs of their own which they looked to their children to fulfill. Somehow, despite their outward devotion, it didn't seem to occur to them that children must receive narcissistic enhancement and nurturance before they can, in their turn, provide emotional food. Consequently, male and female identifications proliferated in my analysands without coalescing into an integrated, gender defined self identity (Socarides, 1978).

However, I do not by any means wish to imply that these women were bisexual. As a matter of fact, I find the construct of bisexuality neither helpful clinically nor provable in developmental terms (Rado, 1949; Socarides, 1988). Freud (1940) himself toward the end of his life noted that he had been unable to conceptualize a developmental course for bisexuality; having first observed, as early as 1896 (1896b), and noted in a letter to Wilhelm Fliess, the interplay of male and female tendencies in people, and having repeatedly observed this duality clinically, he concluded that it must be a biologic force. But increased clinical experience and research, direct infant observation, as well as new theoretical formulations have provided us with another, more useful point of view. The concept of a gender-differentiation process during which both sexes wish for and think they possess the attributes of each other, provides a developmentally based formulation which explains and encompasses the fate of early male and female identifications (Fast, 1984). Infantile omnipotence allows the little girl to assume that she, too, will grow a penis and the little boy to assume he can bear babies. Probably around the second half of the second year, delimitation of possibilities inherent in sexual differences is accepted, along with anatomical sex differences. An appearance of exaggerated bisexuality (de Saussure, 1929; Brierly, 1935) seemed to prevent my analysands from becoming their biologically determined female selves. But this exaggerated bisexuality revealed itself as developmental arrest in the sexually undifferentiated phase which kept infantile omnipotence and ideas of overinclusiveness intact into adulthood. The gender differentiation process did not take place, and my analysands unconsciously and sometimes consciously thought they had a penis, could grow one, or that they did not need a male to impregnate them. While they knew that they were female, they did not know what this could mean.

CLINICAL DATA

At first glance, I seemed to be in the presence of great penis envy and castration fears. But, when the penis was acknowledged consciously as present in males at all, it was viewed either defensively as insignificant or with disgust and fear. According to my patients, "that thing" was not at all necessary for sexual intercourse. As a matter of fact, they all disliked and feared penetration, although I regularly heard detailed reports about how much more evolved and ecstatic homosexual, especially lesbian, sexual encounters were. However, the details reported never concerned themselves with the actual physical manipulations. This only occurred much later in the analysis. At first, I only heard poetic and romanticized versions of body intimacies and temporary fusion. The need to idealize homosexuality stayed strong in these analysands for a long time, and eventually alerted me to the fact that the idealizations were defenses against the terror and fragmentation of not being in possession of one's own genital.

I came to understand my patients as having been unable to conclude the phase of sexual overinclusiveness, as a case history and some clinical vignettes will illustrate. There were other hallmarks as well pointing toward early trauma and resultant incomplete body image formation of a specific type, namely, the lack of schematization of the genitals. Castration reactions were unusually strong and included fears of body boundary dissolution and internal threats of object loss. Occasionally, aphanisis beckoned (Jones, 1927a).

Roiphe and Galenson's (1981) formulations are invaluable here. Their research convinced them that an early genital phase exists.

One of the most conspicuous manifestations of the early genital phase is the preoedipal castration anxiety, a reaction sharply different in boys from what it is in girls: the boys attempt to deny the anatomical difference, the girls acknowledge the difference and become depressed and angry (p. 2). Roiphe and Galenson go on to elucidate: "The preoedipal castration reactions, in contrast to the later phallic–oedipal phase reactions, not only reflect a threat to the infant's sense of body intactness, but simultaneously are experienced as a threat of object loss" (p. 14).

My own clinical findings are consistent with these formulations. While it is, of course, impossible to ever recapture the past in its entirety, derivatives of these impingements on early reactions made themselves felt repeatedly in the analyses I discuss in this chapter. The somatopsychic integrity of my analysands' body selves and their inner representations had been severely affected by many factors, as I indicated above. They failed to make the appropriate intrapsychic separation from their mothers and were given to merging and fusing mechanisms as a way of dealing with their preoedipal castration anxieties and threat of object loss. The deficiencies in their body images predisposed them to the same difficulties as their male counterparts in that the threat of object loss and castration were secondary to the lack of genital schematization. Socarides's (1979) unitary theory of perversions is most applicable here. He categorizes the merging and fusing phenomena, increase of primary and secondary aggression, disturbance in body self schematization and other mechanisms that result in the faulty development of self–object representations and fear of engulfment present in all perversions.

I have already mentioned that among my patients there was a distinct distaste for penetration, although, at first, in some of them, this was unconscious. While most of the women allowed fingers and devices to enter their vaginas during homosexual loveplay, they did so as an act of masochistic surrender. Some even felt that penetration prevented orgasm. The wish was to be held and stroked, to be made gently aware of the entire body periphery. The message to their lovers, and to the world, was: Mother didn't teach me who I am, therefore, another like myself must show me that I have a sexual self. But the mirroring they received from their female lovers was as distorted as their primary, maternal experience had been, locking them into the never-ending cycle of the repetition compulsion and the imperative need for homosexual body intimacies. Penetration, when it did occur, aroused murderous fantasies which were then secondarily sexualized and elaborated.

When the compensatory and reparative functions of some of these fantasies were interpreted, dreams and manifestations of early castration anxiety occurred. For instance:

Delilah began to suffer from lower back pains and extreme anxiety states and exhibited heavy armoring across the chest, resulting in constricted breathing patterns. She withdrew from friends. Work inhibitions made her life difficult. This was followed by a dream in which terrorists with guns invaded an igloo in which she lived. To ward off the fear of body dissolution, Delilah tried to scrub herself down with a loofa sponge and to masturbate while in the shower. After interpretation, Delilah reported that she "had begun to experience the mystery of being a woman. All those little mounds and hills, sliding around them with my finger and thinking my lover's penis could fit well in here."

Beatrice experienced terrifying headaches, a need to move about, and to be held by someone. She began to look for women in bars. Eventually, she had a dream of "being pulled apart and snapping back together, like rubber ribbons." This was "very frightening and crazy." Nevertheless, when she woke up, she had a feeling that something new had been added. When she took her morning shower, she felt her vagina was like a "blossom, tender and satiny, and very fragile."

But I am talking here of women who had already in analysis become aware that there was a dead spot where their genitals should be.

Freud (1905) wrote about the supposed inability of little girls to gain a sense of vaginal awareness until they reached puberty. In 1924, he again wrote about the vagina's exclusion from the awareness of both boys and girls. In contrast, my clinical findings demonstrate that the classic view about the young female's lacking awareness of her vagina is a pathological rather than a normal development. Many analysts disagreed with Freud and added to his observations. Greenacre (1950) postulated that cathexis of the erotogenic zones had a direct relationship to body-ego formation. Kleeman (1976) also was of the opinion that early vaginal sensations affect body schematization and differentiation of self from other. These sensations during the first years of life are pleasurable. Between fifteen and twenty-seven months, there is an increase in excitement, which includes vaginal lubrication and self-stimulation of the lower vaginal canal, the clitoris, and the labia. Kestenberg (1956) and Greenacre (1950) held that the vaginal sensations of infancy also serve to discharge psychological stress. As early as 1932, Brierly noted clinical evidence that females have sensations in the vagina at an early age, a finding expanded in 1935.

The treatments I conducted left me with the impression that all these clinical and theoretical formulations were correct but do not include another important aspect: When infantile vaginal sensations are not greeted with conscious and unconscious approval by the parents, the little girl must conclude that these sensations are not appropriate or may be harmful. Therefore, she is prohibited from using them to complete her body image. She may be ashamed of them and become angry that she has these bodily sensations at all. These events take place when the little girl is no longer a baby but has not yet become a big girl. She does not know how to make sense out of sensations, perception, and feelings. But the resulting overflow of tensions must be externalized under the guidance of an empathic holding environment that includes a mother available for identification. If appropriate tension discharge and imitation in play do not occur, a developmental arrest occurs.

Doll play helps to externalize and to master vaginal tensions as does play in general (Kestenberg, 1968; Siegel, 1986). Interestingly, not one of the homosexual women I treated could remember ever playing with dolls or creating the usual games of house and family. They substituted gross motor activities instead.

In the service of having a mother or caregiver at all, my analysands had to keep their naturally occurring vaginal sensations during infancy split off from their organizing, regulating, and structuring functions. Thus, the vagina denied both consciously and unconsciously was not the issue. It simply had not been cathected. Instead, the vagina unknown became the "dark continent" to be analytically understood and constructed.

The relationship to the clitoris was ambivalent as well. Although in their sexual games the women often stimulated each other clitorally and supposedly reached heights of ecstasy, the analysis showed that the clitoris had been included in the lack of cathexis. Delilah became aware of a "dead spot where my vagina should be" during heterosexual intercourse and discovered both clitoric and vaginal sensations during masturbation after a transference had been established. The other patients reported similar experiences. But it was only after the ego-syntonic and stabilizing functions of the homosexual acts had been analyzed that this developmental arrest could be undone. Prior to this, homosexuality had been an absolutely necessary state of being in the world for these women. Interestingly, the reports of ecstasy and delight turned out to be enactments of fantasies of warding off the penetrating lovers. The physiologic stimulations immediately aroused unconscious fear and rage, culminating in gyrations and bodily arching interpreted by both partners as passionate responses. However, I heard reports that the clitoris was "raw," "the bitch nearly tore it off," or "she is a dyke, she hurts me like a man would." This focus on pain at first hid the lack of libidinal cathexis of the clitoris in these cases. My impression is that a partial cathexis of the clitoris did take place but was experienced as unduly strong by comparison with the lack of sensation in the rest of the genital area. The ability to use the clitoris as an erotic organ seemed to wax and wane in accordance with certain fantasies of having a penis and being robbed of it. It was always at the height of feeling castrated and robbed, in fear of disintegration and fragmentation, that the homosexual act was resorted to for its reassuring functions.

Menses presented a special problem for these analysands as well. For instance, Tanya, preoccupied with her homosexual tensions and thinking that these were controlled by the analysis, suffered cramps each month. She tried consciously to hold back the flow of blood. Often, she confused her own odors with those of the analyst, who, she thought, menstruated at the same time she did. When Tanya menstruated, she feared loss of life and mourned the "dead part of me" and later "the babies I could have had." Carla insisted on cunnilingus when her flow was heaviest. Analysis revealed that she feared being eaten and by offering her blood hoped to forestall cannibalistic orgies. The fantasies of mutilation and revenge attached to menses were formidable and, at times, seemed endless. Many of my patients hated the sight of blood and did not eat red meat. Menstruation was felt to be an attack, a mutilation, and, finally, a dissolving of body boundaries. Obviously, such impaired body images led to uneven ego development and to inadequate object relationships. The class of conflict was object relational rather than tripartite (Dorpat, 1976). Nevertheless, object relationships were possible. Although object choices were uniformly narcissistic, they still represented a true object relationship, that between mother and child (Socarides, 1978, 1988).

Naturally, the transferences took a long time to establish and went through many prestages. I identified six steps in treatment before a transference neurosis proper arose. (1) The search for the ideal mother. Like young children, the analysands at first expected to be unconditionally gratified and felt rejected and humiliated by analytic neutrality. Acting out was ubiquitous and served to ward off and to deny growing feelings for the analyst. (2) Hypochondriacal concerns. As these women became more aware of their potential connectedness to the analyst and more openly began to ask for gratification and nurturance, there was usually an emergence of somatic delusions. There were reports of imaginary bugs crawling all over one patient, thermal awareness went awry with another, constipation or vaginal secretions were experienced as grave insults, and so on. It was as though these analysands needed to reassure themselves by their bodily preoccupations that their bodies existed at all. (3) Denial of the need for a good-enough mother and the simultaneous need to recreate the mother–child dyad. During this phase, the analyst was experienced defensively as part of the grandiose self, as having no identity of her own. This helped to stave off the desperate longing for contact, and the analyst was unconsciously asked to give the analysands a completed body image. (4) Projection of body image distortions onto the analyst. The demand here was to "have an analyst like themselves" and this included their derogation of the genitals or the acquisition of a penis. (5) Analyst introject fantasies. At first, the analyst clearly was not perceived as a person at all but as a commodity. During the analyst introject phase (Dorpat, 1974) some reparative internalizations occurred. (6) Homosexuality as a defense against transference. Homosexual acting out once again increased when the analyst was perceived as important and the analysis as potentially growth-producing. This realization aroused panic because inner structures were still incomplete.

The following case history more completely illustrates what I mean.

CASE EXAMPLE

When Rowena presented herself for treatment, she was thirty-five years old and had left her husband of fifteen years to live with her female lover. Leaving behind two teenage sons, she was nevertheless surrounded by an apparently joyful, excited aura which made her appear younger than her years. Basically an attractive woman, she wore her hair cut very short and clothing so tight it accentuated every flaw in her short, square figure. A kinesiologist who was also responsible for teaching anatomy at a university, she was well known locally for her innovative program. But despite her good work, funding had been cut for her department, making it necessary for her to terminate employment for some of her staff members. She appeared more distraught about having "to let go some sister-women" than about the fact that she had been passed over for advancement. She saw the lack of appreciation for her work as "typical for male dominated academia." As an antidote, she belonged to a feminist group fighting for women's rights. Much to her surprise, Rowena found herself uncomfortable in this supposedly supportive surrounding. "Uncomfortable" is how she described herself in general. Therefore, she was surprised to find herself "comfortable or feeling nothing" about leaving her family. She further described herself as "cold, without passions. I was a dutiful wife and mother. I had my first orgasm when a woman kissed me five years ago. I suspected that I was homosexual since childhood. This confirmed it. I would have left [the marriage] earlier but the boys were too small, and my parents would have had a fit if I deserted my children. Now, the boys do very well without me." Her husband was not mentioned.

Rowena also thought of herself as a good organizer and a hard worker. Work brought her much satisfaction. She felt that part of her mission in life was to "evolve a female mode of getting things done." She wasn't quite sure what she meant by this phrase but it was clear to her that "male domination should not be replaced by female domination." This notion brought her in conflict with both her female lover Carmen and the members of her feminist group. They wanted to create a nation of women only. But this conflict didn't bother her. She was used to "thinking things through and acting from her head." In her interaction with her lover, this passionless state "annoyed" her. She didn't like the void where, she thought, feelings should be. In analysis, she hoped to find her feelings. As an aside, she mentioned an attack of dizziness and near fainting, with associated palpitations and breathlessness when boarding a train with her husband. A neurologic exam had revealed nothing pathologic but psychotherapy was suggested. Her group advised therapy with a woman but counseled against Freudian psychoanalysis. Dutifully, Rowena interviewed a Gestalt analyst, a Jungian analyst, a transactional analyst, and, finally, myself. She had a contract for eight weeks in Gestalt therapy but thought that she could see me at the same time. I told her that by working with two such divergent approaches she might become confused and internally divided. To prove me wrong, Rowena decided that she wanted to see me anyway. I advised waiting until either the Gestalt contract was fulfilled or until she felt ready to commit herself to psychoanalysis. Whereupon Rowena, correctly, I thought, pointed out to me that she saw it as my job to help her resolve her dilemma. We agreed on a schedule and an interaction ensued that was to last nine years.

Developmental History

Rowena was the second child and first daughter among six children of a fundamentalist clergyman, the Reverend Mr. A. and his wife, "the Mrs." The father insisted on being called Reverend, although this was not usual in his denomination. He also expected his congregation to be very respectful of his "Mrs." who taught Sunday school and was involved in many parish duties. They lived in a fairly affluent Northeastern timbertown where an old-fashioned value system was not only preached but rigorously adhered to. Fire and brimstone threats of punishment in an afterlife permeated the very air Rowena and her siblings breathed. But she adored her demanding, exciting father anyway when she was little. She was his avowed favorite. He took her along on visits to the old and infirm and showed her off as "his little beauty." The old folks were allowed to pinch the child's cheek, to fondle her, and to cluck over her frilly clothes. Rowena came to hate the fussy ribbons and bows she was decked out in and beseeched her parents for jeans and slacks. But her father sternly forbade such garments for "his little woman." Rowena's older brother, Jacob, however, was permitted to climb and run and to carry on what were considered to be male pursuits. He was not chided for coming home dirty or when he had fights with the town children.

Rowena thoroughly detested dolls and games of family and preferred to jump, run, and climb also. She had already begun to think of herself as different from other girls and felt certain that her boisterous behavior distressed her mother whom she idealized as supremely gentle and feminine. Later, she thought her mother was frightened of her.

As an adult, Rowena had a curious, warding off gesture in which she made her arms stiff and turned her hands palm outward whenever she disagreed with something or felt threatened. We eventually discovered that this gesture had to do with holding her father at bay. When she was two or three years old her father seated her on the railing of their porch and demanded that she jump from this high perch into his arms. He wanted to make her fearless. The frightened child complied and learned to hold in what she really felt. Curiously, she re-membered these early happenings after the analysis helped her to uncover "the flimmering behind my eyes and my heart beating so fast and my breath almost stopping." Her mother used to hover close by but did not interfere. Father and daugh-ter were united in devaluing mother by calling her "scaredycat." Mother did interfere when Rowena "touched herself" in fear and in anticipation when father announced that it was time for the "flying game." Rowena was taken to the toilet, and when she couldn't urinate, was examined for signs of "contamination." Rowena thought contamination meant feces in her "front." She puzzled about why mother thought her "front" would produce matter she knew came out of the "back."

Another game father liked was to load his children on a sled, harness it to his car, and then to careen the screaming children down Main Street. This won the approval of his pa-rishioners but frightened the children out of their wits. "Almost all of us peed in our pants when he did that" Rowena reported. "Mother even told him to stop but he said, 'If you provide what they need at home, they don't go thrill-seeking elsewhere.' So mother just cleaned us up and made sure we went [to the toilet] before he loaded us on the sled. She thought we screamed with joy."

The panic and loss of body boundaries, as well as the mem-ory of lack of physical and psychological control caused by these dangerous games were to surface in various derivative ways in the analysis many times.

A young brother, Joseph, was a particular burden to Ro-wena. Only eighteen months her junior, he was sickly and a whiner. Rowena felt he got the lion's share of mother's atten-tion. Even when they bathed together, mother washed Joseph "between the legs" while Rowena was handed a washcloth to attend to herself. By the time Rowena was four years old and Joseph about two-and-a-half, father happened to notice that the little boy had an erection in the bath and forbade the "com-munal ablutions." Rowena thought this must be her fault some-how, and felt deeply resentful that her only physically commu-nicative time with her mother had been taken from her. She now had to bathe alone and mother no longer towel-dried her.

She yearned for hugs and kisses from her mother and became more resentful and sullen each time she was handled and fondled by the aged parishioners on the visits with her father. She intuited that the old folks pawed her for reasons of their own and wanted her father to rescue her. But he never seemed to notice her distress. At about this time, mother became deeply withdrawn and had many fainting spells. In the analysis, it was reconstructed and then confirmed by the mother, that the unfortunate woman had suffered a miscarriage and a year later gave birth to a child that only lived for seven days (both of these were female). Officially, Rowena and the other children knew nothing of this. In the analysis, there was for a long time an amnesia, a dead spot Rowena complained about. Somehow she knew that this was the time during which the inferiority of the female sex was imprinted on her as a fact. Concomitantly, the father, in deep mourning for the dead infants, stopped paying attention to the living children and immersed himself in the study of the Bible in order to understand what sins he had committed to call such terrible punishment down upon his head.

He came to the conclusion that his own sins were not involved but that some unspecified "perversions" in his ancestors were being visited upon him and his family. "He worked so hard to prevent us from being perverse that he bred a pervert—me!" Rowena exclaimed. She thought this humorous, and only late in the analysis recognized the tragedy involved in such unconscious acceptance and search for perversion in her parents (Socarides, 1978).

At the time, Rowena again thought all this preoccupation with sin must be her fault and that it had to do with her femaleness because she was now required to keep her bedroom door open and, on occasion, woke up to find her father staring at her. Her mother kept admonishing her "not to touch herself." For a while, Rowena thought mother meant not to get herself dirty while playing and turned into "Miss Priss," an extra careful, doleful, and obedient child. Her reward was that mother fussed with her hair, producing Shirley Temple curls, and bought black patent leather shoes for the little girl. In later years, when Rowena had fully evolved into the positive and energetic persona she retained into adulthood, her parents often harked back with regret to this time when Rowena was "good." They had been unable to recognize that in actuality Rowena was depressed. Despite the ever present vigilance of father, Rowena saw herself as unprotected and alone. She felt empty. In order to comfort herself, she began to sing to herself after being sent to bed. She discovered that if she sang loudly enough, her parents would sometimes come to the landing and listen. Another, more important discovery for Rowena was that with her singing she could stop the noises coming from the parental bedroom directly across the hall from her own room. That door was also kept open, ostensibly so that mother could monitor everybody's toileting. During the analysis, Rowena remembered sneaking to her parents' bedroom door to investigate the origin of the strange noises. She insisted that she did not know what was going on when she saw bedclothes moving and body parts exposed. She assumed that father was terrorizing mother as he terrorized his children. She began to feel deeply sorry for her gentle mother whom she wished she could protect.

By the time Rowena was seven years old, three more siblings had been born in rapid succession, two boys and a girl. Rowena was called upon to help take care of the babies and heartily despised them. Even as an adult, she spoke of her siblings as puny, stupid, and demanding. She was surprised halfway through the analysis to find that her brother and sister admired and envied her "spunk" and often sought her advice. Recalling the upbringing of her younger brothers and sister allowed Rowena to investigate her own infancy more fully. Her mother nursed all the babies until six months of age, then fed them gruel, oatmeal, and milk until they were two years old. This was in "order not to arouse the evils of the flesh too early." At first, Rowena rationalized these feeding procedures as good for the maturation of the digestive system, a view shared by some contemporary pediatricians. Then she began to understand that from early on, aggression was quite literally forbidden in her family. Even biting food was prohibited early and sucking was considered too sensuous. Rowena also recalled several other crucial events that sharpened her aggression and precluded her identification with her mother. During all of the pregnancies her mother had fainting spells. The tiny, panic-stricken Rowena would then run for her father and, if he was not there, put blankets over her mother and try to pray for her. Fantasies of mother dying and being revived by her little daughter began to solidify into defensively omnipotent assumptions that Rowena could rule life and death. Later, these early experiences were sexualized and replayed in homosexual encounters.

When Rowena was a toddler, she and her brother, Jacob, were placed for play in the fresh air into a wire fence enclosure. Jacob soon learned to climb out of it and to reappear when mother called. Rowena tried to emulate him and got caught straddling the fence, hurting her genitals. Mother came running and frantically washed and put lotion on the little girl's vagina. Rowena even as an adult analysand could not understand her mother's frenzy about an organ that was otherwise disavowed, devalued, and even abhorred. "It felt completely numb, so why worry about it," she said. A little after the wire fence incident, she saw a statue of a stone dwarf in a neighbor's garden. She was enchanted by this because it reminded her of pictures she had seen in her fairytale books. She ran up to it, straddled its shoulders and "rode on it." Her father saw her and immediately brought her home to be washed, prayed over, and admonished. Rowena was again amazed. She had been busy imagining herself in a wonderful world full of dwarves and elves where everyone played with her and let her run at will. What did father's prayers have to do with the numb place between her legs?

There were many other developmental traumata that befell Rowena. I have presented only the most crucial events of Rowena's preoedipal years. Living in a chronically restrictive, punitive atmosphere she was forced to construct an imaginary world in which "only nice, pretty ladies like my mother could have nice, lovely babies. Girls like me were nothing and had nothing."

One other, crucial event must be mentioned. During Rowena's latency years, the local sawmill caught fire and many workmen and their would-be rescuers were killed. Rowena's mother and siblings watched the conflagration, prayed, and tried to evade the stink of burning flesh. Her father tried to help the rescue attempts, came home exhausted, cried, went back to help and sank into a blank stupor from which he would not rouse himself for many weeks. Rowena perceived things in her own way: "I knew definitely then that I was different, and always would be. Everybody was sad and afraid and cried or prayed. I was mad that nice people got killed and that those doddering old fools were still there to pinch me. I hated everybody, and especially my father who had more time for old people and dead bodies than for me."

Not only Rowena's internal world seems to have been decisively altered after this catastrophe. Rowena described the once lively and prosperous little town as sepulchral. She herself became wild, but she was devastated when an adored female teacher considered her behavior chaotic. She teamed up with the "bad boys and made a lot of trouble." Her father occasionally roused himself from his depression to buy her clothing and to dissuade her from her wild ways. She said: "He always bought the things I didn't want, never asked me what I wanted, and then told me my legs were too short and my butt too big. It was true, too, and I hated him for telling me."

College was a relief to Rowena. She was an outstanding student, receiving grants and scholarships. She met her husband-to-be as a graduate student. According to her, he was "muscular, blond, handsome, very quiet. He had never been with a woman before, so I thought he would be perfect for me because he wouldn't notice my being different. We experimented sexually but he had a hard time penetrating me, and I didn't lubricate much. I had read all I could about sex since I was a kid but nothing I experienced was like the books said."

There was some difficulty in achieving pregnancy which was quickly and efficiently overcome by following the rules of infertility specialists.

Rowena thought her husband was satisfied with their sex life. He obediently kissed her through veils and made love while she kept her body covered. Her lover, Carmen, however, "lifted her to heights." They made love in front of open windows, on quilts on the floor, in the back of cars, and in the bathtub. But

Rowena "knew this life was not for me." She felt superior to the "dykes and creeps who can't be trusted." She had already put Carmen on notice that she might move out when she started analysis.

The Course of Therapy

The Search for the Ideal Mother: Rowena, at first analytic glance, seemed to be an oedipal homosexual (Socarides, 1978, 1988) possessed of penis envy and all its derivatives. She unconsciously appeared to wish for the male role with the mother. Included in this stance were incomplete feminine identifications. The homosexual act was not at all ego alien to her. Although clearly driven to it by forces beyond her control, she rationalized it as "curiosity about what women do."

Rowena's many ego strengths, including outstanding intelligence and devotion to hard work, as well as the ability to see different projects through to their successful end, at first hid the fact that fixations occurred before the age of three. In the transference, however, it became clear almost immediately that she had been unsuccessful in traversing the separation–individuation phase, thus showing that she had been unable to reach the oedipal phase. A subtype of an idealizing transference developed (Kohut, 1971; Siegel, 1988).

The early sessions were taken up with a shy courting of the analyst. Rowena brought beautiful homegrown roses and later, vegetables to the analyst. Attempts to analytically understand these gifts were met with hurt silence. She had produced something beautiful and wanted to share it with the analyst, period. Her verbal flow ceased. She wanted to be accepted, her gifts were to be accepted and that was that. But there was one question that plagued Rowena. She wanted to know if the analyst were homosexual. When asked why she thought so, she remarked that the analyst "seemed to know all about cunnilingus." Then she dropped this line of inquiry and confessed instead that she feared her husband might give her cancer because he was uncircumcised. She could not acknowledge the hostility expressed in this thought, nor did she see any connection to events in her past. Confusingly, Rowena's first dream again seemed to point toward oedipal castration anxiety while all her other productions appeared much less evolved. She dreamed that a surgeon probed her eye with a knife but didn't hurt her. While bicycling fast, a black police car overtook her and warned her that she was going too fast. Where she was going, there was no bed for her to sleep in.

The first association that jumped into her mind was that she must be a dead body on the couch, viewed from the analyst's position. She thought her lover, Carmen, might be the surgeon probing her eye. The many deaths her father had officiated at came to mind, and the Oedipus myth. But why was she being sought by the police? Rowena thought her life quite free from shame and guilt, using feminist political ideology to rationalize the abandonment of her children. The dream and its associations threw her into turmoil from which she found it hard to emerge. She claimed to feel whole and good only during her sessions. The analyst was felt to be the source of all soothing goodness. Even Carmen could not hold a candle to the analyst's charms and omniscience. It didn't seem to matter much what the analyst said, as long as it was delivered in a soft and neutral way. Any change or shift in position of the analyst in her chair was heard and commented upon. Often she "checked out" what she heard by turning around on the couch and looking. The possibility that the analyst might also represent the probing eye surgeon was contemptuously scoffed at, as well as the idea that seeing herself as a dead body on the analyst's couch might be an identification with her fainting mother or her father's dead parishioners. Rowena refuted everything by informing the analyst that the analyst's function was to listen and to be "there." Carmen became more important than ever. She introduced Rowena to a group of women who liked to wear tight jeans in order to constantly stimulate their genitals. They promised untold ecstasies to Carmen and Rowena but Rowena was reluctant to participate in group sex. She feared she might pick up some disease that way. She also felt that Carmen was pressuring her too much and decided to move back to her family. She claimed to miss her house and gardens, not her husband and children.

Hypochondriacal Concerns with the Body Self: Rowena was deeply disappointed that she was not praised by the analyst for moving back home. She began to experience excruciating headaches, abdominal tensions, and states of dizziness. She was doubly upset when medical examinations revealed no ailments. She insisted that she had migraines and possibly cancer of the cervix or the beginning of muscular dystrophy. She acknowledged that there "might be a psychological component" to all this but was "at a loss how to link it all up." She absolutely and positively denied feeling rage or in any way negative toward the analyst. The only person who possibly could make her angry was her husband, who accepted her return as silently as he had accepted her departure. He often approached her sexually. She tried to "show him what was pleasant but did not succeed." He also suffered from unspecified and uninvestigated muscle spasms which disturbed Rowena's sleep. He had to leave her bed after sexual intercourse. She was very angry about this. She said that "once again she was deprived of nonsexual affection and body contact." Carmen had provided more of that. Yet this homosexual affair was now relegated to the realm of "experimentation." Her husband was viewed as an unfeeling monster who did not give her any money which, on second thought, she didn't want from him anyway. She preferred to earn her own money and to be independent. Cautious analytic inquiry as to whether she perhaps felt displeased with the analyst also for not providing body contact, was dismissed with a haughty sniff. She claimed that she understood the analytic rules, didn't expect to break them, and wondered why the analyst was so self-centered as to think she, Rowena, would need body contact from the analyst. She began to pamper herself with special diets, vitamins, and stress reduction techniques. With these new preoccupations she could hardly find time to fit in her sessions; as a matter of fact, she only continued because unpleasant dreams added to her headaches. Still, a working alliance had formed and Rowena's hypochondriacal preoccupations bound aggression sufficiently to stave off further fragmentation. It helped her to suppress rage at both her husband and her analyst.

She dreamed that two ugly, narrow-faced youths who spoke French, a language she did not understand, were in my waiting room. The door to my office was open, and I was not tall and blond but small and dark, speaking in an incomprehensible tongue. Some abstract paintings fell from the wall and broke. She referred two children to me who were covered with hair from the waist down, like fauns. I was dressed like a charwoman. I called her mother and betrayed her.

The recitation of this dream was accompanied by complaints about sleep disturbances and a carefully executed schedule of when and how often her sleep had been interrupted. She perseverated about the impossibility of establishing a true measurement of the length of time she was forced to stay awake. She seemed not to hear a question by the analyst as to what she thought the dream might mean. Finally, she said that she had read Freud's *The Interpretation of Dreams,* and felt that her dream reversed reality, that's all. She didn't recognize her hapless sons in the two lanky, hard-to-understand youths. What mattered was her physical well-being. Nor was she able to look at the devaluation of the analyst. Equally unacceptable was the idea that the hairy, faunlike children could symbolize her sexually immature sons whom she wanted to hand to the analyst for mothering along with her own sexually immature self.

Rowena, at this time, was vociferous in the cause of sexual freedom for women. This, rather than other ideas, interested her.

Rowena, like other homosexual women in the same phase of treatment, needed her hypochrondriacal preoccupations to feel her body boundaries and to stave off acknowledgment of her incomplete body image. However, fantasies of bodily mutilation heralded the emergence of preconscious knowledge about this.

Penetration by her husband was always followed by an increase in symptoms, which finally culminated in a dream of wearing a tailcoat, being naked from the waist down, while a man yanked a chain that was fastened around her neck.

Rowena's rage became intense when the analyst asked if she felt controlled. She brought in another chart in which she traced her husband's sexual behavior, timed his thrusts, and finally explained her own lack of responsiveness as caused by his supposed premature ejaculations. With the execution of the chart, Rowena directed her rage away from herself to her husband. As a result, the hypochondriasis diminished.

Denial of the Need for a Good-Enough Mother and Simultaneous Need to Re-create the Mother–Child Dyad: By this time, Rowena felt that "she could not do without the analyst." Some recognition had dawned that she felt better after ventilating her disappointments. She was often tearful, usually when she felt misunderstood. When it was interpreted that she must have felt very hurt by being misunderstood, she was startled. Her affect vacillated according to whether she felt merged with the analyst as part of her grandiose self or whether she felt deserted. Some childhood memories emerged, and she began to talk of her parents. She dreamed that two bald eagles frightened a flock of birds and that her mother fell into a brook, slipping on a mossy stone. She associated to mother's fainting spells but also absolutely denied feeling frightened and helpless then or now. The analyst reminded her of an Indian in ceremonial robes which, on second thought, was "a projection." Rowena had decided to help the analysis along by reading a lot of semianalytic books and by keeping a dream diary. She had heard that famous people did that and later published the results. Which famous people? Freud's early analysands! So while the analyst was now like Freud, she was also totally useless and needed help. Rowena's reactivated grandiose self held sway everywhere in her life. Her husband and the boys practically disappeared from her reports, and the emphasis was on career advancement and on finding a new woman to love.

Projection of Body Image Distortions onto the Analyst: Three years into the analysis, Rowena had begun to experience summer breaks and minor absences of the analyst as a painful loss of part of her self. She sometimes called separations a "rape of the soul." She cried about being alone and then contemptuously said that she didn't need the analyst anyway, she needed the rest. She had decided on a career change and settled on medicine as her next profession. Her previous training uniquely suited her for this change, she felt. There had been an alleviation of symptoms. Rowena was able to recall many childhood

incidents and acknowledged some of her hurt and disappointment in her parents, in particular, that they had preferred boys
to girls.

When the next summer break loomed, Rowena wanted "to
die voluptuously." She thought death would be like having an
orgasm and spoke with great disdain of the "ridiculous Freudian idea" that there is such a thing as a vaginal orgasm. She
spoke of a lack of nerve endings in the walls of the vagina and
of the impossibility of feeling anything there. She bemoaned
her husband's inability to please her sexually, and stated that
only a woman could physically fulfill another woman. The question of whether the analyst had ever had a homosexual encounter was raised again but with a new facet. This time around,
Rowena thought the analyst might be bisexual, although she
phrased this delicately, claiming to have seen a man enter the
analyst's living quarters. She asserted that she "just knew that
this was the analyst's husband." She also claimed to smell men-
strual odors in the office and questioned whether they were the
analyst's or her own. She was sad that the analyst might have a
husband and yearned to be the analyst's best friend.

At this point, she had been accepted in medical school
and had started classes. She immediately became furious with a
female professor who seemed to favor her. Why? The professor
must be homosexual. When the analyst cautiously inquired as
to Rowena's current sexual orientation, she was told: "It's obvious. A real homosexual doesn't sleep with men. That life is not
for me." She became coldly furious at this question, but insisted
that she and the analyst were "entirely the same." This meant
that "sexual differences didn't matter to a truly evolved human
being."

Simultaneously, she confessed that after the heated one-
way arguments she engaged in on the couch, she lubricated
copiously. Aggression was sexualized.

She ardently pursued and abhorred the echoing–mirroring presence of the analyst (Kohut, 1968) when the omnipotent
and grandiose fantasies of having both a penis and a vagina
surfaced. She again berated "Victorian Freudian dogma" when
the analyst interpreted that perhaps she needed to imagine

herself in the possession of the attributes of both sexes in order to hide from herself the lack of feeling in the genital area.

Analyst Introject Fantasies: Although deeply involved in the analytic process and the analytic setting, Rowena had not yet reached a self to object transference. Her incomplete body image and faulty self representation still prevented her from taking in the analyst as a person. Transference interpretations were felt to be ego-alien intrusions into a closed-off world of pseudointimacies (Khan, 1979). Yet it was clear that an internalization process was also taking place. As Dorpat (1974) put it, a reparative internalization process takes place which evolves from a stage of a fantasy relationship involving imitative identification with the analyst, to a later stage of selective identification with the analyst (p. 183).

Rowena now aped the analyst's syntax and accent, grew her hair longer, and wore similar fashions. She began to boast about her analyst to others, and was pleased when a common chance acquaintance commented on the similarity in clothing. In the sessions, she now strained mightily to "give the right answers, to say what you want me to say." She could not recall that just a short while ago the analyst had been viewed by her as unempathic, even cruel. But she was able to make a link between this phase and the time in her childhood when she had so desperately tried to please her mother. She also reported having imaginary conversations with the analyst who was her "make-believe best friend."

Homosexuality as a Defense Against Transference: All these new feeling states aroused panic in Rowena. The reality of the analyst in sessions felt different to her from the analyst of her fantasies. She began to dream of aphids invading her vagina, trees being uprooted in a storm, herself tearing out saplings and of finding little, desiccated kitties in cubbyholes. She herself linked all this to the inability of her parents to nurture her femininity appropriately. She mourned their emotional unavailability but became frightened at the thought that she might feel as though "the analyst were her second mother." She felt an "emotional earthquake" was devastating her and spent many

sessions in cathartic sobbing. She eventually accepted an interpretation that she was becoming aware of feelings in her vagina
and was perhaps in the process of giving up the wish for a
penis. "All people are androgenous" she countered, "why do
Freudians think that trees are penises and boxes and kittens
are vaginas?" Despite this disavowal she thought there might
be something for her in these thoughts because (1) "they felt
right even though they were junk." She could feel it in her
body; (2) "if you substituted female power striving for penis, it
was true." Now Rowena became convinced that "something she
didn't even like in analysis" forced her to exchange "the longing
for power for warm feelings in her vagina." She thought this
might be an uneven but inevitable exchange. And no, she was
neither resigned nor depressed, merely realistic, she said. The
formerly disdained woman professor was giving her a lot of
attention. She was better informed than the other students. Her
husband and sons were leaving her alone. Her life was just fine
and in perfect order now, she claimed. If the analyst didn't
persist in making these self-centered transference interpretations, she'd be in good shape. Finally, she recognized that "the
professor was putting a move on her." Appalled, she was nevertheless aroused. She noted that she had sexual feelings, lubri-
cating both in the presence of the professor and the analyst.
Rowena was acutely ashamed of this phenomenon. She fantasized about palaces filled with flowing draperies and a dais of
flowers on which the analyst held court, with herself as hand-
maiden. She still refused to see this as a repetition of a certain
phase of her experience with her mother who was viewed as a
beautiful, fragile queen whose babies did not all thrive. But
slowly an awareness dawned that a mother whose babies died
and who removed herself from her living children could be a
difficult model to follow. Rowena now became filled with a
passionate longing to know if the analyst had children, a husband, and lovers. She wanted to be a woman like the analyst.
The feelings in her vagina became acceptable to her. She also
began to view her husband with greater kindness and felt compassion for his emotional ineptness and, in particular, for his
sleep disturbances.

An intensely emotional period followed during which Rowena thought she literally smelled the analyst and gauged her responses in accordance to what this often fantasized smell conveyed to her. This could be perfume, presumed menses, cooking odors, or flowering plants. Finally, a link to the burning timber mills of her childhood home was understood. The deep fear surfaced that the analyst, too, might be taken from her by catastrophe, as well as the wish that the analyst might burn in hell as Rowena burned in a hell of her own. After this was worked through, Rowena had clearly taken the quantum leap into a transference neurosis in which her developmental traumata could eventually be replaced by new and more beneficial internalizations.

DISCUSSION

It took another four years to reach the conclusion of this particular analysis. I have focused on the long and stormy initial five years in order to call attention to the fact that patients like Rowena are forced by arrested development to form incomplete self and object representations. The arrest is a specific one. The body image is incomplete and its completion is sought for in the homosexual encounter.

For women like Rowena this inevitably means lack of genital schematization, not always fully visible at the beginning of treatment. The Rowenas of this world are usually full of praise for their sexual adventures, not realizing that they farm out their vaginas to others like themselves in the hope of garnering any feelings at all. The familiar complaints of emptiness, loneliness, desperation, of the black hole that can't be filled up or which opens into a void, is regularly traceable to the inability to traverse the early genital phase (Roiphe and Galenson, 1981) and the resultant lack of schematization of the genital area. Merging and fusing mechanisms are resorted to, as can be seen in the way Rowena used her partial transferences in treatment in a way that was reminiscent of the incomplete relationships she had with significant others of her past. Self-involved parents who tried to force her into the rigid mold of their own narrow world unwittingly increased her aggressive drives by withholding narcissistic enhancement and support. Rowena adaptively developed ego strengths which allowed her to survive intellectually. Nonetheless, she was enslaved by her faulty self and object representations which drove her into homosexual encounters in the search for the missing part of herself, namely her uncathected and unavailable vagina.

Countertransference Responses: This report about Rowena is by no means complete. Space constraints make it necessary to emphasize only those aspects which are similar in Rowena's case to those of others I have treated. This includes my countertransference responses to these women. In my opinion, many psychoanalytic treatments of homosexual patients fail because analysts too are imprinted with societal restrictions, fears, and taboos. For myself, that initially meant abandoning so-called liberal ideas about the state of homosexuality in our society. My patients taught me that there was no choice involved for them, that they were driven toward homosexuality by internal forces they did not understand until very late in their analysis. Far from being especially liberated and free, these women revealed themselves to be particularly enslaved by their sexual needs and deprivations. Their passionate demands often left me feeling drained, even persecuted. I constantly felt challenged to define femaleness and femininity, in particular my own. It was not until I understood some of my somatic responses as part of the countertransference patterns evoked by these patients that I was able to get on with the interpretive work. For instance, the affect storms many of these analysands experienced were often part and parcel of oral aggressive fantasies and rages which slightly nauseated me. Not surprisingly, I do not relish being viewed as something eatable, even though I understand intellectually that little children think–feel concretely: I will swallow that important person, then I will have her forever. This phenomenon occurred when a very early transference had already been established but was disavowed by the patients. My nausea did not disappear until the analysands had understood their wish to devour me. I was not pleased to note that, at first, I wanted to counterattack with some aggression of my own in the wish to stop analyzing and to start counseling. It was only when I acknowledged my temporary helplessness when faced with Rowena's wish to bite my cheeks and perhaps my breasts that I could let nausea surface and to keep on interpreting.

Another countertransferentially difficult phase arose when I was endowed by my analysands, among them Rowena, with a fictive penis. I felt sleepy, irritable, and put upon until I realized that the fantasized phallus was projected onto me in order to block out the possibly disintegrating need for the maternal breast. As long as mother was felt to be malevolent, her milk was also poisonous. In the transference of these women at that point, I became the feared mother who dispensed poisonous interpretations. This combined attack on my ability to mother and on my analytic skills made me cranky indeed. Strangely, I did not understand this until I noticed that I often found myself going for a walk before Rowena's sessions, barely making it back on time for her. I clearly wanted to run from her. There were other somatic responses, such as a cough and the need to exercise strenuously, which alerted me to nonverbally transmitted primitive needs in my patients and in myself. For instance, I could understand Rowena's olfactory symptoms and need for olfactory incorporation only after recapturing the smell of bombed-out cities in wartorn Europe where I grew up. The stench of death was in my nostrils also.

It is not helpful in such cases to speak of one's own incomplete analysis or of the unanalyzability of the patient. Investigation of how to deal analytically with deeply regressive demands, and how to allow for temporary regression, including somatic responses in the analyst, will bring better results. The countertransferential conviction that Rowena, too, could grow out of her incompleteness helped me to provide the analytic holding environment so desperately needed for symbolization, internalization, and finally, structure, to arise.

CHAPTER 4

Homosexual and Preoedipal Issues in the Psychoanalytic Psychotherapy of a Female-to-Male Transsexual

WILLIAM S. MEYER, M.S.W.
CHARLES R. KEITH, M.D.

INTRODUCTION

In this paper, we explore the history, dynamics, and psychoanalytic treatment of a thirty-seven-year-old white female who identifies herself as a female-to-male transsexual. We contrast female transsexualism with homosexuality and propose that in transsexualism there is a blocking of the homosexual developmental line. The case we present is particularly unusual because of the length of time (4 years) this patient has remained committed to exploratory intensive psychoanalytic therapy in the motivational context of desire for anatomical change.

FEMALE TRANSSEXUALISM: A REVIEW OF PSYCHOANALYTIC CONTRIBUTIONS

The *transsexual,* a term first coined by Cauldwell (1949), is defined by Socarides (1970) as a person who suffers from a psychiatric syndrome characterized by: (1) an intense and insistent wish or desire for sexual transformation into a person of the opposite sex; (2) the conviction that one is "basically" a person of the opposite sex; (3) imitation of the behavior of the opposite

75

sex; and (4) the insistent search for physical transformation into the opposite sex, even to the point of self-mutilating acts.

Lothstein (1983), who has evaluated and treated over fifty-three female transsexuals, states that such patients can be placed on a spectrum of psychopathology. On one end are those with the most impaired ego functioning in nongender areas of their personalities. Such patients evidence minimal self–object differentiation; many are overtly psychotic. On the other end, which contains the overwhelming majority of female transsexuals, are those with a borderline personality organization representing a variety of schizoid and paranoid disorders.

Socarides (1970, 1978, 1988) believes that transsexualism, like almost all other sexual perversions, represents a primary preoedipal fixation. This fixation, he says, occurs between eighteen months and three years of age, and is the result of a basic nuclear conflict: the wish for/dread of maternal reengulfment. This conflict results from a failure to successfully traverse separation–individuation phases, a disturbance in gender defined self-identity, and varying degrees of pathology of internalized object relations. Children who later become transsexuals suffer from overwhelming anxiety, body-ego deficiencies, fears of engulfment, and paranoid fears of attack (Socarides, 1975).[1]

Volkan and his coauthors (Volkan and Bhatti, 1973; Volkan, 1974; Volkan and Berent, 1976; Kavanaugh and Volkan, 1978–1979; Volkan, 1980; and Volkan and Masri, 1989) support and expand upon these ideas. In the female transsexual, they too note the presence of severe unresolved preoedipal conflicts related to psychic separation from the mother. They document six themes characteristic of the female transsexual: (1) The mother has been martyred, depressed, and sexually hungry, and her child has developed intense rescue fantasies. (2) The child has unconscious fantasies that she could save her mother only if she were male. (3) The child places something between her legs to symbolize a penis, which psychologically links her to her mother and assuages separation anxiety. (4)

---

[1]In 1988, Socarides suggested that there are various forms of transsexualism (oedipal, preoedipal, and schizotranssexualism) depending on the patient's level of fixation.

Simultaneously, the symbolic penis serves to separate the girl from the depressed mother who lacks a penis. Thus such symbols both link *and* unlink the child's self representation with that of the object representation. (5) The child has suffered an actual physical trauma which is congruent with or echoes the girl's unconscious fantasies about her genitals. (6) At the oedipal age, the girl yearns to be loved and rescued by her father from the intense relationship with her mother. When this fails, she identifies with him, thus consolidating the preoedipal image of child with phallus.

Stoller (1985) comments that during childhood the female-to-male transsexual impresses observers as being masculine, often passes undetected as a boy, plays only with boys, and takes a boy's name. Pauly (1974), who reviewed eighty such cases throughout the world, described how remarkably similar were the histories of female transsexuals.

This paper will explore the history and provide case material concerning Ms. Jones (pseudonym), a woman who identifies herself as a female-to-male transsexual. Ms. Jones is a biologically normal woman according to physical examinations and laboratory tests performed by an endocrinologist at a university hospital. Ms. Jones has been seen three times weekly for over four years in intensive face-to-face psychotherapy. While in treatment Ms. Jones decided to receive testosterone injections and has been living as a male for two years.

CASE PRESENTATION

Ms. Jones, a thirty-seven-year-old white single female, came for treatment to get help with her feelings of extreme fear and neediness. She presented as a bright, articulate, highly anxious woman. She was small and thin, her hair was short and disheveled, and her style of dress gave an androgynous appearance. In one of our first sessions I[2] noted that she was wearing girls' black patent leather shoes, men's gray slacks, and a boy's green jacket. Usually she wore a baseball-type cap and tended to resemble a latency-aged boy. She was a graduate student who

---

[2]First person references to the therapist refer to W.S.M.

rented a single room not far from the campus. Because of multiple fears, she often avoided going out among people.

Ms. Jones stated that many of her problems were rooted in difficulties related to gender. Since early childhood she held the conviction that she was actually a male residing in the body of an anatomical female. In her early twenties she had assumed a male identity for approximately two years. However, pressures from family and others in her support system prompted a return to the previous life-style in which her appearance reflected gender ambiguity.

In our fourth meeting, she reported the first of many dreams. "I have come to a doctor's office for a physical. The doctor never shows up so I do the procedures to myself. I take my temperature, but I am unable to take my blood pressure. I sit down and begin playing a piano. The piano makes weird noises, and suddenly I am transported somewhere else. An earthquake is occurring. My mother is being buried alive; she yells for me to get her out. I don't want to. Then I wake up." Another dream, several weeks later, reveals conflicts of similar intensity: "I am in a trailer with my wife. They were both me. We were fighting and yelling at each other. She started throwing things. I picked up a plank, swung it, and hit her in the stomach. I meant to kill her. I think I did. Then I woke up. I'm supposed to be female. Sometimes it feels right but my identity sure feels male." As we were to discover, themes related to killing the mother had played a prominent role in Ms. Jones's fantasies since early childhood.

As treatment has unfolded the clinical data points to some interesting findings: (1) that Ms. Jones has merged psychic images of her own anatomy with those of a "bad" mother representation; (2) that she has chronically experienced these juxtaposed representations as loathsome and dangerous; (3) that she has been involved in an ongoing battle since early childhood to "kill off" these representations; (4) that such struggles have filled her with anticipatory separation anxiety and an overpowering sense of guilt which accompany these symbolic "murders"; and (5) that in fantasy, she imagines herself as a boy sexually linked with his mother in an attempt to maintain a connection with the "good" mother representation.

In the next section we will present information, all of which has been obtained from Ms. Jones, about her family and her early development. We have organized the material by developmental phases and will later highlight those factors which likely contributed to Ms. Jones becoming a female transsexual.

The Family

Ms. Jones was adopted at age three months by an upper-middle-class couple who already had a six-year-old adopted girl. Ms. Jones described her adoptive mother as a shallow, insensitive woman who was gregarious and charming in public, but embittered and depressed at home. Her mother ruminated about vague physical complaints and spent most days either in bed, or lying around the house in her bathrobe. Ms. Jones's father was sexually impotent, and he and his wife stopped trying to have sex after the first year of their marriage. Ms. Jones remembered her adoptive father as a sensitive, but quiet and reserved man who was dominated by his wife.

Infancy and Early Childhood

Ms. Jones's early history is remarkable in that immediately after her adoption she was intermittently quite ill. In quick succession she contracted measles, chicken pox, and then nearly died from an allergic reaction to sulfa drugs. Ms. Jones also remembers an injury she suffered between the ages of two to three years. "I sat on a fence post and injured myself. I think I split open my clitoris. There was a lot of blood. I was petrified, but too young to be able to express myself verbally." Ms. Jones related that later in her childhood she had constructed a fantasy around this incident; namely, that she once had a penis, but lost it.

Ms. Jones feels that she received mixed messages regarding her gender identity from her mother. Overtly, her mother attempted to enforce a feminine appearance upon her. The mother, in describing her own childhood, said that she never had any dolls and that she had always dreamed of having girls who were dainty, delicate, and who would wear white furry coats. Ms. Jones felt humiliated and treated like "a thing" when her mother insisted that she wear white pinafores, petticoats, and curls.

On a deeper level, Ms. Jones felt that her mother rewarded her for being masculine. If she were playing with dolls or other girls, she remembers her mother withdrawing emotionally; if she were playing with boys or boy games, her mother showed interest. "I've always had the idea that if I had a penis my mother would hold me and love me and that deep down she wanted me to be a boy." At age three, Ms. Jones decided she was a boy, and she was certain that her destiny was to grow up male, marry a woman, and become a father.

While Ms. Jones feels certain that she and her mother once enjoyed closeness, her most distinct memory is of her mother turning her back or pushing her away. She remembers her mother as always having a cigarette in her hand which resulted in a frequent fear on Ms. Jones's part of being burned. Throughout early childhood, Ms. Jones had a speech impediment. Until much later when she had speech therapy in elementary school, her mother was the only person who could readily understand her. This made it necessary for the mother to be involved in all verbal interactions between her daughter and anyone else.

The Oedipal Period

Ms. Jones was quite ill between the ages of four, when she had a tonsillectomy, and seven, when she had an appendectomy. Both surgeries were traumatic, and experienced as life-threatening. In between these surgeries, she had ongoing problems with stomach pains, constipation, and refusals to eat. Her mother routinely administered suppositories, an experience Ms. Jones hated and found humiliating.

Ms. Jones recalled that due to her illnesses, she stayed at home and felt trapped by mother much of the time. She described a fantasy of being in a room that had a window but no door. While the window allowed her to magically leave, the absence of a door kept her mother from coming in. She remembers feeling that her mother was oblivious to her emotional needs and relentless in "coming after me." She remembers turning to her father for protection. "I remember thinking, 'Dad, I'm helpless, but you are not. You have a penis and you can protect me.' "

Ms. Jones idealized her father. Sometimes when she was in pain he rubbed her back or stroked her hair while she sat on his lap. "I never got past the idea of my father being a God. He was always bigger than life. Sometimes I would look at my father and feel like I was looking at perfection. But he was just there. We would work together and he wouldn't talk. I never remember a discussion with him about how he felt about anything. He would always be off in the distance someplace. Maybe that's why I hung around him so much—because I kept wanting something from him. I rarely felt validated by him. I remember feeling, 'Look Dad, why don't you notice me? Can't you see I'm just like you?' "

Her early heroes were cowboys. She imagined going home with Roy Rogers and being his son. Between the ages of three and five, her favorite possession was a cowboy hat. She "lived in it" and took it everywhere. One day, her mother told her that her father had burned it because it smelled so bad. Ms. Jones has painful and bitter memories associated with this incident.

She remembers shadowing her father around the house. They played ball or checkers and watched the fights together. He had a number of playful, but decidedly masculine nicknames for her, such as "Jack," "Hyram," or "Shoot-Luke." She senses that it was not so much that he wanted her to be a boy, but rather that he felt uncomfortable that she was a girl. At age five she took on a boy's nickname. In her early twenties she made it her legal name.

The Latency Period

Ms. Jones's latency years were, relatively speaking, less traumatic. She was not as sick, played ball with the boys, went fishing with her father, and excelled at school. Occasional painful reminders of her gender problem arose, however, such as not being allowed to play in the Little League.

During Ms. Jones's latency years, not a day went by that she did not pray for or fantasize about having a penis. She also reported that while she would never touch her vagina, she had masturbated daily since she was eight years old. "I would touch myself everywhere—except my vagina. I must have known more than I let on to myself, because I was very clear where I drew the boundaries, as far as touching myself. I was scared; as though if I touched my genitals a guillotine would chop my head off."

Ms. Jones felt enraged when others didn't understand about her mother's intrusiveness and insensitivity, telling her how lucky she was to have such a wonderful mother. "There are things about my mother that no one understood. For instance, when I was eight or nine I was really into stamp collecting. One day I walked in and there was my mother putting my stamps in *my* book! It was like every time I turned around there she was inside of me."

Ms. Jones reports having the following fantasy when she was about seven: "I imagined that I was one of a set of multiple births, or that I was from a very large family. My father liked me sometimes, but then sometimes he didn't. One of the reasons he didn't like me was that I had killed my mother."

Puberty and Adolescence

Ms. Jones felt certain that as a girl she was a profound disappointment to her father. She recalled an incident from the time she was eleven illustrative of how she may have distorted her father's sentiments. She had been in the shower, and called for help to turn on the water. Her father came in and upon viewing his naked daughter, told her to put a towel around herself. "I felt embarrassed. I felt like he was pushing me away. I felt like he was angry—as though he were saying, 'I don't like the way you are; don't remind me that you're not a boy.' " Throughout adolescence she had a recurrent beating fantasy: "My mother had died a long time ago. A neighbor's barn had burned down, and the neighbor—thinking I had done it—caught me and began beating me. My father was there, but he just stood silently and watched."

Ms. Jones felt horrified when her body began changing along its inexorable path toward physical maturity. "Somewhere between the ages of twelve and fourteen my body started changing. I tried to hide it, and not to notice. When my period came . . . I had to notice. When I started menstruating I felt like I had committed some crime. I wanted to die. I felt trapped."

She described her junior high school experience as "horrible." "I had no one. When I had to take a shower for swimming I felt like I was somewhere I didn't belong. I tried not to think about it; I would change clothes and leave as quickly as I could." In an apparent attempt to disassociate herself from femininity, she would neither use deodorant nor comb her hair. Other students referred to her as "Mouse" or "Bone."

Ms. Jones continued to be plagued by physical problems. At age thirteen she developed her first stomach ulcer. She also had a protruding lower jaw, which was of particular concern to her mother. The parents had a brace devised for her that was very uncomfortable, and at age sixteen she had a piece cut from her lower jaw. Ms. Jones believed these procedures were linked to the needs of her mother, who, Ms. Jones felt, was attempting to fix her defective child.

On a few rare occasions Ms. Jones dated boys, primarily due to family and social pressures. She remained relatively isolated throughout much of her adolescence. She retreated into books and fantasy, but avoided any books which might have sexual themes. During her senior year of high school, she went to a private, all-girls school. In college, she became increasingly reclusive, although as always she did well academically. At age nineteen she had her first experience of sexual intercourse with a young man. It marked the first time that Ms. Jones consciously recognized that her body contained a vaginal opening. She graduated from college the following year.

Young Adulthood

After college, Ms. Jones decided to present herself as male. When she told her father he wept and said he could imagine how painful life must be for her. Her mother, reportedly, was unmoved and chatted about reports of transsexual surgery in

Europe. Ms. Jones found a good job and developed several relationships without anyone knowing she was female. She has since described this period as, "The one time in my life I knew what it was to be alive."

Shortly thereafter her father died. Without his support, Ms. Jones caved in to pressure from family and acquaintances and agreed to stop trying to pass herself off as male.

She rented space in the house of a wealthy, older, married couple. In time, she and the husband began to secretly have an affair. Ms. Jones enjoyed the relationship, although only for the "closeness" it afforded her. She imagined herself a young boy who was doing his father's bidding. The relationship continued, but, after a time, only on the condition that he agree not to penetrate her. This condition persisted with other men in several subsequent brief relationships. While her primary sexual attraction had been to women, she had thus far not had a sexual relationship with a female. She claimed that her female anatomy would make the relationship homosexual, and she was raised to believe that homosexuality was immoral.

Preoedipal and Oedipal Themes in the Case

Theoretical Background: To explain the complexities of adult psychopathology by reconstructing the remote past is an exercise fraught with pitfalls and, at best, can only result in crude approximations. It is nonetheless striking to note how comparable are the dynamics and how similar the histories of female transsexuals. We have only to look to the first such in-depth clinical report in which Redmount (1953) described the dynamics of a thirty-three-year-old female transsexual. He noted that a male identity seemed to be the only type of adjustment in which his patient felt any degree of security and protection. Further, this identity seemed to provide her with "a way of relating to the idealized mother whom she needed" (p. 110). These themes have since been echoed and elaborated upon by nearly all subsequent investigations into the dynamics of this condition.

Severe disturbances in early development are characteristic of the histories of girls who go on to develop female transsexualism. It is not surprising that such severe conflicts related to a girl's feminine identification would be rooted in problems associated with the earliest stages of the mother–daughter relationship. In each of the histories of fourteen such patients studied by Stoller (1975b), there was a reported "rupture" in the mother–infant symbiosis. This was due either to the mother's depression, or to a lengthy separation between mother and infant with no adequate provision of a mother substitute. Mahler (1975), while allowing for some influence from the constitutional makeup of the child, surmised that the road toward transsexualism could only begin if there was severe trauma and conflict during the baby's earliest stages.

Greenacre (1967) states that when an infant is unduly threatened by early experiences of object loss and body dissolution, this can result in an unstable formation of the body image and uncertainty about the outline of the body. This is particularly true for the genital area. Roiphe and Galenson (1981) found that severe disturbances in the pregenital phase were correlated with profound castration anxiety in the phallic phase. Indeed, in eight of thirty-three girls they studied who developed intense preoedipal castration reactions, *all* had experienced an important threat to either their developing body image or their maternal relationship during the first year.

We do not have any preadoption information about Ms. Jones. We can speculate, however, that the change of caretakers at three months, followed by multiple physical illnesses, contributed to a premature differentiation and a strained, if not traumatic, early development. The adoptive mother's inability to relieve the baby's pain and discomfort would have likely compromised however much of a good object she was capable of being. These unfortunate circumstances could reinforce aggression toward and consolidation of the "bad" mother "bad" self image (Abse, 1980). Kernberg (1975) cites "vicious circles involving projection of aggression and reintrojection of aggressively determined object and self images" (p. 27) as major factors in the development of psychosis and borderline personality organization. And it is out of many such images that the child gradually creates self and object *representations* which endure (Sandler and Rosenblatt, 1962).

Jacobson (1964) describes how during the first years of psychological development, the child's self and object images have introjective and projective qualities. Such primitive mechanisms produce the earliest types of identifications which correspond to *fusions* of self and object images. Such fusions disregard the realistic differences between the self and the object. Jacobson notes Melanie Klein's observations that very young children and primitive personalities may at times experience their mental functions *or their body organs* as foreign bodies which they want to expel. Jacobson explains that while such notions are temporary and reversible in small children, such ideas in psychotics may turn into fixed, delusional convictions.

The female transsexual is similar to the borderline in that despite her use of defensive splitting she does, for the most part, differentiate between self and object representations. The female transsexual, however, has one particular feature which more closely resembles the psychotic. The female transsexual experiences her own feminine anatomy as though it were *fused* with the representation of the dangerous, engulfing mother (Abse, 1980). Thus the girl must vigilantly deny the reality of her body in an effort to remain safe from the fused, split-off bad mother/genital representation.

The need to defend against the representation of the engulfing mother was later reinforced by the circumstances of Ms. Jones's illnesses and speech impediment, which resulted in an unusually prolonged dependence on mother. The need to ward off the intrusive mother could have contributed to Ms. Jones's problems around eating. Volkan (1980) wrote of another case of a female transsexual who refused to eat as a child, which he linked with the child's attempt to defend herself against mother's penetration. In the case of Ms. Jones, however, such defenses were likely overpowered by the mother's use of suppositories. This would only strengthen the image of mother as invader while further compromising Ms. Jones's body integrity.

Ms. Jones looked to father to help extricate her from the intense dyadic struggle with her and mother. The father's perceived absence during this phase, either in the physical or psychological sense, is considered a contributing factor in the development of female transsexualism (Volkan and Masri, 1989).

The female transsexual yearns to be loved by the father; yet she feels that as a girl she has failed him. "Sadly bereft of her father's love, she consoles herself by identifying with him" (Volkan and Bhatti, 1973, p. 277).

Stoller (1985) states that fathers of female transsexuals stimulate their daughters toward precocious ego development so that the daughter will serve in their place to comfort the depressed, unreachable mother. Later, as in the case of Ms. Jones, the father takes the daughter as his buddy, and encourages her masculine behavior and interests.

The latency period of the female transsexual is active (Volkan and Masri, 1989). The girl cannot put to rest her unnegotiated developmental tasks nor her object relations conflicts. Her ability to use repression is severely compromised by reliance on the splitting of contradictory images of the self and other.

The function of Ms. Jones's daily masturbation, which began in latency, might best be understood by the work of Galenson and Roiphe (1976). The infant, having been held, washed, powdered, and so forth, associates stimulation with the image of the mother. Later, when the child actively stimulates herself, she is maintaining not only a relationship with her own body, but a link to the image of the mother as well. Masturbation can then be used as a means to assuage loss and separation anxiety. Thus, while fantasizing herself a boy, Ms. Jones's masturbation served to both unite her with the "good" mother representation, and relieve her of the anxiety of being one with the representation of the "bad" mother. Ms. Jones's central masturbatory fantasy lends support to this notion:

I am a normal boy, and I am in sort of a prison camp. I am naked and there is a woman—either a mother or a baby-sitter—who is ordering me around. I obey only because I am threatened with punishment, usually by a man who looks on from the distance. Then the woman begins to masturbate my penis. This fantasy leads into the next, or sometimes, vice versa. In the second fantasy I am in charge of the woman and I threaten her. If she doesn't do what I order then I will lock her up in a box. I have her hold onto my penis and I spank her very hard. [Another fantasy]: A number of women hold me down and stimulate me until I have an erection. While I am on my back, one of the women mounts me. I use my hands to explore this woman's body while we have intercourse.

Transsexualism Vis-à-Vis Homosexuality: Some authors have viewed female-to-male transsexuals as simply an extreme form of homosexuality. This generalization does injustice to the complexities of transsexualism. Further, we would argue that there is a homosexual developmental line which has been blocked in the female transsexual. In the case of Ms. Jones, we believe that there has been a massive developmental disruption and resulting fixation of this homosexual developmental line.

If we begin with a general definition of homosexuality as love for the same-sex object, we can map out a developmental line for homosexuality which begins with the girl's attachment and love for the mother. Around twenty to twenty-four months of age girls enter into an active, dyadic preoedipal phase which has been described as "phallic–narcissistic" (Edgcumbe and Burgner, 1975; Rees, 1987). We will elaborate on this further below.

As development proceeds, increased self–object differentiation ushers in the capacity for triadic relationships, necessary for the full development of rivalrous negative oedipal strivings. Roth (1988) contends that while the negative Oedipus can function defensively against the positive oedipal situation, it is also a normal developmental process. "The girl attains a sense of feminine competence by feeling attractive to mother as a sexual figure, eliminating mother's need for father, nurturing her, and sharing a fantasied child with her. Once she feels equal to mother, she can then attempt meaningful rivalry with her in the positive oedipal period" (p. 54). With further development, sublimation, and neutralization, the normal latency-aged girl develops strong, same-sex peer relations while retaining the underlying tie to the mother. Negative oedipal themes continue to be reworked through the developmental milestones of adolescence, career, marriage, pregnancy, birth, and child rearing (Roth, 1988).

In the normal phallic–narcissistic phase, children tend to believe that both males and females have phalli leading to what Freud described as the "phallocentric view of the universe."

This occurs when there is a relative lack of self–object differentiation. In girls, a dyadic phallic competitiveness, based largely on voyeurism and exhibitionism, emerges between mother and daughter. This stage fuels competitiveness with mother while enhancing identification with her (Edgcumbe and Burgner, 1975; Rees, 1987).

We believe that Ms. Jones has suffered a massive developmental disruption, resulting in a fixation at this phallic–narcissistic phase. She has maintained a quasi-delusional belief that her magical phallus can maintain a safe libidinal tie with the mother while at the same time it can prevent merger with the engulfing, "cancerous," destructive maternal imago. This intense perseverative preoccupation has blocked her forward development into the subsequent stages of penis envy and eventual acceptance of the reality that she has female genitals.

Most homosexuals, both male and female, generally accept on conscious and unconscious levels that they have genitals congruent with their biological and socially assigned gender. In treatment our patient has revealed strong superego injunctions against homosexual activities. When she is able to entertain a "lesbian" fantasy, she is jarred by the fact that the fantasied woman lover would discover that the patient has the disavowed female genitals. Thus we believe that Ms. Jones has experienced a serious fixation at the phallic–narcissistic phase which has blocked further emergence of a homosexual developmental line.

Course of Treatment: The initial treatment focus had little to do directly with concerns about gender confusion. Rather, the overriding task was to establish an alliance and create a holding environment for this very disturbed patient. In the first months, Ms. Jones talked about her near-constant feelings of fear and vulnerability. During one of our earlier sessions, Ms. Jones was startled when I crossed my legs. She said, "It doesn't make sense, but sometimes when you change positions like that, I'm afraid you'll come and hit me. I remember once having crawled out of my crib, only to hear my mother coming up the stairs. I tried to crawl back in the crib but couldn't. She had a look on her face like she wanted to kill me."

At the next session she reported the following dream: "I am in a car, but I'm not driving. The driver was a nice looking man, but I thought, 'I shouldn't be driving with this stranger.' Suddenly he tried to strangle me with his necktie. If I shifted my position to kick him, I'd be unable to keep the noose away. At first I thought the driver was you, but the more I thought about it, he had my eyes."

At a later point in the first year of treatment, Ms. Jones, rather than fearing me, began to see me mostly as her protector. "At night, I imagine that you're with me, and then I don't have nightmares anymore." She imaginatively elaborated upon this theme in the months to come. For example, "At night I clutch my pillow. I pretend that it's a stuffed tiger that you gave me. It makes me feel better. I don't care if I grow up—I just want you to be my father." Some weeks later, "I fantasize that you're my father and I live with you. It's the nicest fantasy I've ever had. At night I have you come in and say good night. You always make sure I feel safe. You see that I'm tucked in and that I have my tiger." (Volkan [1980] points out that the female transsexual lives in a world she regards as dangerous. She does not know that much of what she fears is, in actuality, an externalized part of herself. Hence she experiences an urgent need for allies to protect her.)

The wish that I be her protective father persisted throughout treatment. At times, the fact that this could not actually be enraged her. She would plead with me to take her to my home so she could live with me. She would become infuriated when I would suggest that we explore and try to understand the meaning of the request. This issue became especially difficult when I was away, however briefly. It upset her so much, she told me, because it reminded her that I was really not her father; for if I was she would be going with me.

During my earliest absences she appeared psychologically depleted and disoriented, with gross impairments in her ability to function. She invariably called and requested an appointment with the female colleague who provided back-up coverage for me. Upon my return, extra phone calls and additional appointments were necessary to help her reintegrate. On several occasions hospitalization was actively considered.

Later in treatment she revealed that during my absences, or whenever she sensed anger to or from me, her image of herself was more distinctly male. We came to understand that any feeling of vulnerability prompted within her an intense need to be "attached" to or identified with a male.

During the second year of treatment she struggled with questions about her self identity. She said, "I'm involved in some activities with all these guys. But I don't know if I want to be one of them any more. I feel like Gregor in Kafka's *Metamorphosis*. Gregor spends his whole life trying to please everyone. One day he wakes up and his body is changing into an insect. All the people he's taken care of begin to ignore him and he starves to death. Mostly he dies of loneliness."

Shortly thereafter she told me, "I want to be sure of two things [regarding her decisions about gender identity]; one is that my feelings are mine and that I'm not just trying to please you, and second is that you won't leave if I don't please you." I worked hard to respect her autonomy in this matter. She stated that treatment had become the most important part of her life because, she said, it was the only place she felt like she existed.

She dropped out of graduate school and began teaching courses at the college level. She became more social and increased her involvement in church and community activities. She began living with a family: a woman, who was newly separated from her husband, and her two children, a boy and a girl. She consolidated warm and caring relationships within this family.

Several months prior to the third year of treatment, we talked about various issues as they related to Ms. Jones's lack of self-care. Among them was the fact that Ms. Jones had not seen a physician in years, and she had never received a full medical workup. I facilitated a referral to a recommended university-based endocrinologist. Several weeks later, to my consternation, Ms. Jones informed me that she had decided to begin taking testosterone injections under the guidance of the endocrinologist.

I did not try to prohibit this, but did stress the importance of our exploring her motivations. However much her decision was inspired by fears related to a deepening of the transference, she steadfastly maintained that her decision to take testosterone was based solely on a newfound confidence in herself. She no longer felt, she said, that she had to pretend to be anything but what she experienced her true self to be. To this day, she continues receiving injections.

In the weeks to come, Ms. Jones began assuming a male identity. In spite of my recommendations to wait and think through all the implications of her decision, she decided to let others know that she was now a male. To acquaintances she knew less well she would say, "My parents had to make a decision when I was young [suggesting that there were biological ambiguities]; unfortunately they made the wrong decision." Ms. Jones reported that people were far more compassionate if they thought the problem a physical one.

There was a dramatic improvement in Ms. Jones's physical appearance and expressions of self-confidence. Although the testosterone caused her to break out in acne, she began taking better care of herself physically. She began wearing a coat and tie (the styles she chose were strikingly similar to my mode of dress). She claimed that she now felt good about looking in the mirror and seeing facial hair and muscle mass. Further, she acknowledged taking more showers.

Ms. Jones described what appears to be a common view of a transsexual toward herself: "I've been reading about transsexuals. Sometimes I'll read about someone like me who is, I think, inappropriately referred to as a woman and a homosexual. My identity is male, not a female who wants to be a male. Sometimes I liken myself to someone who went off to war and had his testicles shot off. That person would be no less of a man."

In spite of this apparent "resolution" in the third year of treatment, the clinical material and related transference themes revealed severe inner turmoil. Four topics repeatedly emerged: (1) uncertainty about her gender; (2) hatred and fear of the mother; (3) intense penis envy; and (4) fears of sexuality.

Two of her dreams suggested a deep uneasiness about her decision: (1) "I was with this guy named Tony. At one point he put his hand in my crotch and said, 'There's nothing there. You're a fake.' " (2) My minister came up to me and whispered in my ear, 'You've made a mistake about your gender.' " A later dream portrays the morass of confusion she felt: "I am in the waiting room of a doctor's office. Sitting next to me is a little boy who is sickly and has bad teeth. It was unclear where his mother was. I spoke with him and felt a sort of identification with him. He had to go to the bathroom so I took him. He said he was four years old, though he looked younger. He was wearing a diaper. He sat down to urinate, but I told him he didn't need to—that he could stand. He stood and joyously urinated all over the room. I was upset with him and gave him a water hose to clean the room. He did but then he was suddenly wearing a dress and he threw up all over himself. I picked up the hose and tried to clean him off."

Ms. Jones developed a growing awareness of longing for, and hatred and fear of her mother. She reported fantasies of hitting women and active death wishes toward her mother. "My mother is the spider who encases you in a silken web and you can't get out. I've always been afraid of her. She's the black widow ready to devour the male. She always intruded upon me and never acknowledged that I existed in my own right. It was as though I had no identity. I think that's what upset her most when I started living as a man—that she couldn't take control of me anymore."

A dream elaborated: "I am on a bicycle, and I pass by what I think is a corpse on the ground. I am hesitant to look at it because I don't want to be the one who found it. Suddenly, it turns into a large bear and I think I must look this bear in the eyes. The bear comes at me to hug me and I notice the bear's long claws. I think even if the bear is kind, it's likely to harm me. When I awaken I think that the bear must be my mother."

Longings for a penis and her sense that she was profoundly defective without one were unmistakable, as illustrated in another dream: "I was about to write something on a white board, the kind one writes on with felt-tipped markers. As I started to write I became concerned that my father would come in and see what I wrote and I would feel humiliated. Ultimately my father did come in and although he did not laugh at me, I kept thinking that he would. Part of this had to do with my sense that there was something defective in the marker I was using."

When I suggested her concern seemed to be about feeling humiliated if she revealed something, she remembered a subsequent dream from the same night: "I was masturbating. When I looked down I was pleasantly surprised to see I had a long, thin penis."

Fears of the penis as a powerful destructive weapon repeatedly surfaced in her dreams: (1) "I was in the sixth house in a row of houses. There was a man in a car that I think was you. I felt certain that the man was going to ram his car into my front door. I was carrying a cat and petting it—reassuring it that everything was going to be all right. But I was really quite afraid." (2) "I am in a car circling around, and you're there with a gun—a bazooka. I got out of the car and you started shooting at the cars that were going by. When you'd hit them they'd explode. I tell you that I don't have a gun, but that I have a knife, although I really don't know how to use it."

In the fourth treatment year, our work increasingly focused on what appeared to be the core underpinnings of Ms. Jones's psychopathology; namely, that images of the bad, engulfing mother had been merged with her female anatomy. This framework enhanced our understanding of her urges to rid herself of her feminine body which she had heretofore experienced as cancerous, loathsome, and devouring. My initial explorations of this theme, however sensitively ventured, evoked intense anxiety as the following dream illustrates:

"Someone was trying to get into my apartment to kill me, and I tried to wake the dogs to defend me. But the dogs were sleeping. They had a hypodermic needle stuck in their flanks [an allusion to the testosterone injections?], and they couldn't be aroused." Associations: "I have been reading *The Lord of the Flies* and was struck by the children's fear of the Beast. I know I have my own fears of the Beast. It's as though if I pull down the zipper the Beast will be there."

Immediately following such sessions, when Ms. Jones felt particularly frightened or threatened, she would become all the more resolute about living as a male. It is difficult to convey how unwavering and intense was her conviction that she would never consider "going back" to being a woman.

Yet doubts would inevitably appear in subsequent dreams and associations. Although it upset her considerably, I brought these doubts to her attention. She once raged at me, "All you want to do is burst my bubble. I feel like screaming at you and hitting you. No one has ever accepted me for who I am. For forty years I have been male and I want you to be someone who says, 'Yes, you are who you say you are!' "

Following such instances—and there were many—I felt guilty and wrestled with the question about switching therapy to a more supportive approach, one which would accept the seeming finality of the patient's decision to live as a man. The material in subsequent sessions, however, invariably revealed that Ms. Jones's decision was unmistakably an ambivalent one. Then, when her anger at my interventions subsided, she said that even though she didn't like it, she supposed it was all right even if I did see her as female, and that on some level she found my consistent approach reassuring. During one such contemplative moment she said, "Sometimes I feel like the tapestry of who I am is all woven into place, except for one loose thread. Sometimes I wonder, will this thread be woven neatly back into the tapestry, or, if we start pulling on it, will we unravel the whole thing?"

As we enter the fifth year of treatment we are unable to predict the outcome. There are no existing reports (Stoller, 1985) of patients who have successfully resolved such problems through intensive psychotherapy or psychoanalysis. Yet, Ms. Jones continues with an unfailing commitment to treatment. She possesses an uneasy awareness that ongoing intensive work can only further illuminate the hopes, fears, and conflicts which underlie her struggle to reconcile the gender discrepancy that exists between her mind and body.

SUMMARY

In this paper we have presented the case of a woman who identifies herself as a female transsexual. By examining the patient's history and treatment we have tried to illuminate some of the determinants of this condition. We have proposed that Ms. Jones has been fixated at the phallic–narcissistic phase of development which has blocked further emergence of a homosexual developmental line. If treatment is able to progress and help her development resume its forward thrust, we might then observe not only emerging heterosexual positive oedipal fantasies but also homosexual fantasies and interests indicative of the negative Oedipus. Thus we would view the emergence of homosexual issues as progressive forward movement if they were accompanied by beliefs that she was engaging in the homosexual activities as a woman with female genitals.

Addendum: Much has occurred in the two plus years since this article was written for publication. Ms. Jones is doing very well. She continues in treatment, has stopped taking the testosterone, and is living as a woman. Updated clinical material will appear in a future article.

CHAPTER 5

The Narcissistic Imperative and Therapeutic Alliance in the Opening Phase of the Analytic Treatment of Male Homosexuals

HOWARD B. LEVINE, M.D.

INTRODUCTION

Every act of psychological relevance serves an adaptive purpose. This is particularly true in the narcissistic sphere of mental life, where considerations of adaptation can go beyond the very important dimensions of instinctual gratification (pleasure–pain motivations) to issues of psychic homeostasis. By the latter, I refer to the various regulatory mechanisms of the ego that modulate affect and self-esteem and maintain a stable and coherent organization of the self and object world, including a fundamental inner sense of attachment to primary objects. Where patients cannot autonomously provide an effective level of psychic homeostasis, their emotional comfort and adaptive capacities may remain precarious at best. In such situations, effective regulation of psychic states may be contingent upon interpersonal transactions that are experienced by the patient as nonnegotiable needs. These, in turn, can give rise to chronic behaviors that appear to an outside observer as dependent, controlling, self-centered, or entitled. Failure of the object to act in accordance with these needs produces states of personal

97

distress and interpersonal conflict. In such instances, therapeutic technique requires that the level of ego dysfunction and the symptoms to which it gives rise must be addressed interpretively, as a prerequisite for the successful engagement and maintenance of a stable analytic setting.

The issue is a complex one. For some patients, the object relationship with the analyst can serve a stabilizing function in and of itself, which permits the treatment process to move forward in a way that is truly analytic. To the degree to which an analysis unfolds in just this fashion, we can speak of the analytic setting providing the patient with a holding environment (Modell, 1976), within which the relationship to the analyst offers sufficient support or the conditions for silent growth needed to foster the development of a therapeutic alliance (Zetzel, 1958). It should be noted that this provision is often inadvertent, in that it may require no special activities on the part of the analyst other than those which fall within the bounds of ordinary analytic technique. It is more a matter of the use to which the patient puts the analytic relationship and situation independent of the intention of the analyst. That is, while the analyst may wish to analyze, the patient may, for a time, prefer, or need, to draw emotional succor from such factors as the presence, stability, acceptance, and nonretaliating stance of the analyst.

In those treatments in which a therapeutic alliance and analytic process are not established, we do not have a therapeutic setting conducive to true analytic progress. Rather, such an analytic situation may only allow for an unstable equilibrium based on the use of the analyst as "sustaining object" (Levine, 1979). In such instances, further psychotherapeutic work is needed to help the patient develop a stability and capacity for engagement in a true analytic process (Corwin [1974] has attempted to conceptualize the progressive aspect of this mode of relationship within the therapeutic situation as a "narcissistic alliance.").

In either case, whether the analytic relationship and setting fosters the development needed for the analysand to engage in a true therapeutic alliance or functions for the analysand as a refuge from the world or an auxiliary, homeostasis-regulating ego (i.e., a narcissistic alliance or sustaining object relationship), it is ultimately of great importance, *if possible*, to analyze (articulate and explore) this use and the needs (i.e., ego deficits) from which it springs. Failure to do so, no mattter what the cause, can result in severely limited therapeutic results or interminable treatments.

For some patients, the functions of self-regulation and psychic homeostasis may be so precariouss that such analytic work may not be possible until the later stages of treatment. This can make for a prolonged and difficult opening and middle phase, because it is precisely these issues of threatened psychic equilibrium that hold the potential for serious disruptions in the treatment process, and, indeed, in the lives of our patients, and which often take therapeutic precedence over other areas of potential analytic scrutiny. Failure to accord them such precedence can create insurmountable perturbations in the analytic field, as the claims of these issues are experienced by the patient, either consciously or unconsciously, not as wishes, but as needs felt to be essential for existence—matters of life or death. It is for these reasons of felt urgency and therapeutic precedence that I have termed this dimension of psychic functioning *the narcissistic imperative*. I will here examine its importance in the opening phases of the treatment of male homosexuals who come to analysis with the manifest goal of changing their sexual orientation. Before I do so, however, some further clarification of the problem of homosexuality is in order.

THEORETICAL CONSIDERATIONS

The emergence of homosexuality in the personality of a given individual is a complex process and involves many factors. What I am concerned with here is not necessarily related to development, but may refer more, or perhaps even exclusively, to dynamic factors that operate only after the homosexuality has been established as a behavioral pattern or fantasy system. What I wish to call attention to is the way in which some patients use homosexual fantasy and/or behavior in the maintenance of psychic equilibrium and the implications which that use has for the opening stages of a treatment that includes the analysand's expressed wish to change his sexual orientation. Thus, what I will describe may have relevance to the treatment of only some homosexuals. I am not necessarily making a claim for the universality of this phenomenon, other than to say that I believe that bearing the concept of the narcissistic imperative in mind can be generally useful in thinking through the problems of treating any symptomatic manifestation or fantasy system that has become incorporated into the analysand's psychic regulating functions. Perhaps to say this much is simply to call attention to and emphasize a general point that has relevance for the analysis of certain features of the narcissistic part of any personality.

Beginning with Socarides (1968b), psychoanalytic authors have noted that for many patients, homosexual thoughts and behavior can have an "obligatory" quality. That is, homosexual acts and fantasies attain the status of automatic regulatory mechanisms, employed at times of stress to provide affective relief and to help modulate psychic equilibrium (Goldberg [1975] presents a self psychological view of this phenomenon, which he suggests has relevance for the perversions as well). Patients in whom homosexual acts and fantasies have become obligatory find themselves in the unfortunate position of feeling, or acting as if they felt, that they could not live without them. Thus, no matter how strong the conscious motivation to change one's sexual orientation or life-style might be, a homosexual patient who begins analysis with the goal of developing a heterosexual life-style may find himself in the difficult position of feeling that movement toward this very goal is tantamount to being asked to give up something that is seen as essential for (emotional) life, if not literally life sustaining itself. The result is apt to be a very deep, often unconscious, ambivalence about treatment and its goals. This can look very different to different aspects of the patient's mind. From the point of view of conscious motivations and the analysand's desire for change, treatment is seen as an ally. However, at a less conscious and more emotional, behavior-determining level, treatment may be viewed as a real threat to a precarious psychic equilibrium. It threatens to disturb existing compromises and security measures and to throw the patient into a state of serious panic and/or threat. This situation must be attended to by the analyst, if the treatment is to effectively proceed.

The prospects of changing a patient's sexual orientation, weaning him from an obligatory homosexuality toward a life of heterosexual fantasy and behavior, is difficult even in the best of circumstances. Not every homosexual patient who seeks therapy or analysis does so with the wish to change his homosexual orientation. In addition, even among patients who do have such desires or who develop them in the course of a treatment, the work of facilitating that change is very difficult. It is my contention that one important factor in the opening phase of analytic treatment that will determine the success or failure of cases in which there is a wish to attempt such a shift away from homosexuality lies in the domain of the relationship between homosexual fantasies and behavior and the narcissistic imperative. In many cases, successful analysis of the various functions and meaning of the homosexuality must begin with the exploration and elucidation of the purposes, in terms of psychic equilibrium, that the homosexual acts and fantasies serve and the degree to which the underlying weaknesses and/or deficiencies in ego functioning (i.e., the dysequilibrating ego structures and conflicts); the absence of alternative means of providing psychic homeostasis; and the forces that have combined to select the homosexuality as the equilibrium preserving feature of the mind can be analyzed. It is the analysis and working through of these security issues in their genetic, dynamic, and transferential contexts that allows for the unfettering and development or strengthening of alternate means of providing a psychic equilibrium, thereby reducing one set of factors that makes the homosexual behaviors obligatory. What then remains to be analyzed, which will include issues such as fears of damaging or being damaged by the mother—woman or castration threats posed by the father, can be done from a freer and less life- and homeostasis-threatening perspective.

A parallel illustration of the clinical operation of the narcissistic imperative comes from the treatment of patients who have a problem with obesity due to overeating. It is very common to learn that such patients eat to regulate and control affect states, such as anger, depression, or boredom. They also may eat from a generalized sense of deprivation. Such issues as isolation, longing, and low self-esteem are commonly noted to occur as preliminary affective determinants of the moment to moment states which precede or accompany their eating binges. In these cases, the eating is obligatory in the service of affect tolerance and the maintenance of self-esteem. It also has the added advantage of being self-contained and independent of the participation of another object. This is often important, because the genetic precursors of the states of deprivation have to do with strain trauma (Kris, 1956) induced by a primary object, who was experienced by the patient as depriving or unavailable in some other important way. Thus, one message behind the eating is often something to the effect that, "You are so unreliable that I must and will do this entirely by myself." Obviously, the eating and its concomitant fantasies and behaviors will have additional meanings which will be specific for and congruent with the life history of any given patient. These meanings, too, will have to be pursued within the analysis. The eating behavior will be very difficult to relinquish insofar as it augments basic ego functions used to regulate affect, self-esteem, self-organization, and primary object attachment. The consequences of relinquishing this mode of augmentation may be perceived by the patient to be potentially catastrophic, in that it can produce a severe depression, intolerable aloneness, a precipitous drop in self-esteem, the mobilization of a destructive and frustrated rage directed toward a needed primary object. Attempts at analysis may be experienced by the patient as an attacking or stripping away of desperately needed defenses until the regulatory need and the fantasies that accompany it (i.e., the narcissistic imperative) is articulated and explored in its dynamic, genetic, and transferential contexts.

To return to homosexuality, a patient who wants to change his sexual orientation needs a currency within which to begin the exploration and analysis of the issues. The classical formulations of Freud (1910, 1914) emphasized the retreat from the threat of castration anxiety and the wish to reproduce the love relationship with the mother. There is clearly much wisdom in these formulations and much work to be done in the analysis of homosexual patients around these issues. However, my sense is that in many homosexual patients one cannot effectively get to these issues in a meaningful way until one has helped the patient to consolidate his self-regulating, self-esteem maintaining, and affect tolerating capacities. If these mechanisms are not firmly in place, then, as noted above, the development of a therapeutic alliance may be impossible. Any attempt on the part of the analyst to help the analysand move in the direction of the wished for change will be experienced by the latter as a threat to this beleaguered ego. Under such circumstances, the patient will inevitably remain heavily defended against the possibility of change. Therapeutic impasses, in the form of states of unrelatedness and distrust, false compliance, únmodifiable negative transference, and negative therapeutic reactions, will prevail.

CLINICAL ILLUSTRATION

Marty was a thin, bright graduate student who presented for treatment wishing to change his homosexual orientation. Although he was clearly intelligent and accomplished—he was a musician, an ethnologist, a serious collector of art, and had just begun graduate work at a prestigious university—his self-esteem was remarkably low. He did not suffer from depressions, but gradually, as our work together unfolded, we discovered that his homosexual relationship with Bill, a friend and colleague, was, among other things, serving the function of protecting him from a deep and abiding sense of inferiority; that is, his homosexuality was important in regulating self-esteem.

The early part of treatment was marked by a stand-offish attitude in relation to me. Although he clearly wanted to be helped to change and although I came well recommended to him and he seemed to like me, he did not relate to me in a warm or open manner. Partly, this seemed to be an aspect of his compulsive character style. He tended to talk exhaustively about any topic that he was trying to relate to me, but I felt after a while that there was more involved. He complained frequently to me about his lover, Bill, and the effects of Bill's selfish and unempathic orientation toward Marty and the rest of the world, in a way that I found exasperating. This contrasted quite distinctly with Marty's own way of dealing with others, including Bill, which was often quite sensitive and in tune with the needs and feelings of others. In fact, it was Marty's capacity for empathy (which he did not boast of, but which I came to recognize in the many reports of various events in his life that he brought to treatment) that began to alert me to the distance that was in our initial relatedness. When I thought about him outside the sessions, I felt that he was a very nice and likable fellow. I experienced a paternal affection for him and pride in his accomplishments, which contrasted strongly with his own father's negative response to him, particularly since he had revealed his homosexuality. (I considered that the latter also may have contributed to his initial distrust and caution in approaching me, whom he might have seen as another potentially rejecting male authority figure.) Yet, when I was with him, I found that I felt little of anything, was often bored, and sometimes felt as if we could begin to quarrel at any moment, although in fact we never did.

After several months, I became aware that he seemed quite unwilling to talk about his homosexual feelings or thoughts. I considered the possibility that this was partly motivated by shame—he felt and reported many instances of past experiences in which he felt defeated or humiliated by his failure to feel and respond as a heterosexual man or because he was immersed in homosexual thoughts. (He never went through a phase of promiscuity and, in fact, Bill had been his only homosexual partner.) As we began to explore his reluctance to talk with me about his homosexuality, it turned out that Marty had a deep ambivalence to changing, one that was as unexpected for him as it was for me. His surprise at learning that his intentions were divided stimulated his curiosity about himself and aided us in the treatment.

We explored this ambivalence—which sometimes became manifest as a downright refusal to change—and discovered that it had many determinants. For example, there was a part of him that felt outraged that he had been "dealt such a hand." He didn't ask to be homosexual; it wasn't fair. Why should he change when others, most notably his brother and sister (sibling rivalry issues entered strongly here), did not have to? However, what we came round to uncovering that seemed to be the most useful in helping Marty to change the level of his engagement in the treatment was the feeling that homosexual thoughts or behavior gave him something that he desperately needed for his self-esteem.

Marty had read some analytic literature about homosexuality and had become convinced on his own that his homosexual activities were somehow important to his establishing a sense of manhood or heterosexuality. Based on his affect and my own countertransference sense, I felt that this self-discovered insight was genuine—neither a compliance nor an intellectualization. In addition, I began to interpret to him the way in which the homosexuality served in the regulation of his self-esteem, in ways that extended beyond the consolidation of his manhood and masculine self-identity. Thus, the part of him that wished to change his sexual orientation and which was attempting to become allied with me in the treatment task was being opposed by another part that feared the dire consequences that would result if he didn't have this means of regulating his affects and esteem at his disposal.

As we worked on this fundamental conflict that restricted the depth of his analytic engagement and sapped the strength of his therapeutic alliance, we discovered that there were other behaviors that were not so societally and ego dystonic, but were just as necessary for Marty's sense of well-being, and that he acted as if he could not do without them. For instance, Marty felt tied to Bill by the similarity of their interests, which in his case were quite specialized and not liable to be encountered in many other people. As we explored this sense of being bound, we learned how much Marty felt that he couldn't do without someone close at hand to share his interests with. It was as if such sharing was vital to some psychic interest and had to be achieved at any cost. This discovery shed light on why it was so important for him to talk to his parents after each art purchase. (The parents were also avid collectors and were very knowledgeable and often enthusiastic about his latest purchase or discovery. Marty used his own funds for this, so his parents weren't really needed for financial backing for his hobby. He just needed someone to tell his adventures to.) When they weren't available, he found himself sharing the details with Bill. But when Bill, too, was unavailable, he would fill the sessions with descriptions of what he found and bought. These could be quite lengthy and often supplanted any room for other analytic "work" to take place within a given session. However, rather than simply being a *resistance* in the common, dynamic sense of the term (i.e., talking about something less meaningful, because he was avoiding getting down to talking about something that would be anxiety provoking) I felt that he was also enacting an important transaction within the transference. Telling me about the antique trips *was* in itself meaningful for him at that moment. Moreover, it was obligatory, although I cannot say what the consequences would have been had he not told me of his trips. Nor could he explain that to me, as he didn't really know it himself. He knew there was a powerfully strong urge to tell someone about the trips, and with his parents and Bill away and out of reach, I was next in line. The telling had to be done, for reasons that neither of us could yet put fully into words, although he was later able to come to identify the positive changes in his mood that being able to do so produced.

Still later in the treatment, Marty began to observe and clarify the extent to which his need for (homo)sexual activity—be it actual or imagined, with Bill or masturbatory—was determined by his moods. If he was worried about exams or if things weren't going well in his research, he would find himself admiring an attractive male, seeking out sex with Bill, or masturbating "to relieve the tension." With such observations, the homeostatic gain of the sexual behavior began to come into focus in the treatment.

Another important reference point in regard to this development in the therapy was the first time that Marty noted that he did not resort to homosexual fantasy or action in the face of disturbing affects and threats to his self-esteem. This was told to me in an excited fashion. Marty was bursting with the news, which seemed to reflect a variant of the need to tell the parents, or someone, about the art collecting trips. Only now, I was the one with whom he wanted to share this news, an indication, I felt, that he was beginning to be more deeply engaged with me in the search for his heterosexuality and confident masculinity within the treatment. This took place in the second year of treatment, a time frame that reflects the difficulty with which such issues are broached and engaged in by patients who have the need to protect themselves from these terrible states of vulnerability.

DISCUSSION

I have attempted to illustrate an important dimension of the dynamics underlying a young man's unconscious ambivalence in relation to his wish to change his homosexual orientation, and to describe working through this ambivalence on the way to better therapeutic engagement in the opening phase of analysis. The example selected focuses on the fact that the patient's homosexual thoughts and behavior are inextricably linked to homeostatic functions of the ego, and on the dynamic and technical consequences of that linkage for therapeutic alliance formation.

For this particular patient, the areas of homeostatic ego functioning that had become linked to and supported by the homosexual acts and fantasies included self-esteem regulation and affect modulation. It is in the connection between homosexual act and fantasy and the routine mechanisms of psychic regulation that a powerful motivational source for the patient's resistance to change his sexual orientation can lie. It is my conjecture that this is a frequent, although not necessarily universal, issue encountered in the opening phase of the treatments of many homosexual men, who present wishing to change their sexual orientations.

The dynamics of this issue (i.e., symptomatic action or fantasy subserving a primarily adaptive and ego regulatory function) are by no means exclusive to the psychic functioning of homosexuals. Rather, this phenomenon can underlie many different kinds of symptomatic presentations, whenever an analysand suffers from limitations in certain fundamental ego capacities, such as affect regulation, self-esteem maintenance, organization of the self or attachment to primary objects. Hence, what I have described here is simply a specific instance of a more general issue, which I have termed *the narcissistic imperative*. To the extent to which the claims of the narcissistic imperative are present, the failure to analytically address their demands and to give them precedence in timing over the interpretation of other important issues can have serious consequences for successful analytic engagement and therapeutic outcome.

CHAPTER 6

Transitional Phenomena and Anal Narcissism Controlling the Relationship with Representations of the Mother and the Father: The Transference in a Case of Latent Homosexuality

WILLIAM F. GREER, JR., Ph.D.
VAMIK D. VOLKAN, M.D.

It is not unusual for heterosexual men to report homosexual fantasies in the course of psychoanalysis or intensive psychotherapy. Although these fantasies may in some cases be accompanied by erotic arousal, they usually are not.

The term *latent homosexuality* was originally applied to otherwise heterosexual men who entertain homosexual wishes and fantasies. Freud borrowed the notion of constitutional bisexuality from Fleiss in the 1890s, and references to its importance appear in many of his papers as he related bisexuality to dreams (1900), the Oedipus complex (1923a), neurosis (1928), and mental conflict (1937). He regarded latent homosexuality as an expression of the feminine component of man's inherently bisexual nature.

Ovesey (1969), however, was dissatisfied both with labeling as latent homosexuals all men with such wishes and fantasies, and with Freud's explanation of the phenomenon. Accordingly, he made a distinction between a latent state of true homosexuality and one of pseudohomosexuality on the basis of whether or not homosexual fantasies were accompanied by erotic arousal.

After a critical review of the classification systems used by earlier psychoanalysts dealing with homosexuality, Socarides (1978, 1988) developed his own distinction on the basis of three major criteria: (1) the role of conscious and/or unconscious motivation; (2) the developmental stage at which fixation had occurred; and (3) the degree to which internal object relations were pathological. Using these criteria, he identified, differentiated, and defined five forms of homosexuality. The most germane here are the oedipal and preoedipal. The former involves failure to resolve the Oedipus complex and castration anxiety. Because of his anxiety one so classified regresses to secondary identification with the mother, and assumes a female role vis-à-vis another man. The preoedipal form indicates failure to have negotiated separation–individuation from the preoedipal mother. In this case homosexual activities occur in response to a wish for and dread of symbiotic fusion with the mother's representation. Socarides identified within these two types a class of individuals whom he called latent homosexuals because they rarely or never engage in overt homosexual activity. He described two patterns within this type differing from one another in the degree to which the man is conscious of being attracted to other men. The first includes those who have elaborated unconscious homosexual fantasies, the significance of which they may or may not grasp. The second includes those conscious of their sexual fantasies but who, with few exceptions, abstain from overt activity. Some even function heterosexually, although with little pleasure or sense of fulfillment, and prefer to stay single, gaining sexual satisfaction from masturbation to homosexual fantasies. The rest abstain altogether from sexual activity. Socarides holds that the latent homosexual has the same basic intrapsychic structure as his overtly performing counterpart. He acknowledges that the preoedipal homosexual, whether overtly or only latently homosexual, may have unresolved oedipal problems, but he puts his main etiological emphasis on what he calls the "nuclear conflict"—the desire for

and simultaneous dread of fusing with the mother's representation.

Here we present the case of a latent homosexual in treatment with one of us (W.F.G.). Although he could afford no
more than twice weekly sessions and more intensive treatment
would have been better, when he entered his fourth year,
enough material became available to shed light on his psychodynamics. Those reporting on his case here discussed its progress
throughout, and such continuous observation was invaluable.
In spite of Socarides's view that all such patients have the same
intrapsychic structure, we demonstrate that in our case this
patient was fixated at a point between his desire to merge with
the representation of his preoedipal mother and fear of doing
so, and between a desire to reactivate the oedipal struggle and
a dread of its reactivation.

There seemed two possibilities for him to move out of his
fixation: (1) he could engage in *regressive* activity dealing with
separation–individuation from the mother's representation, or
(2) engage in *progressive* activity dealing with identification with
that of the father. Carrying out part of the second course, he
sought an idealized father, seeming to feel the need to engage
in an oedipal struggle with a strong male figure; this motivation
was played out in his treatment. However, since his search
brought anxiety, he kept open his involvement in regressive
activities in order to move beyond his fixation point. The psychodynamics of this one latent homosexual illustrate that his
main intrapsychic operation centered around the task of keeping a balance between preoedipal and oedipal moves. We alert
other analysts to these psychodynamics to see if such patterns
can be found in other cases of latent homosexuality.

IDENTIFICATION OF THE PATIENT

Henry was a thirty-year-old Protestant clergyman, handsome,
articulate, self-possessed, and artistically gifted. Modestly experienced as a pastoral counselor, he disclosed with textbook clar-
ity the symptoms that had prompted him to seek treatment.
They fell easily into two categories that seemed to him unre-
lated. The first had to do with depressive episodes in which he

felt listless, bored, and lonely, experiencing an ineffable sense of emptiness and hunger that nothing seemed to satisfy. He gorged himself on sweets, flipped aimlessly through the television channels, or masturbated while looking at pictures of nude men, engaging in the latter activity several times a day. Of television he said, "I turn it on for company as much as anything else. It mesmerizes me so I can fall asleep."

The second symptom was concerned with homosexual anxiety. He had tried for years to resolve the question of sexual preference but felt he would never succeed in doing so. He had just about decided in favor of men, but wanted to explore this decision before openly declaring himself to be homosexual. His sexual activity was up to this point limited to masturbating while looking at the pictures of male nudes in pornographic films and magazines. Except for a few dates in school and college, he avoided women other than those he saw in the practice of his profession. He said he avoided them because of fear of a sexual overture; he had never had sexual intercourse with a woman, but had twice engaged in homosexual acts with men. His sexual satisfaction came only from masturbation accompanied by homosexual fantasies in which partners "pinched each other's nipples and slapped each other on the buttocks."

History

Both Henry's parents had been married before coming together in a discordant relationship into which Henry was born as an only child, and they separated when he was a year old, divorcing when he was two. The mother won custody of the child, and the father returned to his parental home not far from where Henry lived with his mother. Although he had rights of visitation, the father was seldom involved in their lives, and his work as a mechanic meant he could contribute little to his son's support. Needing to work, Henry's mother left him with baby-sitters. When he was six, his maternal grandmother moved in with mother and child, and Henry remembered her as a warm and loving woman who devoted herself to him in his mother's absence. He recalled with special fondness snuggling under an afghan with her on cold winter nights while they watched their favorite television programs. Her death after a brief illness when he was twelve was a great loss to him, as she had been by far the most devoted of his caretakers. Her death left Henry with a mother he described as rather rigid and duty-bound, very insistent on good manners, obedience, and conformity to social convention. He saw his father so infrequently that he had become little more than a fantasy figure.

Henry's mother had told him that as an infant he had been allergic to a number of foods and had received desensitization shots. She also spoke of a hernia operation that had taken place when he was two. At the age of five he had a corneal ulceration that damaged his left eye so badly that he was declared legally blind. In the following year a corneal transplant was performed; it was the first ever attempted on a child, and it proved to be a complete success, restoring his sight. It had been necessary to immobilize him for a week or so, and his convalescence was lengthy. He recalled a period at about that time when he had been terrified by thoughts of snakes and vampires.

He described himself as a boy as having been quiet and obedient to a fault, and perhaps overly sensitive. He thought that in his early pictures he resembled Shirley Temple. He remembered his mother degrading his father throughout his boyhood, and said that he could always tell by the tone of her voice when it was his father calling her on the telephone. As he grew, his mother claimed that Henry resembled her first husband, whose death Henry thought she had never fully mourned. When Henry began driving she would say that, like her first husband, he "could always find that empty parking space."

He always thought of himself as being different from other boys of his age—odd, inadequate. He claimed to have been stodgy, awkward, and unathletic, avoiding the sports other boys enjoyed because he was ashamed of his poor coordination and afraid of being injured. His envy of boys with a "good build" and athletic ability was so great that he would walk past their homes just to get a glimpse of them without shirts. He made invidious comparison between his body with its "little breasts, straight shoulders, and rolls of fat around the waist" and theirs.

Seeing other boys doing things with their fathers made him acutely aware of his own father's absence from his life.

He felt excruciating shame and humiliation when obliged to take part in games and sports, and came to dread recess, making excuses to get out of it whenever possible. His aversion to athletics persisted into adult life, except for racquetball, which he came to enjoy.

A review of his relationship with his father disclosed that after the divorce the father had limited his visits with Henry mostly to birthdays and holidays, in spite of living nearby. He was in the habit of bringing his son gifts on these occasions. Henry's excitement over a visit would be somewhat dampened by his awareness of his mother's scorn for her ex-husband, and this animated a dormant conflict of loyalty. He sensed, beneath the formal pleasantries his parents exchanged, that they were separated by a vast emotional chasm.

Henry was conscious of an irrepressible fascination with his father's body when the two were alone; he wanted to be close to his father, see him without a shirt, and roughhouse with him. His barrel chest and muscular arms were the epitome of what his son wanted to develop, but Henry was afraid that he would never have hair on his chest like his father's. In spite of being fascinated, Henry felt an undercurrent of discomfort when with his father "because I was never sure what was going to happen." Since there was no daily interaction between father and son, the man remained a stranger to whom Henry felt unconnected "either biologically or psychologically." He said thoughtfully, "The man was and still is a mystery to me." It should be noted that his mother found her son's aggressive play with his father boorish, and strenuously objected once when she found them "lying around the house in their underwear." Dismayed by her indignation, Henry began to conceal his masculine interest and strivings from her.

When Henry was in latency, his father took him on summer vacations to places of historical interest, but the boy was inexplicably anxious when alone with him, even more so after his mother confided that the father was an alcoholic. Henry recalled feeling panic when his father once ordered beer with his meal; he had thought that he would "get out of control" and his mother would have to be called. No problem developed, however, and he never told his mother.

His father's visits became increasingly infrequent after his grandmother died. Henry was almost exclusively in the care of a mother whose life revolved around the church. On the few occasions when his father did visit him, Henry responded to him with ceremonial respect that both concealed and expressed the rage he felt toward him, which he vented in a diary he kept throughout most of his adolescence. One entry was memorable; Henry paraphrased it as "Dad has no business in my life now. It's too late!"

In his late adolescence Henry's mother insisted that he visit his father and his paternal grandparents. In compliance he made occasional visits to their home, the deplorable condition of which shocked him; the house was dark, dank, and ill-cared for. His father's family drank well into the night and slept most of the day that followed. His father lay about in his underwear, only dressing to go to work. (In retrospect it was clear to Henry his father was sinking into chronic alcoholic deterioration.) After Henry left for college at eighteen, his paternal grandparents died within a year of one another; Henry wept at the news of the death of his widowed grandmother "not for her but for him [his father] because I knew he would be completely alone." The garage where his father worked closed soon after this, and, unable to find other employment, he quickly succumbed to the ravages of alcoholism.

Henry saw his mother as an efficient, conventional proponent of lofty morals who had tried since his infancy to inculcate her standards in her son. Henry could not recall her ever having been physically affectionate; she disciplined him by using guilt, which she re-enforced by Biblical injunctions whenever necessary, to bring him to heel. She often told him that God would not look with favor on a son disrespectful toward his mother. Portrayed as punitive, her God became a wrathful tyrant meting out horrific punishment for the least transgression. Henry envisioned Him enthroned in His heavenly mansion poised to dispatch him. On the rare occasions when Henry defied her, his mother dissolved in tears of self-condemnation, wailing, "Where have I gone wrong?" Since it upset him to see her so distraught and vulnerable, he was quick to repent and contritely submit to her wishes.

Nothing seemed to please her more than the thought that he might one day enter the ministry. Being steeped in the religious ideals of her faith and the regional awe of the clergy, she impressed him with the nobility of a career in the service of the church. He came to consider it his bounden duty to "rescue her, make her happy, and be her consolation in life."

As he approached puberty, he became increasingly preoccupied with his stodginess and what he thought of as his poor muscular development. He bought body-building magazines and gazed for hours at the pictures of muscular men. When his mother found them hidden under his mattress, she berated him for "sneakiness." Not long after this she found among his toys in the attic drawings of naked men he had made as a younger boy, and again scolded him for his lurid imagination, insisting that he pray for forgiveness. Intensely self-conscious about his body, he ordered a set of barbells to build a more muscular physique; when his mother refused to pay for them, he paid for them himself from his allowance. It was probably not fortuitous that she selected this time to speak of how deeply moved she was by the story of Christ's crucifixion.

While in high school Henry won the admiration of his teachers and peers for being an accomplished violinist and scholar, and a student leader. This compensated in some degree for his inactive social life, and his dependence on his mother, but much later, when a patient, he still recalled his envy of "the jocks." This period of his life was difficult and painful for him because of his feeling of being alienated from the interests of other young people.

As he began his freshman year in college he resolved to change and improve on the kind of experience that had been his in high school. A clean slate lay before him. He was stunned by a sudden physical attraction to his roommate, "a handsome, well-built athletic fellow who wore tight shorts around the campus." Although he had felt different from other boys in high school, he had never had homosexual fantasies or wishes, but he now started to masturbate to fantasies of sexual activity with his roommate. Abashed and confused, he sought the help of a "gay counselor" off campus, who urged him to experiment with homosexuality, offering himself as a partner. He carried on a relationship of mutual masturbation and fellatio with the counselor for several months, but abruptly broke away, and abstained for the rest of his time in college. He feared being branded "a faggot," and became what he called "a sham heterosexual" to conceal his lack of interest in girls from his male peers. After graduating with honors, he was accepted at a prestigious seminary.

As a seminarian he kept up the academic excellence he had shown throughout his schooling, and abstained from any homosexual activity. He dated occasionally but found little that was appealing in heterosexuality; he could fondle a girl's breast, but without making genital contact. Masturbation to homosexual fantasies of Adonis-like men gave him the only orgastic satisfaction he had.

After seminary, he had a one-year internship in pastoral counseling. He became depressed and consulted a pastoral counselor on the staff of the establishment in which he was interning. With his supportive care Henry's depression remitted sufficiently for him to carry out his responsibilities.

Henry had his second homosexual experience in the interval between his internship and the assumption of his first pastorate. On a trip to a large city he went to a gay bar where he met a man toward whom he felt an immediate, strong attraction. After some idle talk he agreed to go with him; he was so obviously flustered by the invitation offered him that his new acquaintance asked if he were sure he wanted to accept. They masturbated each other, but his partner told Henry to work out his inner conflict about homosexuality before trying it again. Henry left with this advice and, despite occasional temptation, remained abstinent thereafter.

His preoccupation with his body and those of other men nonetheless became obsessive as he assumed his pastorate. He complained endlessly about being "too rounded, flabby, and soft," and worried that he might be gynecomastic or have some other endocrinological disorder. A casual observer would have found nothing unusual in his appearance when he was clothed, but he felt obliged to undertake a program of regular exercise, not just for fitness, but to build muscle.

Treatment

Although Henry had ostensibly sought treatment to relieve his depressive symptoms, during his first several weeks with his therapist he displayed concern over the latter's attitude toward homosexuality, asking if he viewed it as an alternative life-style or a symptom of mental conflict. Since he thought Freudian theory opposed homosexuality, he expressed anxiety over being indoctrinated with "Freudian dogma." He was sure that homosexuality was the expression of an innate constitutional disposition to which experience contributed nothing. His comments and questions on the subject were made aggressively, but the therapist listened attentively and quietly. As Henry became more insistent on having answers, the therapist reminded him that he had described his experience with the homosexual counselor as traumatic, and that the therapist's way was to work with a patient by being curious, along with the patient himself, about what would be disclosed in his free associations. This response seemed to reassure Henry, who began settling into a typical therapeutic routine.

Henry began pensively to describe his feelings about himself and his life. He was "a cripple—wandering, limping, and lonely." He had recently been unsettled by the possibility that his call to the ministry had been inspired more by his mother than by God. With shame he revealed that he masturbated ritually each morning in the shower with a pornographic magazine propped against the door so he could gaze at the picture of a male nude. He played with his nipples, and masturbated to fantasies of having chest muscles as developed as those of the man in the magazine, and also focused on the penis.

> I look at his body and I want it so badly. It seems as if this would solve something. I want to look like them, not make love to them. I want masculinity and to feel secure about myself. I don't feel masculine like men are supposed to feel.

He recalled his boyhood fascination with his father's chest and his nightly prayer that he might some day have such a manly chest himself.

His sessions during the next several months were filled with detailed descriptions of men whose bodies he coveted. Sometimes these were men he knew, had seen on the street, or had simply conjured up in his fantasies. He became exquisitely sensitive to the firmness of his body, adopting diets and Spartan exercise programs whenever he felt he was too heavy. When exercising he wore "daringly bold racer swimsuits" in an effort to enhance a spurious sense of manliness.

Although the therapist did not grasp the meaning of all this so early in the treatment, he empathized with Henry's desperate search for a strong man and the fear that went with it. Henry explained: "If I become a man I'll become strong, muscular, ready to have sex—an animal, a male prostitute. . . . Therefore I'm afraid I'd feel crippled with women and humiliate myself."

Playing with Visual Images: After the first six months of therapy, Henry's intense preoccupation with the muscular bodies of other men seemed to fade and his associations became interspersed with fragmented visual images, some sessions being given over to them altogether. The therapist thought of them as variations on the theme of transitional phenomena as described by Volkan (1973), who had reported that a narcissistic patient he was analyzing had used certain repeating fantasies in a special way as intangible representations of transitional objects. Volkan called these "transitional fantasies" and reported that his patient had acted as though addicted to them. Since he had complete control over them using them gave him the illusion of having a similar control over the environment and its interference with his inner adaptation.

Now Henry seemed to create his visual images to play with like a child playing with his toys. The images were formless, and their content did not matter; what he did with them was the issue. As Henry "played," his therapist felt outside Henry's world, in a fog bank as it were. However, as he became more accustomed to his patient's unusual mode of communication the therapist's feeling yielded to curiosity. He thought that perhaps the visual togetherness Henry had enjoyed with his grandmother, who had been such a comfort to him when he was a child, might be echoing in this phenomenon, but he recalled Volkan's warning that it is the function of these phenomena rather than their content that needs interpretation. When the function is interpreted, the patient is ready to understand the meaning of the content. Accordingly, the therapist conveyed his feeling that playing with visual images interposed a buffer between the patient and his therapist, and asked his patient what he thought might be causing his anxiety.

After his interpretation Henry had fewer visual productions and began talking about a sense of emptiness and a longing for affection. One day he announced, "My head fills up with a stream of pictures." The therapist began to see another meaning: not only were the visual images being used as a buffer to control object relations conflicts, but also as nutrition. The therapist had seen a search for a masculine male—an ideal father image—but, at the same time, a need to control awareness of being hungry for affection, and a desire to be filled by a maternal representation. He began to sense that Henry was imprisoned in an imaginary room in psychic space in which he found himself between his father and mother, wanting to open the door to each but thinking it too dangerous to do so. He seemed doomed to stay in the room, managing by playing with his visual images as though they were transitional objects. This soothed him, and helped him keep at bay the danger lurking behind each door. He could conjure up images of idealized fathers and mothers without ever leaving the room. By never leaving to face dangerous parental representations, he could keep both idealized.

When the therapist spoke of his understanding of Henry's preoccupation with being between mother and father, Henry offered a dream in which someone broke into his house and terrified him. The therapist's remarks were the day residue of this dream since his understanding had intruded into the imaginary room Henry must defend at all cost if he were to survive psychologically. At this point he did not hear his therapist's remarks as interpretation but as a threat. During the next few sessions he withdrew and played with his visual images. He also became more frantic outside his sessions about keeping his territory intact. He bought pornographic videos and repeatedly masturbated with them. Eroticizing his anxiety became his chief defense.

He began coming late for his sessions, sometimes skipping them altogether. Once he spent his session time at a Revolutionary War battlefield. He had visited historical sites with his father, and here he was seeking his idealized father and coming close to him after his therapist had intruded on his inner world and threatened his way of dealing with conflicted object relations. His associations pointed to identifying his therapist with Great Britain–mother from whom he wanted to become independent. He thought he could accomplish this by being with his father, but to succeed he had to engage in a battle in which someone could be killed. The therapist's understanding of this enactment allowed him to tell Henry that perhaps he could put the situation into words rather than actions. The therapist felt that when he became the mother representation Henry not only raised a protective barrier but initiated a relationship with his father's representation. His dilemma was that the search for the idealized father was symptomatic and unresolved since the father's image might turn out to be rejecting, humiliating, or frightening.

Henry experienced turbulence at this point, and felt a heightened interest in men and a desire to incorporate their penises. One day he was asked to help landscape the grounds of the church, which was an extension of his mother. He had been asked because none of the members of the property committee was strong enough to operate a rototiller. As Henry used the machine, he became conscious of being manly "with this throbbing member between my legs." It seemed as though he were involved in a symbolic attempt to identify with a strong father and to repair his mother by making the soil better so he would not have to be so afraid of her. In any event, imitating either parent made him so anxious that he went back to his visual images, apparently deciding that it was safer to stay in his metaphorical room.

In time his images began to have form and content. For example, he saw a cat with kittens crowding at her teats to root and suck. This image expressed a wish for being fed, but also anxiety over the possibility of being engulfed by the mother's representation.

Besides eroticizing his anxiety, Henry's homosexuality was defensive adaptation to the unresolved struggles with representations of father and mother. As treatment began to uncover what was behind each door, Henry visited some actively homosexual college friends. On his return he announced that he was going to live "a gay life" and end his treatment. His friends had told him that his therapist undoubtedly was trying to make him a heterosexual. Also, he was tired of waffling on the issue and wanted to settle it once and for all. He strongly denounced the therapist as an unenlightened perpetuator of psychoanalytic myths about homosexuality. After Henry composed himself, his therapist commented that he had noticed for some time that his patient had increasingly come to regard their association as unworkable, but he urged that they explore together why this was the case. After pondering for a minute, Henry agreed to continue and to see what could be learned about himself.

The meaning of his resolution to acknowledge his homosexuality so vigorously emerged slowly. It turned out that he was so afraid of his therapist as the dangerous mother and father representation that he wanted a title, a name, or a classification in order to quiet his mind at last.

A Young Woman: Toward the end of his first year of treatment, Henry met a woman he described as a lovely, softly feminine divorcée whom he found very attractive. He began seeing her regularly, viewing her as "a nurturing person," although he added, "I'm so afraid something will be taken away from me." As their relationship evolved, she told Henry that she cared for him and hoped he shared her feeling. Thoughts of romance swirled in his head as their emotional relationship intensified. There was no talk of sexual intercourse, but he was afraid she would propose it. His anxiety increased to the point that he stormed into the therapist's office, walked past the couch, and took a chair facing him. His face was contorted, and he announced that he wanted to terminate at once. His anxiety had driven him back into limbo where he was neither fully man nor fully woman. Two weeks later, he reported a dream in which he drove a truck with his mother seated beside him. They came to a dangerous turn over a bridge, and, caught in a storm, the truck went into the water. The bridge "decapitated" the truck, but he did not remember being drowned.

This dream brought a memory of a childhood phobia of bridges. It represented, among other things, his desire to have a big phallus, and the danger this suggested. He had come to an important turning point and had to decide if he were going to possess a truck–penis, or submerge in water–mother. His castration anxiety was evident in the dream of the truck's top being torn away. His childhood phobia about going over bridges had both oedipal and preoedipal constellations condensed in it.

His relationship with his woman friend became more turbulent as his perception of her became increasingly contaminated by the representation of the drowning, smothering mother. He could sometimes keep his friend relatively free from this distortion by splitting, displacing it on older women in his church whom he thoroughly disliked, calling them "parasitic, possessive women . . . who suck blood out of you." He connected them with his mother, saying, "I was afraid of being swallowed up by her and being unable to get away. She could be cold, biting, and cruel." Sometimes he expected his woman friend to be like this, and through his relationship with her he reexamined his mother's representation. He was able for the first time to verbalize directly his fear of women.

In spite of therapeutic work on his contamination of this young woman with his internal representation of his "bloodsucking" mother, Henry shied away from her, expressing affection physically only by an occasional kiss that gave him little pleasure. He found his fantasies far more exciting; in them he saw himself as "a macho man—aggressive, forceful, but not raping her." He sometimes had sexual intercourse with her in fantasy, although he was far from ready for it in reality. He spoke of his conception of the act as being violent and sadistic. His friend announced that she was accepting a position in another city. Perhaps she would not have taken it had Henry been more receptive to her, but he felt relief, and came to realize that a part of him wanted her to go so he would not be swallowed up.

In the midst of the crisis brought about by her departure, Henry spoke again of terminating. This time, however, he said spontaneously that he wanted to continue to learn "what he might be running from." He had become identified with a therapeutic function. "I now have this little voice in my head that tells me I'd better take a look at what I'm doing," he said.

Increased Self-Observation: Although Henry still had to protect the space between mother and father representations by remaining in limbo, he was now better able to observe the processes involved. Along with improvement in his ability to observe himself came improvement in his ability to tolerate anxiety, depressive affect, and frustration. The therapeutic alliance was nevertheless eroded whenever he was stressed since his main adaptation to life was control. This was exemplified around Christmas in the second year of his treatment.

His senior pastor was unexpectedly called away over the holiday, and Henry was left in charge of the church services. When his mother decided to spend the holidays with him, he interpreted this as being left alone with his mother by an absent father. This situation had two dangers: (1) symbolic oedipal triumph and (2) his being left with a "blood-sucking mother." He became acutely symptomatic, experiencing a resurgence of homosexual fantasies along with a renewed determination to exercise regularly. For the first time he became obsessive about cleanliness, clearing off and reorganizing his desk, vacuuming the floor of his living quarters, washing the dishes, and tidying up on a daily basis.

He described his state as "like being in a pit where you look around and see this shit you're stuck in. You can see around you like you're in a foxhole." The therapist thought of the possibility of seeing his patient's situation between father and mother representations in a psychosexual light. It was as though Henry were reaching down (regressing) from phallic–oedipal dangers, but at the same time reaching up (progressing) from oral dangers to anal defenses and adaptations. His control was now accomplished by formed obsessional mechanisms rather than by the more global control seen earlier in his treatment when he had used reactivated transitional phenomena.

An Event in the Therapist's Life: After New Year's Day, when his mother had gone home, Henry had an unexpected invitation from his woman friend to visit her in her new home. Although he accepted, he was dismayed at the thought of physical intimacy with her. On his return he spoke of being relieved that she had slept in her bed and given him a sofa to sleep on. He explained, "There was a good feeling about being attracted to her, being a man, but the thought of sexual intercourse scared me to death. I didn't want to rape or force her." He had wanted very much to explore her body, something he had never done with a woman, but his inhibitions prevailed and they never went beyond a warm embrace.

While work on Henry's perception of a relationship with a woman as rape went on, the therapist's father died. He phoned Henry to tell him that he had been called out of town, giving no details, but Henry learned of the death from an obituary in the local paper and offered his condolences at his next session. Thanking him, the therapist assured Henry that he was ready to continue their work. In the following session Henry reported a dream:

> I was in a large house that had layers of floors and a secret passage. There was a man after me. It was Lex Luther, the archvillain in Superman. Superman had made him go bald but Luther was after me. I try to escape. I lock some doors but discover I've made a mistake. The weapons available to me were locked away. I had locked myself out of the weapons room. I ran to a college campus which I got to by going over a bridge. It looked like a bridge located near your office. Luther is in pursuit of me saying "I want to see you, I have a bone to pick with you."

Henry's associations were to an earlier dream he had had soon after becoming involved with the woman with whom he had just spent the weekend. In that dream he was being chased by a man with a shotgun who was understood at the time to represent the alarming father–therapist. He reasoned that, since it had always been his ambition to be "strong, virile, and attractive," he must be Superman and Lex Luther, the father bent on revenge. "It was definitely a life and death situation," he said.

The symbolic oedipal triumph inherent in his father's departure after his divorce may have left Henry with fantasies of a father to be feared. When the therapist's father died, the notion that when a father goes away it is because his child wanted to be rid of him was reactivated in Henry's mind. Perhaps it was this wish that brought the great danger he had felt in his dream, but it should be noted also that Henry seemed to want to connect with the therapist as a good father.

At any rate, Henry regressed after this death, in spite of interpretations. It was unfortunate that he learned of this death at a time when he was experimenting with becoming a man vis-à-vis his woman friend. When she fell in love with someone else and married, Henry was devastated for a while but had to acknowledge that he had not really pursued her.

The Desire to Find a Loving Idealized Father: The therapist's vacation interrupted Henry's treatment. When the therapist returned, Henry insisted once more that he wanted to terminate because he was "ready to try it on his own." He particularly wanted to see if he could have a "healthy relationship with someone of the same sex," but his identification with the therapist was so strong that he said, "This voice in me tells me to be patient and work longer." He then announced that he planned not only to terminate but also to leave the ministry and enter medical school. The therapist felt that Henry was going to close the door on conflicts involving therapist–father and church–mother, and identify with the therapist as a healer in order to remove himself from an untenable position between his two parental representations. When asked for his thoughts on all this, the therapist suggested that Henry was seemingly going to resolve in action something that needed further understanding. After a moment's reflection Henry agreed to continue.

Feeling a need to buffer the therapeutic interchange, Henry reintroduced a myriad of visual images, now somewhat formed and coherent, with which he played. He used one image to spin out a tale of his being in a historical town where a dilapidated house was undergoing renovation. In view of his knowledge of Henry's having visited historical places with his father, the therapist suggested that he was in search of a concerned and friendly father who would make himself available to help his son build the kind of structure that would enable him to separate from the mother representative.

Another image illuminated the reason why Henry restricted his homosexual activities to idealized fantasized men. In it he saw himself on an arid African grassland while horned gazelles roamed around him. After telling this, he fell silent for a moment and then exclaimed, "I have surrendered so much power to you. I have hated coming here because I am under your control. It's as though you were my antagonist rather than my therapist." He then compared the therapist to his father, who seemed such an imposing figure to him. He recalled how much he had wanted his father to teach him to swim when he had been a boy, although he had rejected his offer to do so "because I was too scared to let him."

The therapist felt that Henry wanted to become identified with him in order to restructure himself, but that he still needed controlling transitional relatedness because he was afraid of being hurt. However, Henry then expressed for the first time without putting up a buffer his desire for getting help. He was apparently considering the possibility that the therapist might be different from his internal representation of his father. His father was so much a figure of fantasy because he had had such intermittent real experiences with him as a child. The oedipal period thus dealt primarily with fantasies that were given a sense of reality by the operation on his eye. Anxieties from this period were greatly intensified by his symbolic oedipal triumph; the anticipated punishment being reflected in his phobia of snakes. He was disclosing again in treatment his desire and simultaneous dread about finding a good father with whom to redo the oedipal struggle, but now he was permitting his therapist to join in the effort within the functional working alliance.

His wish for, and dread of, involvement with a strong man emerged in a dream about a high school classmate who had been on the football team, and with whom he found himself sitting on a pink picnic basket and being tenderly affectionate. His associations indicated that this man was short, which made him less threatening. The friend had, as it happened, followed in his father's footsteps professionally, and Henry envied this. What he remembered most vividly about the dream, however, was his desire "to be touched skin against skin."

He realized that what he wanted more than anything else was to be like this man. He lamented that he had never been "one of the guys," and went on to say, "I feel like a mirror that only reflects stuff back. When there is nothing to reflect back, there is no substance." His wish to touch this man expressed his desire to fuse with him and become a man himself. The therapist was able to interpret the progressive meaning in his homosexuality: besides being an adaptation to preoedipal and oedipal conflict (i.e., separation and castration anxiety and its erotization) it was also in the service of identification with a man. Although Henry wanted this identification, he also feared it, as was clear in the fact that the subject he chose had to be short (i.e., partly castrated).

Henry's thoughts in the next session were about the theological question of theosody, which is concerned with the extent to which God participates in temporal affairs. The therapist suggested that perhaps Henry was also interested in whether or not God–father would allow him to absorb his power, and to do so without punishment. The dream of the previous night indicated that Henry had begun to flirt with becoming a man. In this dream an effeminate homosexual acquaintance of his was shot to death. He interpreted this dream himself as being an expression of his wish "to eliminate his homosexuality." He was persuaded that the homosexual in the dream represented that part of himself that lived in such a controlled space and was, in consequence, a source of shame and humiliation to him.

An Alteration of the Therapeutic Frame: Because Henry missed a session, the therapist departed from his usual routine of handing him a monthly bill and mailed it to him instead. He was unable to discern in this any unconscious reasons. In any event, the bill was delivered when Henry's mother was visiting him, and she saw it. Again, an external event precipitated a triangular situation with profound intrapsychic implications. Henry had not told his mother that he was undergoing psychotherapeutic treatment and had indeed denied it when something had aroused her suspicions and she questioned him. When he came to his next session, he was very upset and inveighed against his therapist's betrayal. Having planned to await a propitious time to tell her about his treatment, he was enraged that his mother had been empowered "to invade his territory." The working alliance of therapist and patient was strong enough, however, to hold. Henry pulled himself together and became genuinely curious about what this incident really meant. The therapist shared with Henry his impression that by sending the bill he had represented contrary images of the father, being the man toward whom Henry felt such rage for his failure to help with the struggle to separate from his mother—but also the father who intruded into the symbiotic pull toward her.

Soon Henry reported a dream that gave a deeper appreciation of where he was in his intrapsychic work of individuating from his mother's representation. In it, he was behind the wheel of a car much more costly than the one he really owned. He was surprised by its elegance since he had always criticized those who drove so conspicuous a vehicle. He suddenly realized as he drove along that he was in the parking lot of a grocery store and that he had never left it to go out on the highway. His associations indicated a desire for a more functional penis and the stature of a man. The therapist suggested that the grocery store represented his mother and that he had to put a symbol of her in his dream in case he became hungry when separated from her. Henry was still in his metaphorical room—the parking lot—between mother and father, although he had better equipment (the car) to proceed elsewhere.

We are reminded of Glover's (1955) patient who was impotent. According to Glover:

> When he began to report consistently that he could *now* engage the gears without much difficulty and that the cars no longer shrank to small proportions when he sought to drive them, I decided to terminate his analysis, in spite of the fact that he had

not yet had any opportunity of proving his sexual potency [p. 158].

Similar intrapsychic changes appear in both cases. It may be that Glover decided to terminate because of other unspecified material, but we felt that Henry's dream of being in a better automobile than he in fact possessed did not necessarily mean that he had resolved his conflicts.

Between Phallic Narcissism and Castration: Anna Freud (1952) observed while treating male homosexuals that after a period of progress:

> I had to realize that what analysis had restored in these patients was the fantasy of phallic narcissism before their regressive aban-donment of the oedipal conflict. They were caught up in a nar-cissistic overvaluation of the phallus, a position in which most of their libido was not available for the formation of true emotional relationships. Women were welcome so far as they served their phallic needs and helped to create an illusion of masculine po-tency. They still represented dangers due to the demands made by them that aroused anxious oral fantasies of being sucked dry, impoverished, etc. [pp. 255–256].

Henry's restored phallic narcissism was apparent in his renewed determination to build "the perfect body." More regular and energetic workouts did bring physical changes in which he took great pride, telling his therapist about them not only because he wanted admiration but also in order to have someone share in his own admiration of himself.

While full of phallic pride, he reported a dream about being in physical danger. Although he called for his mother, his calls went unheeded, and he felt desperately lonely and afraid. Another dream that came a little later provided, along with Henry's associations to it, a clearer idea of the content of his anxieties. In it he had lost a tooth, and those left were so loose that he feared losing them also. This prompted thoughts of a toothless old man who had fallen far short of realizing his potential, and this led to thoughts of a man who had repeatedly run for President without ever being elected. The therapist made the interpretation that Henry was running for manhood but that the race stirred up so much castration anxiety that he felt compelled to castrate himself to allay the fear of punishment. Besides, his real father was a humiliated alcoholic, and Henry was afraid of being like him. Moreover, he was told that, on a lower level, he must infantilize himself to defend against the cannibalistic rage he felt toward both parents if he were to protect them from being destroyed. If this were true, all he could ever be was a clownish caricature of a man. In developmental terms, a phallic narcissistic little boy is only a caricature of a man!

More on the Father Transference: In Henry's third year of treatment, his bill once more came into the therapeutic story. He had failed to pay it for more than two months, and when this was called to his attention, he had "a confession to make." He had lost the last two bills and had been too embarrassed to bring the matter into his associations. Bills had become sexualized, so losing them was equated with the symbolic castration of the therapist. When this was interpreted to Henry, he became so anxious that when he asked for replacements he chortled, "You'd better strike while the iron is hot and give me all three at once." He just wanted to get his punishment over at the hands of the therapist–father he sought and feared.

Besides the wish to castrate the therapist–father, another wish and defense lay behind his behavior: his desire to become a man and his fear of doing so. He gathered up his bills only to lose them again because of his expectation that the therapist would be angry and rape him. To become a man through incorporation of another man's penis inspired fears of retaliation from its owner. Also, such an incorporative act would deprive him of a man with whom a mature identification was possible. It was clear that his father's representation had been invested with Henry's projected aggression. Identification with such an aggressive representation was impossible for fear of mutual destruction. In these circumstances it was not hard to see why Henry endlessly and futilely searched for an idealized man in his fantasies.

Physical Illness: Toward the end of Henry's third year in treatment there was an outbreak of a virulent strain of influenza in the area, and Henry contracted it and was confined to bed for nearly three weeks. Too sick to care for himself, he had his mother stay with him. When he resumed treatment, he associated at length: "Here I was all dependent on her . . . and she didn't smother me. She didn't even hover over me. I was close to pushing the panic button, but I didn't. I entered the jaws of the lion and came out. I could stay in the same room with her and not be destroyed."

This illness had considerable psychological significance for Henry inasmuch as it brought him into close bodily relation with his mother. Regressed, he symbolically and with self-observation redid his separation–individuation. The therapist wondered whether his paroxysmal coughing might not represent, over and above the effects of the flu, a psychological effort to expel the smothering maternal introject.

Henry's symbolic reference to the jaws of the lion indicated his conceptualization of symbiosis as being eaten. On a higher level it represented the female genitalia as vagina dentata, implying that the mother was a castrator. After this, Henry seemed to have better mastery of anxiety over separation from the woman and castration by her. This was a good example of the condensation of object relations with psychosexual conflicts.

Interpretation of the psychological meaning of Henry's illness became the day residue for a dream in which he saw a salmon-colored shirt with an alligator emblem. This was in reality a favorite of his, and in his dream it was being ripped apart. Henry associated to sexual fantasies in which he ripped off his clothing and that of the other man because it felt so masculine to do so.

He spoke of the pleasure he took in the firmness of his body and of his pride in his progress in weight reduction. "It feels good to change that image," he said. The therapist used his dream to explain his unconscious fantasy of separation–individuation as a savagely aggressive act in which he must literally tear himself away from his mother. He was shedding his identification with a highly aggressive representation of her. These fantasies are consistent with Apprey's (1985) observation that: "In the unconscious mind separation is perceived as a tearing away from the object and thus shedding blood at the site of separation. As a result there is considerable anxiety regarding the consequences of leaving the self or object lacerated" (p. 164).

The Meaning of the Church: Not long after this work on the meaning of separation–individuation, Henry began to rail at the church's sanctions against homosexual clergy, and he again expressed curiosity about the therapist's attitude. He was convinced that the therapist harbored a prejudice against homosexuals and objected, saying, "I have a therapist who won't allow it, so like a parent who says you can't do something, you must be challenged." The therapist saw his aggression as another version of separation–individuation from the mother's representation represented by the church. Such aggression was in the service of psychological progress, and interpretation to that effect prompted Henry to recall a dream from several nights earlier in which he stood naked in a Gothic church where his mother was in the congregation. It occurred to him that he might be rebelling against his mother by mocking the sacred; it was clear that church and mother were connected in his mind.

After a visit to his mother he reported that she had patted him on the knee and called him "her boy," and that he had felt outraged. His homosexual desires increased, with the most violent fantasies he had ever had, involving bondage, domination, and violence, "but not butchery." He confided, "It's arousing to be a victim, tied up, strung up, and forced to have sex." His mother's implication that he would never be a man mobilized tremendous aggression in him. He eroticized it in masochistic fantasies. He tried to repress his rage by eroticizing his aggression and by denying his strivings to individuate away from the maternal representation. This, moreover, had the benefit of turning a bad representation into a good one that gave him pleasure.

After the therapist interpreted these masochistic fantasies, Henry expressed concern about his career. As the church became to him freer of maternal symbolism, he reaffirmed his commitment and abandoned the idea of going into medicine.

He said that he was being considered for transfer to a church elsewhere that ministered to the poor and homeless. Were he to go, his treatment would necessarily end within two months.

The therapist tried to help him sort out what was intrapsychic about his symbols from what was real, especially emphasizing his substitution of physical for intrapsychic separation which let him avoid going through either door of his metaphorical room and which would leave much unresolved with both mother and father representations. After a moment of reflection Henry reported a visual image in which he saw himself at the bottom of a huge container of water, seated beside a woman with whom he shared a breathing apparatus. Removing this apparatus, he surfaced and saw a balcony full of people applauding him. The therapist commented that although Henry was now better differentiated from the smothering representation of his mother, he was still not out of the water.

Henry is still in treatment, but he now gives much evidence of observing his internal world. He needs more work to get him out of the water–mother as he further identifies with his therapist as a good father.

DISCUSSION

Interaction with the Childhood Environment: The familial environment in which Henry grew up is typical for the prehomosexual male (Socarides, 1968b, 1988). Socarides saw the particular constellation of parental character organization and marital interaction so consistently by means of analytic reconstruction and direct observation that he came to refer to them as homosexogenic. The typical mother had low self-esteem, was possessive, and tended to treat her child as an extension of herself. It seemed not unusual for her to interfere with his early strivings for individuation and gender-appropriate identification. The fathers tended to be weak, inadequate, and unavailable, failing to exercise the kind of parental influence that might counteract the mother's, and failing also to offer an acceptable model for identification. Such parenting disrupts the process of separating from the mother and individuating, and of identifying with the father. The child in this case is left "structurally deficient and developmentally arrested" (Socarides, 1988, p. 265).

Henry's mother fit the prototype rather closely, consistently interfering with his strivings for separation–individuation from his early years on. She divorced her husband when Henry was two and constantly devalued him thereafter. As Henry grew, she demanded obedience to her will with reference to God's punishment of the disobedient. She treated him as a boy even after he was grown.

During the time he was trying to "get out of the water," she told Henry of having had a dream in which he rebelled against her, and she threatened to abandon him. She interfered with his growing masculine strivings, thinking of him as another Shirley Temple. She criticized his roughhouse play with his father and refused to help him buy weights with which to work out. She spoke movingly of the crucifixion of Christ, and her account undoubtedly had an unconscious meaning for the already deeply traumatized boy. She took no pride in his masculine development and actively discouraged his attempt to identify with his father in those ways that Stoller and Herdt (1982) found essential for normal gender identification. The grandfather's death just as Henry was entering adolescence, and as infantile conflicts were being rehashed in conjunction with the process of second individuation (Blos, 1979), kept these difficulties alive, and deprived him of a chance to work out his fear of women.

Not only did Henry's father have problems of his own, being himself unindividuated from his mother, alcoholic, and weak, but, as Goldstein, Freud, and Solnit (1973) have pointed out, "A visiting or visited parent has little chance to serve as a true object for love, trust, and identification" (p. 38). His repudiation of his parental rights and duties left his son without anyone to turn to for help in achieving intrapsychic separation from his mother. There was no father's love to compensate for the loss of the preoedipal mother, so Henry had been deprived of something that might have ameliorated his anxiety enough to allow him to maintain his individuated state and become identified with his father. Summarizing the findings of a report on the role of the father in preoedipal years, Socarides (1988) notes that:

> The father's libidinal and aggressive availability is a major requirement for the development of gender identity in his children, but for most all prehomosexual children the father is unavailable as love object for the child. Nor is he available to the mother as a source of emotional support. If physically present, he rarely limits or prohibits, and is often exquisitely passive [p. 266].

Clearly present in Henry's life were the two elements of parental interaction Socarides (1988) considers critical in identifying the homosexogenic family—a mother who smothers her son's strivings toward separation–individuation and masculine identification with the father, and a father who permits this.

Actual Trauma

Although in agreement with Socarides, we suggest that a like background can be found in persons who are basically heterosexual, particularly if the personality organization is borderline. Further clinical research seems indicated to determine what factors other than the early environmental constellation itself tend to promote homosexuality. Volkan, with Masri (1989), points to the importance of the superimposition of actual trauma on a family constellation in the development of transsexualism, such trauma usually involving bodily injury experienced or witnessed by the child. Greenacre (1952, 1958) wrote of primitive "body disintegration anxiety," holding that a serious disturbance of the early body image and its development contributes significantly to fetishism, and noting that actual trauma is likely to cause defective development. Although we do not maintain that actual trauma, whether recalled or not, is a necessary element in the development of homosexuality, we believe that in Henry's case his two surgical operations—one near the genitals and the other on his eye—at the ages of two and five respectively, concretized his fantasies of castration. That castration reactions can occur as early as the age of two finds support in the direct observational research of Roiphe and Galenson (1981) on an early genital phase. One of the boys they studied suffered an acute postoperative castration reaction to hernial repair at twenty-one-and-a-half months. His expectations of castration for his oedipal triumph did not stay entirely in the sphere of imagination; their concretization in external reality intensified them enormously and, perhaps, laid the foundation for his interminable search for an idealized father whom, with few exceptions, he never tested because of fear. It is likely also that Henry was trying to master his castration (eye surgery) passively experienced at the hands of a surgeon–father when he gratified himself with the visual incorporation of idealized men.

Greatly magnified by surgical trauma, Henry's castration fears may have contributed significantly to the severe inhibitions against assertiveness and competitiveness that characterized his years of latency. His fear of injury and his avoidance of athletic competition in this period as well as in later stages of his development becomes exquisitely understandable against this background. This also helps explain why he was always so anxious around his father and never really got to know him. Because of his contamination of all men by the internal representation of a dangerous oedipal father, it is questionable if he could have developed a healthy enough relationship with a surrogate father had one been available to further progressive psychological development. Anna Freud and Burlingham (1943) noted that fatherless children in wartime England were strongly attached to fantasied fathers, their fantasies being crafted out of what experience they had had with a father or, in the case of a father's total absence, from phase-specific material. It is reasonable to suppose that children create representations of an absent father, whether or not he has real existence. Meiss (1952) holds that a fatherless oedipal boy cannot correct a father's representation that is dangerous because of lack of experience with a real father or father substitute. When splitting, projective identification, and other primitive defenses predominate, the father's representation, like the mother's, can be divided into idealized and punitively destructive segments. Henry was safe from the castrating fantasy father (and mother, too) as long as he was with the idealized fantasy father.

The Meaning of the Search for an Idealized Father

The different meanings of Henry's homosexuality that have emerged to this point were present all along. What we illustrate here is how the salience of the different meanings changed as they were interpreted by the therapist.

For the first several months of treatment, Henry's virtual obsession with virile Adonis-like men whose manliness he coveted and wanted to appropriate for himself by fantasied oral and anal incorporative acts, expressed an effort to repair his self-esteem, which had been so badly damaged by his feeling of being deficient in masculinity. As this was understood and worked through, it became more and more evident that his homosexual fantasies served his wish to incorporate a powerful penis that would function as an internal bulwark against the regressive pull toward his preoedipal mother. They served also to reassure him about his father's love at a time when he felt both great need of it and great rage at his parents for being so unavailable. As his aggression toward both parental representations was being remobilized, his homosexual fantasies became more and more floridly sadomasochistic while he sought a strong father to tame it. As his aggression continued to mount, he said, "We've stripped away the excess stuff, and what is left is violence. The only thing left is the erotic nature of it all." The defensive erotization of aggression to which Socarides (1978, 1988) has drawn our attention in the sexual perversions is unequivocal here.

Oral and Anal Control Mechanisms

Henry was neither fully individuated from his mother nor fully identified with his oedipal father when he came into treatment, often referring to himself as androgenous. We offered the analogy of his being in a room with a door at the back and one at the front, behind each of which lay danger. The front door concealed the dangerous father with a sword or a surgeon's knife in hand, and the back door concealed the dangerous lioness mother, jaws agape, ready to devour him. Thus he had to exert considerable continuous effort to keep the room safe for him to occupy. He used reactivated transitional phenomena (Coppolillo, 1967; Kahne, 1967; Kafka, 1969; Fintzy, 1971; Volkan, 1973, 1976, 1987) and, later in treatment, anal obsessional controlling mechanisms to achieve this "safety."

Volkan (1973) wrote about "transitional fantasies" as intangible representations of transitional objects. Like concrete reactivated transitional objects, of which they are a variation, they afford the patient who uses them the illusion of having absolute control over his relative closeness to and distance from the objects. Volkan's (1976) analogy of the lantern will help clarify this motion: "The lantern has one opaque and one transparent side: when the opaque side is turned toward the outside world, the outside world is wiped out in darkness but the other side illuminates it so that it can be known" (p. 201). In this sense transitional fantasies both have a regressive and a progressive side, buffering against and linking with the external world in accordance with the pressure of anxiety.

As Henry's treatment began, he used transitional visual images and fantasies to insulate himself from his therapist, who had become contaminated by representations of his parents. He was using oral-level mechanisms to promote an illusory sense of control between himself and the external world.

We noted that in therapy Henry exhibited a shift toward anal-level defensive and controlling organization. Shengold (1988) has written on anal narcissistic defensive organization as a means of controlling affects and impulses from every stage of psychosexual development. He puts special emphasis on the vital role it plays in managing oral rage. As Henry's therapy progressed, he exhibited a shift toward a more anal defensive and adaptive organization to achieve control over drives, wishes, and fantasies. Shengold (1988) described this anal-narcissistic defensive organization as

[A] panoply of near-somatic body-ego defenses that children develop during the anal phase—that is, between the very early existence of the (most likely physiologically based) stimulus barrier and the later formation of the repression barrier during the oedipal period. Anal-narcissistic defense . . . acts as a kind of emotional and sensory closeable door that serves to control the largely murderous and cannibalistic primal affects derived from the destructive and from the perverse sexual drives of early life. This "door" operates along the body-ego model, as it were, of the control of the anal sphincter. . . . The sphincter-like defensive power of reducing intensities enables the individual to modulate unpleasure and pain, to avoid overstimulation, and to diminish and evade conflict ridden feelings associated with object ties [p. 24].

This shift toward an anal-level organization represented progressive movement for Henry who had, for so long, utilized more primitive oral-level mechanisms to defend against object relations conflicts. With this movement toward a higher, more integrated level of structural integration there was noticeable improvement in his capacity to discriminate external from internal reality. This improved capacity for discrimination between the two was accompanied by a diminution (but not complete elimination as yet) of his need to control the space between himself and the therapist.

Questions Raised by Henry's Case

The dangers inherent in the intrapsychic relationship with the representation of each parent are observable in Henry's case. But the fact that he would be classified as a latent, as opposed to an active, homosexual raises a question. An active homosexual of the preoedipal type fuses with the representation of the partner—good mother part of himself through the homosexual act in order to maintain psychic survival and a sense of self. He is addicted and must have his fix—the homosexual act. The oedipal homosexual submits himself in the homosexual act to the oedipal father in order to avoid castration, while at the same time trying to defeat the partner—bad oedipal father. We see in the clinical treatment of active homosexuals various combinations of preoedipal and oedipal issues side by side, one often dominating the other.

In Henry's case, the genital sexual act was inhibited. He greatly feared castration by his father and mother (through vagina dentata), and had anxiety about separation issues. One wonders if he had greater anxiety than an active homosexual.

Although this seems doubtful, it is possible that as a latent homosexual Henry had certain peculiar ego strengths that affected his clinical picture. Did he have enough to keep him from needing fusion with the good mother's representation and requiring a "fix"? Did he have enough to create an idealized father, and to be at all times ready to identify with him without having to submit himself to the castrating father? We are inclined to answer both questions in the affirmative.

When Henry began treatment, his symptoms included a ritualistic visual incorporation of idealized males (i.e., he masturbated in the shower while gazing at pictures of nude men of ideal form). This practice gave him hope of identification with idealized manhood. His other visual activities such as watching television or playing with his visual images brought him mentally in touch with that nonthreatening woman, his grandmother, and helped erase the trauma of lying in the hospital after eye surgery with bandaged eyes. It may have been that while in the hospital he had found that being able to evoke visual images while his eyes were bandaged had kept him from succumbing to the thought that he had been blinded and castrated.

It would seem that it was Henry's ego strength in reactivating transitional phenomena superimposed by his anal narcissism (Shengold, 1988), thereby raising a buffer between himself and the threatening world, that kept him a *latent* homosexual. He was robbing himself of any bodily intimacy with another person, whether homosexual or heterosexual. It was only after having had treatment that he began experimenting with psychologically important bodily contact with a young woman.

We have presented the psychodynamics of a single latent homosexual and raised questions about the similarities and differences between such men in relation to persons actively homosexual. Further clinical research will be necessary if we are to learn whether all latent homosexuals have similar psychodynamics.

CHAPTER 7

Instinctualization of Ego Functions and Ego Defects in Homosexual Men: Implications for Psychoanalytic Treatment

JEROME S. BLACKMAN, M.D., F.A.P.A.

INTRODUCTION

Socarides (1988) has put forward the most complete nosology of perverse disorders since Freud's (1905) "Three Essays on the Theory of Sexuality." One of Socarides's proposed formulations is that ego defects are present in certain types of homosexuality. In particular, he notes "intolerance of anxiety and its erotization" as evidence of "a manifestation of early preoedipal *damage* to the structure of the ego" (p. 15; emphasis added). Viewing perverse symptoms, including homosexual activity, partly as defenses against ego fragmentation anxiety (pp. 531–532), he explains how impulsive sexual behavior in homosexuals is "facilitated by . . . deficiencies in the ego, due in part to a *lack of neutralized energy which has impaired the ability to control immediate responses and instinctual discharges of aggression*" (p. 553; emphasis added). *The Preoedipal Origin and Psychoanalytic Therapy of Sexual Perversions* (1988) integrates concepts from the dynamic–structural–genetic theories of Freud with those from the object relations theories of Kohut and Kernberg.

The purpose of this paper is not to rereview all sides of the controversies surrounding ego psychology, internal object relations, narcissism, and psychodynamics as these relate to homosexuality. In fact, Socarides (1988) provides a comprehensive discussion of the literature regarding these theories. Rather, I hope to contribute a general principle regarding technique with homosexual patients. This principle has some similarity to Volkan's (1987) schematized outline for the treatment of borderline personality disorder, a diagnostic category into which, in my experience, a large number of homosexual patients probably fall.

The underpinning of this general principle is the notion that technique needs to be based on a theoretical understanding of ego defects, as well as dynamics, to be successful in helping homosexual patients in psychoanalytic forms of therapy. In other words, this paper, through the integration of metapsychological constructs with clinical practice, will attempt to clarify two issues often debated both in- and outside analytic circles: (1) What do abstract theories about instinctualization have to do with *actual patients*? (2) What can be done, with that knowledge, to help in the treatment of those patients?

I hope to elaborate on Socarides's (1988, pp. 531–560) suggestions for treatment by providing the following theoretical framework derived from psychoanalysis: In treating the male homosexual, therapeutic interventions regarding ego defects must be made first, even when there is concomitant evidence of dynamic, intrapsychic conflicts. Further, there needs to be a relatively lengthy working through of understandings regarding such defects. Oedipally based dynamic and/or genetic interpretations and/or reconstructions are *contraindicated* until structural damage to autonomous ego functions and ego strengths has been resolved to a reasonable degree.

From a theoretical standpoint, I also hope to add to the understanding of the etiology of homosexuality: namely, the concept of instinctualization of an ego defect (not of an ego function). It is my impression that the confusing picture presented by instinctualized defects often leads to mistakes in technique, which, if not recognized, could cause a therapist to formulate an unnecessarily guarded prognosis for analytic treatment.

Since the Oedipus complex was first described by Freud in 1897, in his correspondence with Fliess (Letters 64 to 71), psychiatric and lay opinions regarding sexuality (including homosexuality) have come under greater scrutiny. Although his direct observations of children were limited, Freud (1905) noted the remarkable fact that both sexual identity and successful adult sexual functioning depended on a large number of developmental factors, beginning in early childhood. More recent studies have enlarged on Freud's discoveries and highlighted the impact on sexuality of preoedipal development (Stoller, 1964; Galenson, 1976; Galenson and Roiphe, 1980), cognitive experiences (Mahler, Pine, and Bergman, 1975; Lerner, 1976), neurobiological development (Money, 1986), and fantasy. Sarnoff (1976) has detailed the interrelations of sexuality and latency, and Blos (1979) has discussed the psychic structure of adolescents in relation to sexual functioning.

Socarides (1988) underlines and clarifies previous ideas (Ovesey, 1969) regarding the symbolism of homosexuality: "the perverted action, like the neurotic symptom, [results] from a conflict between the superego, ego and id" (p. 4). He observes that homosexual proclivities may result from compromise formations deriving from any or all stages of development. From the standpoint of symptom diagnosis, he clarifies that homosexual activity may coexist with all diagnoses, ranging from schizophrenia to psychoneurosis, though he is highly concerned with preoedipal drive disturbances to the extent they influence the repetition–compulsion later in life, and in treatment.

Notwithstanding the importance of differential diagnosis, it is my experience that the vast majority of patients engaged in homosexual activity who voluntarily present themselves for treatment are "in-between" cases: they demonstrate ego defects as well as intrapsychic conflicts (involving unconscious defenses, affects, fantasies, compromise formations) as etiologies for their problems.

DEFINITION OF CONCEPTS

Ego Functions and Ego Strengths

In modern psychoanalytic terminology, an ego defect is generally defined as a loss of or severe diminution in one of the many "conflict-free" functions of the mind. Hartmann (1939) and others (Frosch, 1966) have defined these, and they include: perception, memory, secondary process thinking, psychomotor control, integration (synthesis), abstraction, reality testing, reality sense, intelligence (many forms), concentration, attention, orientation, anticipation, observing ego, ego interests, auto/alloplastic adaptation, and judgment (social, environmental, and personal/body).

Other "strengths" of the healthy ego (Kernberg, 1975; Jacobson, 1964) include: impulse control, affect and frustration tolerance, tension and pain tolerance, resistance to regression, delay of gratification, containment (or "repression") of primary process thinking (and fantasy), development of sublimatory channels for sexual and aggressive drive discharge, regression in the service of the ego, and the use of fantasy as trial action.

Instinctualization and Its Consequences

Some authors include defenses in an assessment of ego strengths and functions, but I prefer to limit the terms *ego functions* and *ego strengths* to the autonomous functions described above. This is neater theoretically, since defenses are often used to impede autonomous ego functioning, once such a function has been instinctualized. For example, in hysteria, memory for certain events includes sexual thoughts and intentions that are guilt provoking. The resulting action of the mind may be to shut off the memory function, which has become "sexualized"; that is, remembering has "been invested with a sexual meaning" (Hartmann, 1955, p. 11). In other words, due to its sexual symbolism ("sexualization"), not only can a single memory be repressed, but the memory function itself can be defensively impaired (what Freud [1926] called "inhibition"). This type of limitation, which not infrequently causes a secondary defect in an autonomous ego function, is plainly seen in children who, before adolescence, have repetitively witnessed sexual intercourse or who have been sexually abused. These children often suffer from an inability to remember what is later taught them, and may be diagnosed as having a learning disability.

Likewise, adults who remain "idealists" (in the sense of the "cockeyed optimists" who "forgive and forget" and always give the "benefit of the doubt") are often people who are unable to judge the danger of certain situations or of certain other people. Although many mental mechanisms may be involved in the production of this character functioning, one of the most important is the unconsciously hostile meaning, to the idealist, of the act of judging. Because of this aggressivization (Hartmann, Kris, and Loewenstein, 1949; Hartmann, 1950, 1955) of the autonomous ego function of critical judgment, guilt is induced by judgmental attitudes. The resultant superego anxiety is defended against by reaction formation, denial, and idealization. These defenses, which if utilized to any significant degree may be life-threatening—as in the idealist who wants to give a psychopathic murderer a "second chance," in order to "save" him—would not be instituted if there were not an aggressive instinctualization of the critical judgment function to begin with. Clearly, persistence of the ego inhibition could again result, secondarily, in a permanent ego defect (in judgment).

Object Relations

Many authors (Bellak and Sharp, 1978) describe object relations, particularly as connected to internal (mental) images of self and others, as "ego functions." I prefer to consider object relations as a separate category, as did Hartmann (1955), who would "differentiate ego function and the representation of the self" (p. 13). The development of self-concept and object concepts relies on perception, memory, integration, discrimination (Mahler and Furer's [1968] "differentiation")—and later, on abstraction, reality testing, and observing ego, all autonomous ego functions. Attitudes toward these images, however, derive from drive cathexes (e.g., "I love you," or "I hate him"), the pleasure principle, and superego impact as well. I feel, therefore, that it is clearer to state that object relations are not themselves ego functions, but aside from id and superego aspects, rely greatly on autonomous ego functioning.

To complicate matters, an overlap of ego functions and object relations exists in respect to the development of ego strengths. In order to "mature" and be able to manage affects and impulses without regressing, a human being needs "average expectable" mothering throughout the early years. Through biochemical mechanisms unknown to us, the infant's brain is usually able to "internalize" the soothing effects of maternal ministrations. In other words, as the internalized images of self and other are constructed, ego strength improves. Spitz (1946, 1965) and Harlow (1975) have demonstrated the failure to develop ego strengths and ego functions in children, and even in monkeys, whose relationships (and internalized object relations) are disrupted. Kohut (1968) describes the vulnerability to psychotic regression in narcissistic patients, though he theorizes in terms of stability versus instability of self–object representations. Kohut tangentially attempted to integrate his ideas with those of ego psychology, but finally decided that his concepts were distinct and that narcissism follows a different, entirely separate line of development.

INSTINCTUALIZATION OF EGO FUNCTIONS

As described above, when instinctualization of an ego function occurs, usually due to psychic trauma in childhood, that function may become embroiled in intrapsychic conflict as though it were an id derivative. This conflict then causes defensive activity in the form of limiting the utilization of that function, sometimes permanently. When the ego function involved is memory, the ego restriction may result in learning impairments. If the instinctualized function is that of judgment, naiveté may result. Sexualization and aggressivization of the integrative function often provoke the institution of the isolation defenses so prevalent in obsessive–compulsive disturbances.

In contrast, in borderline and psychotic afflictions, there appear to be primary defects in autonomous ego functions. In schizophrenia, defective integrative functioning seems to have a hereditary basis. The intensity of other defects varies, and accounts, in part, for the different presentations seen in schizophrenic patients; that is, aside from the integrative anomalies, defects in perception, reality testing/reality sense, abstraction ability, and anticipation are present to different degrees. Hoch and Polatin (1949) stressed that patients presenting with neurotic symptoms often harbor schizophrenic thinking and dereistic life approaches. In the language of ego psychology, this would mean that neurotic symptoms, which derive from the oedipal phase of development, may mask or subtly incorporate ego defects in secondary process thinking, judgment, and adaptation; and that ego strength, especially in impulse control and containment of fantasy, is markedly diminished. Furthermore, in schizophrenics, one usually finds defects in the development of self and object representations. These defects are associated with poor self and object constancy, massive use of projection, and anchoritic behavior.

Although there exist numerous definitions of borderline character, a streamlined formulation (Atkin, 1975) is that, like schizophrenia, it is an illness of primary defects (not just secondary defects derived from defensive ego restriction). In borderlines, the primary defects represent developmental delays, but integration, reality testing, observing ego, secondary process thinking, and abstract thinking are generally less damaged than in schizophrenics. The self–object differentiation problems of borderlines are also not as marked, and drive defusion is not as pronounced as in schizophrenics. Clearly, in both schizophrenia and borderline conditions, the magnitude of the various defects can vary greatly. In the current-day obsessional nosology suggested by *The Diagnostic and Statistical Manual of Mental Disorders (DSM-III-R)*, there is actually a throwback to the late 1940s, when Hoch and Polatin (1949) confronted the reluctance among psychiatrists to diagnose schizophrenia unless secondary (or "accessory" [Bleuler, 1908]) symptoms of hallucinations and delusions were present. Today, from a diagnostic standpoint, it is commonplace to hear colleagues refer to patients as "*very* borderline," or "flaming borderline." In my experience, these are patients with such massive defects in integration and reality sense, that simple schizophrenia or pseudoneurotic schizophrenia seem more appropriate descriptive diagnoses.

Although it is sometimes difficult to distinguish primary from secondary ego defects, I feel there are both important theoretical and therapeutic reasons for attempting to do so. To begin with, defects resulting from defensive activity (such as repression) can be repaired through interpretation of the defenses, the instinctualized symbolic meaning of the ego function causing the defenses, and eventually the multiply determined conflicts that led to the instinctualization.

For example, a sixteen-year-old boy presented with interference in concentration and learning (remembering/retaining) what he was taught. Over two years of treatment, it became clear that his father, a highly educated man with several advanced degrees, was absent, working, until the boy reached adolescence. The boy, it turned out, was furious at his father for this, but also missed him and wished for more interaction. Furthermore, his father openly expressed a desire for the boy to do well in school. It became possible to analyze that the boy's inattention was the result of a compromise formation involving a disidentification with his father (a defense). The compromise formation occurred because (1) he could not express his anger directly due to fear of even more rejection from father; (2) he displaced anger from one object to another, as a defense against mourning over his father; (3) he disappointed his father, as his father had disappointed him, which also unconsciously expressed his anger. Although obviously the overdetermination of this boy's problems was even more dynamically complex, these three aspects demonstrate how intrapsychic conflict led to an aggressivization of the memory and concentration functions. His conflict between his wish for love from his father and his rage at him caused anxiety over loss of love, which then led not only to a shift in the object of the aggressive drive (from father to his school work), but to an aggressive symbolization of studying. Had there been less conflict regarding his father, the aggressivization could have helped resolve oedipal conflicts through providing a sublimated channel for patricidal wishes.

However, because of the intensity of the deprivation and anger, the aggressivized function now came into conflict with fears of loss of love. The learning functions were therefore restricted, partly as a defense and partly as an unconscious expression of the aggressive drive.

Therapeutically, repeated interpretations of these mechanisms led to the boy's being able to rearrange his study habits (freeing his ego functions from instinctualization and conflict), and his grades picked up significantly.

The concept of instinctualization can also be extended to describe certain types of object relations pathology. In such cases, all or part of the self or object representation becomes instinctualized and the resulting defensive activity is to limit object relatedness. Such a process is different from the usual mechanism in neurosis, where conflicting drives and affects toward (or cathecting) an object lead to defensive activity against certain sensations and/or thought content (Brenner, 1975). Rather, defensive operation may actually disrupt the capacity to maintain constant representations of self and object. For example, a thirty-one-year-old, never-married woman reported the following: She had been dating and having intercourse with a man for several months. He had made a date with her for Saturday night at the end of the previous weekend. He then did not call her until the Saturday morning of the date. She found it strange that when he called, she could not picture his face, and she felt like she "didn't know him." Analytic exploration revealed she had been developing wishes to marry this man, but that he had never increased the frequency of their dates—he only saw her on Saturday nights. When he did not call during the particular week in question, she felt frustrated and angry, but had not been aware of these feelings. In fact, although the date was marked on her calendar, it had "evaporated" from her mind during the week. She said, "He kind of disappeared from my head." She felt she had no right to be angry, since he had not promised her anything. When I interpreted her apparent diminution in object constancy as a defense against her guilt over anger at him, she began crying angrily, said she would like to "smash the smile off his face," and could then picture him. She added, "I could kill the bastard for stringing me along like this. I'm too old to be playing waiting games!" From a theoretical standpoint, the complex of functions that maintain the object image had become aggressivized. Because of conflict between her guilty feelings (and fear of loss of the object) and the aggressivized functions, she developed superego anxiety; the resulting defensive activity was to eliminate her object representation of the man. This object representation was reconstructable, along with its aggressive cathexis, once the defenses and affect were interpreted.

In homosexual men, instinctualization of ego functions, ego strengths, and/or object relations is quite common as an etiological factor for the homosexuality. For example, a male patient described an intensification of homosexual desires after his father's death some weeks previously. Later, during analysis, he revealed that what he specifically enjoyed in his sexual relations with other men was the act of rubbing his erect penis against the other man's. He referred to this as "dueling penises." Analysis of his associations to that activity demonstrated that unconsciously he felt competitive toward men; however, his fears of castration and punishment by his violent, critical father had led not only to a reaction formation against his anger, but to sexualization as a defense (Coen, 1981) against his unconscious patricidal fantasies. When his father died, the patient's guilt intensified. "Dueling penises" had become an act of "love," which defended him against guilt over the aggressivized object relation with his father. In addition, his mother had had him sleep with her until he was eleven and began masturbating. Father was relegated to sleeping on the couch in the family room. Therefore, his object tie to his mother never became sufficiently desexualized, as would occur in a normal oedipal resolution. Because of the continual sexualization of her object image, which was later displaced onto other women, any sexual attraction to a woman produced immediate oedipal guilt. Homosexuality, therefore, also defended against the castration and superego anxiety by restricting sexual activity with women. When he attempted heterosexual intercourse, he had unpleasurable premature ejaculation. With men, he rarely experienced an orgasm; this was a defense against unconscious aggressivization of his object image of his father.

Instinctualization of ego functions and of object relations, both due to activation through associative stimulation and due to defensive activity, is a concept familiar to psychoanalysts, though little discussed in general psychiatric presentations. In contrast, teenage girls I have treated seem to conceptualize instinctualization of object relations quite readily in their characterization of certain self-centered, sexually preoccupied boys as "dicks."

INSTINCTUALIZATION OF EGO DEFECTS

Recognizing that instinctualization of ego functions and object relations can cause such secondary ego defects is important for psychoanalytic technique, including technique in analyzing the meaning of certain aspects of homosexual behavior (what Socarides [1988, p. 543] calls "decoding the perverse symptom"). However, the obverse of these etiological factors occurs in situations where the ego defect is primary, and then, subsequently, instinctualization of that defect occurs. The notion that a sexual and/or aggressive valence can become attached to something that is not there, a defect, may seem abstruse and experience-distant (although one sees it phenomenologically in negative hallucinations). However, an understanding of that mechanism can enhance the understanding of homosexual development and make successful psychoanalytic treatment more feasible.

In fact, a frequent plea and/or demand (and an object of considerable technical controversy [cf., Socarides, 1988, pp. 533–535]) by homosexual men entering treatment is that their homosexuality not be "taken away." Although this is an overdetermined anxiety, I feel that their request is often based on a defect in abstract thinking; that is, the notion that something concrete will be removed. Further, they fear that without homosexual impulses, something basic will be missing. In my experience, what is missing includes the ego components of affect tolerance, containment of fantasy, judgment, delay of gratification, tension tolerance, and cohesive self-constancy. For example, those homosexual men who easily become overwhelmed by affect, lacrimate quickly, and hunger for a shoulder to cry on, often describe such functioning as "feminine," or "unmasculine." However, this type of "femininity" has accurately been described as exaggerated and a caricature. A homosexual's sense of "femininity" is a rationalization–intellectualization defending against shame and (annihilation) anxiety stemming from ego defects. In other words, there is massive ego weakness, but the homosexual considers this a "feminine" attribute associated with sexual identifications (with mother).

Another homosexual man I analyzed described "having sex" with another man. What actually "attracted" him to other men were their hairy chests, deep voices, and worldliness, all qualities he considered "masculine." Analysis of his associations revealed that he was harboring a fantasy that he could magically incorporate "strength" through fellatio, where he took the other man's penis in his mouth. He also liked other men to suck his penis, which gave him a feeling of strength (Ovesey, 1969). His initial associations to feeling weak were that he had a small penis and could not compete with other boys during latency. But these associations were bland and intellectual. When I interpreted the isolation of affect, he then expressed fear that he could not "handle" his massive rage toward both his mother and father. He now revealed that due to their arguments, unreliability, violence, and exhibitionism, he had "written them off" during his preschool (oedipal) years. He had substituted his own fantasy life, begun conversing with fantasized figures, and disengaged himself from his parents emotionally. This autistic defensive posture was still present and had actually become stronger, through the years, to avoid ego disruption from overstimulation. Meanwhile, he developed charming, "as if" social skills.

The result of his "disengagement" was a stunting of several ego strengths, especially affect tolerance and impulse control. Although fearful of contracting AIDS, loneliness increased his ego fragmentation anxiety, which he attempted to mollify by finding an external object for tension discharge. He did this by "cruising" public restrooms and seducing strange men into fellating him. Once he left a note with his name and phone number on an automobile he *guessed* belonged to an attractive man he met briefly at a party. When I confronted him with his transient break with reality and his poor judgment, he confirmed this was due to the tension deriving from his inability to tolerate loneliness. His awe at the "attractiveness" of the other man was a sexualization of a wish to obtain ego support (in the form of affect tolerance).

Since not all human beings with ego defects become homosexual, what additional factors make gender an issue and lead to instinctualized repairs? As mentioned, Socarides (1988) covers the psychoanalytic literature regarding identification, symbiotic conflicts, and defensive operations. Another special factor is concretization of the instinctualized ego defect. Due to a defect in abstraction, after the defect becomes instinctualized, the solution sought to it is external and concrete: another body. The sexual acting out of the ego repair needs takes on a concrete significance that borders on the delusional. This concreteness further contributes to many homosexual men's need to "cling" to their sexual functioning, and makes them wary of any doctor whom they perceive as being ready to "take this away." Their fear of therapy is, therefore, often not primarily due to castration anxiety, and often not primarily due to either oedipal or preoedipal transference reactions to the therapist. The fear is that the stopper in the bathtub of their mind may be pulled, and that all the water (their sense of affective stability and of self-image) will be drained out and lost. One homosexual man described his anxiety as a fear his mind would wind up like "hash-brown potatoes," chopped up with no structure.

In some homosexuals the ego defects may become aggressivized. This may lead to fantasies that external forces have damaged their abilities/thought processes, and, in some, to a wish for retaliation. These somewhat more unusual (and paranoid) types look to inflict ego damage on others, especially children. Those who advocate teaching grammar school youngsters about the specifics of oral and anal homosexual intercourse would be included in this subgroup, as well as the pedophiliac men who sodomize young boys. Massive aggressivization complicated by antisocial superego development is common in the homosexual male prostitute.

When aggressivization of defects in object and self-constancy is present, defensive attempts at repair may include the development of sadistic (or sadomasochistic) character traits. In particular, hostile "bitch" attitudes may prevail toward others, in action or in speech. Such hostile control mechanisms create in the subject a gratifying fantasy of replenished self-boundaries, and defend against self-dissolution anxiety.

IMPLICATIONS FOR TREATMENT

First of all, many homosexuals should not be analyzed. When ego and object relations defects are in the severe range, as they often are, the sexual activity of the homosexual man can in reality reduce tension and thereby spare the autonomous ego from "meltdown" due to overwhelming affects. A surprising number of homosexuals have defects that are so marked (especially in integrative function and in reality constancy [Frosch, 1966]), that they need to be considered psychotic characters (Frosch, 1970). Supportive therapy may aim at reducing psychic disequilibrium by prescription of medications to bolster the ego strengths of affect and tension tolerance (e.g., antidepressants and/or anxiolytics, possibly neuroleptics). Suggestion, clarification of reality, and discussions regarding reality and judgment may be needed from the therapist, as well.

In those homosexuals where defects do not appear to play a major role, it is most often a mistake to attempt to interpret oedipally based sexual dynamics, either as they appear toward the therapist or toward other people. The descriptions by the patient of genital organ inferiority, shame, guilt, and fears of affects do have dynamic components. However, if these components are interpreted, the patient, due to deficits in ego strengths, will often become flooded with affects and/or fantasy. Instead of facilitating integration and insight, such flooding leads to further ego dissolution, increased pessimism in the patient, and often bitter disruptions or interruptions in treatment.

Analytic therapy is also disrupted by interpretations of behavior and feelings associated with transference, either oedipal or preoedipal. It is not only transference that causes resistance, but anxieties over ego fragmentation due to expectation of interactions that will disrupt the patient's ego. Only a small part of the anticipation of damage is transferential—the rest is based on the patient's sense of his own ego fragility.

For a lengthy period of time, possibly for years, analytic interventions should focus on the nature of the specific ego and object relations defects, in an attempt to help the patient understand how he tries pathologically to repair them. Actual ego support may be necessary from the therapist in the form of verbalized understanding, discussions of reality, and clarification of motives not only in the patient but also in those to whom the patient has formed attachments. If defects in judgment and alloplastic adaptation are present, it is not sufficient to simply confront them; the therapist also needs to explain and reconstruct the reality of the patient's situation, taking care not to assume omnipotence.

The patient's response to an intervention will clarify the accuracy and helpfulness of that intervention as follows: if attention is drawn to defect repair mechanisms, the patient will experience some sense of relief and understanding, and will then produce dynamically oriented associations, which should be noted and catalogued until the patient's ego strength improves. If dynamic interpretations are made (e.g., defensive avoidance of castration anxiety by repression and running to "intact" men), the patient will usually then report or develop an exacerbation of an ego defect. This may take the form of an increase in dangerous acting out (defects in judgment, impulse control, psychomotor control), blocks in association (interference with language, speech, and integration), missing sessions (avoidance of the ego-threatening situation of therapy), or intense intellectualization of an analytic sort (increase in "as if" or "false self" activity to cover defects in the self-image).

SUMMARY

To assess male homosexual pathology, not only oedipal and preoedipal dynamics, but defects in ego strengths, ego functions, and object relations must be formulated. Although such defects may be secondary to the defensive activity of ego restriction, in many homosexuals the ego and object relations defects may be primary. Instinctualization of the defects will then present clinically as apparent inadequacies in sexual identity or in sexual functioning. The more the instinctualization of defects becomes concrete, the more the diagnosis of the patient shades into the psychotic category, and the less amenable he is to psychoanalytic techniques. In any homosexual man, however strong the ego may appear, care must be exercised by the therapist not to be seduced into what seem to be appropriately timed interpretations of resistance and defenses based on transference. For a very lengthy period of time, extratransference interpretations of interpersonal dynamics, and supportive techniques such as verbalization, explanation of abstract ideas, expression of understanding, clarification of defects, and discussions of reality, need to be instituted to help strengthen the autonomous ego. Improved ego strength may eventually allow transference interpretations without the side effect of severe ego regression, which is both antitherapeutic for the patient and disruptive to his treatment.

CHAPTER 8

Identification Processes in the Therapy of Male Oedipal Homosexuality

ABRAHAM FREEDMAN, M.D.

This chapter deals with the psychology of identification and the vicissitudes of the Oedipus complex in the etiology, and, especially, the analytic treatment of homosexuality. Two cases of oedipal homosexuality, treated over twenty years ago, are presented in detail and other clinical anecdotes are given in illustration.

CLINICAL HISTORIES

Case 1. Mr. B.

Mr. B. was a thirty-five-year-old unmarried white male who was referred for psychoanalysis because of a street phobia which had arisen about one month previously and was getting worse. He was employed as a computer programmer for a scientific publisher (in the days before personal computers and purchaseable programs, when programmers were invaluable) and was now having difficulty getting to work and going about his daily business. He felt a vague anxiety when walking on the sidewalk but had greater fear when he had to cross a street. Before the symptoms developed he had been arrested, had

159

sought legal aid, and had been advised to bribe the arresting officer and arrange to plead guilty to get a suspended sentence. He felt helpless, the situation was intolerable, and he was being forced to do something that was against his ideals and values. He said, "I'm being screwed from behind." When I remarked on the possible implications of his metaphor, he said that he had to tell me that he was homosexual, despite the fact that one of his big fears was that if people knew, he would be disgraced at his job and in his family. In fact, the principal worry in his dilemma was that his situation would become known, either by a public trial or through blackmail by the arresting officer.

He had met the officer when the man was out of uniform, in a public park where they sat on a bench and warily began a general conversation. It seemed to him that the other man was looking for a homosexual contact as he was himself.

They had gone into a movie theater and into the toilet. When he exposed his penis to be sucked the other man identified himself as a member of the vice squad and placed him under arrest. The patient felt that he had been trapped, and thought of having his lawyer plead entrapment, but was aware that a public trial, even though fair and with a finding of innocence, would jeopardize the secrecy of his sexual preference. The only alternative, submitting to blackmail, infuriated him. He also feared that whenever he wanted to satisfy his sexual desires in the future he would risk placing himself in the same untenable position. Any contact on the street with a stranger could bring this about. He would be as helpless as if he were to be hit by a truck.

He felt that the analysis was a form of submission and that I had him in my power, could force him to do anything, and could charge him any amount of money once the treatment got under way; he was trapped in it and there was no reason why I too would not eventually blackmail him. Still he had enough trust to remain in analysis despite his paranoid misgivings, and was actually reassured by my quiet acceptance of his accusations.

It seemed clear to me that his dilemma of how to handle his predicament was a derivative of conflict and that he did not entirely accept homosexual submission to another man. Still, he both performed fellatio and had fellatio performed upon him, so that it seemed that he could accept either a passive or active sexual relationship with another man. This led me to hypothesize that he was in considerable conflict between masculine and feminine strivings, and I then looked for evidence of oedipal conflict.

The patient was the youngest of four children. He had two older brothers with whom he was not close. He was fond of his older sister, felt that she loved him, and he could turn to her when he was in trouble. He suspected that she knew that he was homosexual and accepted it. He felt that his brothers had contempt for him for not being as masculine as they were, and that is why he and they were distant.

When he began the treatment he was living with his widowed mother. He described her as an obese woman with a milk leg. She had suffered from phlebitis at the time of his birth. He felt that he had caused her disability and had to take care of her now. He had always been very close to her and she called him her baby. In childhood his sister usually had something to do outside the home and he was left to be the one to help his mother. Thus he had always helped with the housework and cooking. Now that he and his mother were the only ones left at home, she cooked for him, but he still did the heavier housework, the gardening, and all the shopping and other errands. He felt fond of his mother but resented the fact that he seemed to be controlled by her and she was always telling him what to do. She chided him about the fact that he did not go with women and said that she wanted him to get married. However, when he was younger he did occasionally have girl friends, and his mother had always been critical of them and let him know that they were not good enough for him. He said that he felt like he was "married" to his mother. He resented it but on the other hand it gave him an obvious reason why he did not go out with women or think of getting married: he had to stay home and care for his mother.

His father had been a skilled cabinetmaker and had died when the patient was about twenty. He recalled with considerable anger that he had been in a college class when he was called out and told to go to a hospital where his father was sick.

His father had already died of a heart attack, but no one had prepared him when they told him to go to the hospital. He was shocked to learn that his father had died, but could not understand the depth of his grief because he felt that his father did not like him and he had felt angry with his father for several years.

The father had tried to make all his sons apprentices in the shop. As a young child the patient was assigned tasks such as sandpapering a piece of wood that was to become the leg of a chair. No matter how hard he tried, his father criticized him and told him to improve the work again and again. His brothers teased him in the shop. He hated to go there after school and worked sullenly, hating the other boys but especially his father. At times his father told him he had a talent for woodwork but that did not improve his mood as he labored seemingly endlessly over the same piece of work. He recalled that his father struck him only rarely, but he still had a constant fear that he would be beaten if he talked back or disobeyed him. Therefore he hardly ever protested openly but seethed inwardly and thought he was being treated unfairly.

In earlier memories, he was often taken into his mother's bed and enjoyed the warmth and closeness of her large body. When he saw his father from that position he had feelings of satisfaction mixed with a vague dread. When he was old enough to start school, he was driven there by his father, accompanied by his mother. His mother cried and made it difficult for him to stay in school and face the other children. He was a good student and was praised by both parents. He worked harder and did better than his brothers, who usually wanted to play outside rather than do homework. His teachers had known his siblings before him and always told him what a good student his sister had been, holding her up as a model to be emulated. The pattern of helping his mother in the house and staying in to do his homework began in his early school years.

In prepuberty and early adolescence, he was friends with some school and neighborhood boys. He noticed that he was particularly interested when there was an occasion to urinate together and he was always eager to see their penises. When he could get together with only one other boy, he induced him to masturbate jointly. He noticed that there were a few boys who seemed effeminate and were called sissies. In adolescence he heard about being "queer," assumed that those boys were "queer" and avoided them. He dated in high school as he was supposed to do, but was shy with girls, did not kiss them, and felt revulsion when one girl aggressively French-kissed him. He was a good dancer and could be friendly with girls at a school dance, but he recognized he was not interested in them the way other boys were. He silently resented other boys talking about taking sexual advantage of girls and bragging how they were using them.

In college he was seduced into fellatio by a schoolfriend when they were studying together. He liked the experience and it had a calming effect on him, but he was afraid of being found out. When he felt sexual tension or anxiety from any outer cause or from an unknown source, he sought out another man to have fellatio. The accompanying fantasy was disclosed in the analysis. It had to do with a struggle between him and the other man. It was a case of who was stronger and who would be humiliated. He could not lose! If he performed fellatio he would be taking in the strength of the other man. The seminal fluid was a magical substance that would make more of a man of him. If he had fellatio performed on him, it would be a humiliation to the other man. When he performed anal intercourse he felt triumphant when he penetrated the other man but he felt very uncomfortable about being the recipient in anal intercourse. It was harder to maintain the fantasy of taking in the other man's strength than in the event of fellatio because he could not rid himself of a feeling of humiliation when he was penetrated.

It was many months after starting the analysis that he disclosed that he had a special friend who was homosexual. This was a college professor with whom he shared cultural and intellectual interests. They both liked music and drama. Their sexual activity was infrequent but when it did occur the patient had the same fantasies of overcoming the other man, that is, of either taking his strength or humiliating him. He did not get as much satisfaction as when he did it with strangers because he really liked the professor and felt guilty about his fantasies. It was like he was hurting his friend without the other's awareness.

The conflict over anal penetration came out in several transference transactions. The patient had suffered on and off for many years with backache. His backache became worse when he was on the couch and he often got up at the end of the hour with considerable discomfort and stiffness of his back. (I used a modern foam-rubber upholstered couch which other people ordinarily found comfortable.) I remarked that the stiffness of his standing posture was even visible when he was on the couch. He held himself rigidly while lying on his back with his arms at his sides for most of the hour. He then became aware not only of the rigidity of his back but also that he held his buttocks tightly compressed in order to prevent me from penetrating him from behind. With repeated similar observations and discussion of his fear of penetration, the physical symptom was ameliorated. The fear of penetration was stimulated by my words. He constantly feared that I would suggest something to him to control him.

One morning, as I was driving downtown for our appointment, my car was struck lightly from behind at a stoplight. When the patient arrived, he told me that he had been walking down the same street, had seen the accident, and would be a witness if I needed him. He could not understand how unperturbed I seemed about the accident. I had gotten out of my car, looked at the rear, saw that there was no damage, and had calmly driven away. He would have been furious if it had happened to him but he would have loved to have been able to handle it the way I had. The following night he had a dream in which his car had been crumpled by a collision from the rear and he had awakened in a panic. The car in the dream was not actually his car but a large sedan which his mother had owned from the time of his father's death. His mother did not drive but she kept the car and he occasionally drove her in it. In fact, he had driven it for several years before he had bought his own new car, after he finished graduate school and had a job.

A remarkable event occurred a few days later. He had to go to a business meeting at a local hotel. The parking lot attendant offered to park his car, but he said he would rather do it himself. He had then reversed the car too rapidly and backed it into a stone wall and damaged the rear. He was very upset and could not believe that he had done this. He was furious and depressed for days, and even after the car was repaired he seemed to see the damage when he looked at the rear. The patient readily agreed with me that this series of events was related to some very important things that were not visible from the surface.

The car in the dream was associated to his mother. It had a big rear like her backside. Although he had spoken of the pleasure of being close to her body in bed, he remembered the revulsion he felt whenever he saw her defective leg. It was swollen and discolored. He recalled that the higher up the thigh he had seen it the uglier it became. With obviously very unpleasant affect he recalled the times when he had seen her genitalia or big buttocks under her nightgown. It was like the discolored leg only many times more repulsive. The genital was swollen and dark. He thought of it as even more damaged than her leg. It was made worse by the thought that he had done this to her. She had told him about his birth as early as he could remember. His damaging her always made him feel guilty, and he had to atone for it by taking care of her for the rest of his life. However, he also feared as a child that the same thing could happen to him. His legs would swell and his genitals could become a dark, ugly place. When he began to masturbate he tried to control it for fear that he would damage himself and end up like his mother. He became conflicted over being close to her in bed because he was afraid of seeing the damaged leg. As an older child, adolescent, and young man, he was asked to help his mother when her leg became inflamed and she needed to treat it with wet compresses. He could not refuse to help her but each time he had to contend with the feelings of revulsion. It made his skin crawl; in more detail, it made his scrotum retract.

There were more dreams and other analytic material relating to his fantasy that I would penetrate him from the rear. Even my words and interpretations stimulated those fears. After I repeatedly commented that his fear of being like his mother seemed to be like a fear of being treated by me like his mother (I was thinking of the Wolf Man), he had more nightmares about damage to his rear and recalled being in the room when his mother and father were together. He thought that he must have seen them having sex and especially sex from the rear. He then associated his mother's damaged body not only to his birth but also to the sexual act that had caused the pregnancy. After considerable working through of these ideas, he was relieved of the guilt over his mother's phlebitis.

He took an apartment for himself after much difficulty in dealing with his mother's objections to his moving away. His sister was supportive and encouraged him to move. She promised to visit their mother more often than she had done in the past. The patient hired a woman to help his mother with the housework, and still visited her daily. He did her errands, took care of the grounds in the summer, and shoveled her walks in the winter.

His father's woodworking tools had remained in a workshop in the basement of the house. Although the patient had not touched them when he was living there, he now cleaned them up, sharpened them, and developed a woodcarving hobby. He became sufficiently interested to enroll in a woodcarving course in an evening high school program. He eagerly sought my approval as he described his work to me and occasionally brought in a small piece to show me how he'd finished it. I was reminded of his failed attempts to get his father's approval in the carpentry shop, and I displayed my interest (and approval) by asking questions about the work. He began to talk about what an expert craftsman his father had been. One day he chanced to walk by an auctioneer's shop where some custom-made furniture was being sold. He carefully examined some pieces during the inspection period and found a small chest with his father's benchmark. He was thrilled by his find and successfully bid for it. He developed the collection of his father's works as another hobby. He searched through antique shops and auctioneers and was sometimes rewarded by unearthing something his father had made. He described some inlaid jewelry caskets as exquisite and elegant, and lingered over the description of the curve of the back of a chair. In the analysis he spoke admiringly and even lovingly about his father. He wished that he had stayed as an apprentice and had learned more of his father's craft. He blamed his mother for keeping him close to her and keeping his father at a distance.

He became an industrious analysand, free associating or reporting dreams, and then proceeding to an analysis of the material. He wanted to be able to do it himself and as well as I could. I constantly remarked how he really had wanted to be more like his father than like his mother. There was also a rapprochement with his brothers. He visited their homes more often and wanted to be a good uncle to their children. Previously he had felt uncomfortable with his nephews as if he had some fear of pedophilia, but now he could play with them naturally.

His sister introduced him to some of her unmarried girl friends. She had always tried to get him interested in her friends but was understanding when he had not responded and did not pressure him. The difference was that now he seemed more receptive and wanted to meet women. There was some difficulty with his homosexual lover because of the patient's loss of interest in him. It pained the patient that his friend was hurt by the separation and he tried to be gentle. The patient tried to have a sexual relationship with one woman but distressingly was impotent. This led to a withdrawal from women and a renewed interest in his homosexual friend. However, he refrained entirely from the homosexual cruising.

In the analytic discussion of the heterosexual failure, it became evident that he had castration anxiety. He enjoyed embracing the woman's body and got an erection, but he was frightened by her genital. The actual experience had occurred some time before he disclosed it in the analysis. It developed that he was afraid that I would disapprove of his having sex with a woman and taking advantage of her. He accused himself of using the woman for an experiment. He asked, "How would you feel if it turned out to be your daughter?" This led to further analysis of the Oedipus complex and his fear of his father's disapproval and punishment for sexual wishes. Again, he recalled the scenes in the parents' bedroom when he felt uncomfortable in bed with his mother if his father were there.

When we returned from the third summer vacation, he surprised me by telling me that he'd met a woman through his work who lived in a nearby town and was romantically interested in her. Through dreams about women with long black hair, he connected his attraction to her to his early childhood image of his mother in her nightgown with her hair down. That was the summer I had grown a beard. This patient was included in my paper on the change of analyst's visage (Freedman, 1970). He had a dream about being threatened by a man who seemed to be this woman's father. The man in the dream had a beard. When questioned about the beard he disclosed that he had not noticed that I had one and was surprised to see it when he got off the couch at the end of the hour. However, this material gave him more evidence of his fear of heterosexuality connected with the fear of the father. His uncertainty over the beard had to do with its interference with his identification with me, but also indicated that the transference image becomes fixed in the mind of the patient and is not readily changed by external perceptions.

There was considerable working through of his relationship with this woman, his love of her, his fear of her, and the castration anxiety aroused by the new situation. He took the woman to meet his family members and was enjoying his acceptance as a man by his sisters and brothers. His newly found identification with me, his father, and brothers seemed very important in sustaining him in his reawakened heterosexuality. He terminated the analysis soon after he married her six months later. I have not seen nor heard of him since and there is no follow-up.

Case 2. Harry

I was consulted by the parents of an eighteen-year-old male who were concerned when they were told that he was homosexual. The information came from the mother's hairdresser, who said that her son was going with some of his employees who, he knew, were homosexuals. The mother was a short, plump, fashionably overdressed women who did most of the talking during the interview. She was garrulous and forceful, but also very upset and often tearful. Although I strove to maintain my neutral analytic stance, I sensed that I did not like her. I felt that she was protesting too much over the lost masculinity of her son and had a repeated need to deny any responsibility for it. She also told me that they had an older daughter who had been hospitalized for a short time for what was called schizophrenia, but had recovered and was now "doing beautifully." The father was no taller than his wife but was slim and neatly dressed. He did not have much to say but when he spoke was pleasant, realistic, and much more informative. He deferred to his wife and seemed to look to her for cues when he could speak. I agreed to see their son if they understood that there was no certainty of changing his homosexuality if such were the case, but I would evaluate him and determine what treatment if any was needed.

The young man called for his first appointment. He was about the same height and size as his father. He was moderately effeminate in speech and gesture and had a pleasant nondefensive attitude. He spoke readily and eagerly. He was concerned not about his homosexuality, which he knew worried his parents, but he described compulsive–obsessional symptoms. The useless repetitive acts he undertook got on his nerves but he felt worse if he did not carry them out when he had the urge. He was willing to come for treatment both for himself and to make his parents happy, especially his mother, but he had no interest in giving up his homosexuality. He also knew how the parents had come to find out about his homosexuality and was surprised that it was such a shock to them, as he thought they themselves should have been able to notice his difference from other boys. He could use the treatment to get rid of his other symptoms. Also, he had finished high school, was a good student, and bright enough for college but had no idea of what he wanted to be "when I grow up." He thought that seeing a therapist might help him find himself and make some decisions. In the meantime he was content to help his father in the family business when he felt like it or spend his time as it pleased him. After a few evaluative sessions, I explained the procedure to him and he thought it would be very interesting to find out as much as possible about himself.

Harry had known about his homosexuality as far back as he could remember. Penises fascinated him from the first few years of life. He lost no opportunity to look at his father's or his male cousins' penises. Whenever possible, he got playmates to urinate together so that he could compare penises and the urinary stream. By the time he was age ten, he was going to the park and seducing adult men into fellatio or masturbation. He said that the newspaper stories of child molestation were mostly "bullshit" because he knew that he and a few other boys of his age had been active seducers of older men. He was now having the time of his life because he was the pet of a group of older homosexuals who went around together and had great parties. He seemed to enjoy telling me all the details of their sexual activities. In fact, he taught me much about descriptive homosexuality and homosexual language.

It developed that he was shamelessly hoping to get me aroused so he could seduce me. I would then become *trade* (a homosexual term which means the seduction of a man who is ostensibly straight and would never believe that he is homosexual). The advantage of this conquest is that when one wants to suck the penis of another man, part of the reason is to add to the strength of one's own penis. That is why it is better to suck a big penis than a small one. But if the other penis belongs to a homosexual, no matter how impressive it looks, there is always a taint on its masculinity as compared to "trade" which represents a heterosexual penis and therefore has more masculine strength which can be incorporated.

I suggested that from what he said about "trade," a homosexual had doubts about his own penis as if possibly something had happened to it. Harry thought that this was so obvious that I really didn't have to mention it, but I replied that we ought to find out how these doubts arose. Harry then got into the subject of his relationship with his mother. He was always especially close to her and she seemed to turn to him because she and his older sister were always fighting over something as long as he could remember. He was allowed many intimacies. As a child he could not only watch his mother in the bathtub and on the toilet but also was frequently taken into the bathtub with her. He remembered getting erections in the bathtub when she was washing him and it seemed to him that she paid a lot of attention to washing his penis.

Sometime preschool she noticed that his circumcision seemed incomplete and he was recircumcised and had a tonsillectomy at the same time. He recalled awakening with a very sore throat that he had not been warned about. He also had a burning pain in his penis, tried to touch it, and found that it was bandaged. He thought it was cut off and remembered the appearance of his mother's genitals in the tub and thought that he had been made into a girl. However, his conscious memory was that he took this matter philosophically because by then he had become so close to his mother he thought it would be nice to be just like her. In a few days he saw that he still had a penis, albeit a sore one, and always thought that he had lost a part of it. After the surgery he recalled that he was not as eager to be naked with his mother and was uncomfortable when she bathed him. He also thought that the operations were his mother's idea but blamed his father for not protecting him. Then he thought that his father had conspired to damage his penis because he was jealous of how close Harry was with his mother. Still it seemed, as he grew up, his father was less involved with him and he was turned over to his mother. Around age eight, his father tried to teach him to play ball with him in the backyard, but Harry was clumsy, did not learn how to catch the ball, and "threw like a girl." He clowned around to cover his failure until his father got disgusted and stopped the game. On the other hand, his sister became adept in sports and later was on the high school girls' softball and basketball teams. Harry thought that he had turned over his maleness to his sister and had taken on the privileges of being the daughter.

His mother continued to encourage their closeness. He was taken shopping with her and went into the dressing room in women's stores to help her with fit and taste. When other women objected to his presence, his mother told them, "Let him help you. He has better taste than you have." Sometimes his father feared that his son was being emasculated and tried to stop these activities, but his mother told the father he was being silly. Harry recalled in the analysis that all the while he had the privilege of seeing his mother in her underwear in her bedroom or in a store as if he were a girl, he secretly enjoyed looking at her and had sexual feelings which he kept hidden from her lest she stop the intimacies. He admired his mother's body but he was always careful not to see her genital, though he could have arranged it if he had wanted to.

One day he brought a dachshund puppy into the analytic room. He said that he had just bought it and had nowhere to put it on the way home. He went on to talk about how he had begged his mother for weeks to let him have a dog at home, and in fact he had previously talked about this disagreement with her in the analysis. She finally consented and this was the dog, a female, which he had preferred. Toward the end of this hour, he became upset, tearful, and angry with me and accused me of not caring. When I sought some explanation he accused me of insensitivity because I had not acknowledged that this was our baby. He thought that I would have understood this as soon as he came in with the puppy. The next hour we continued with his fantasy of bearing my child, and in fact he often had a fantasy of being impregnated during homosexual intercourse. The most exciting thing for him was to have intercourse on his back with his legs high around the other man while his anus was penetrated. He had a fantasy that he had no penis and that the other man's penis was in his vagina. This would really make him feel like his mother. By this time I was convinced that his homosexuality was part of a very early identification with his mother and was probably not going to change. Still, the history of the early phallic–oedipal strivings was evidence to the contrary.

By this time there had also been much analysis of his rage, his ambivalence over wanting to be controlled, his masochistic wishes, and his anal conflicts. The compulsive symptoms were subsiding. I also noted that he had taken more of an interest in his father's business and had some creative ideas of which his father was making practical and profitable application.

There was a change in his choice of homosexual partners. He had become less promiscuous and was having one-to-one relationships with lovers lasting many months. Harry was becoming less interested in the promiscuous homosexual life which he had previously found so exciting. He had given me many descriptions of group perversions with urinary and defecatory acts. Now these perversions made him feel more disgusted than before. He had previously witnessed but rarely partaken of them, and now he did not even want to see them or hear about them. He noticed that many of his compulsive acts were used to get rid of the feelings of revulsion that these acts aroused in him. He now preferred lovers who were not so kinky.

Around this time he began to become interested in men who had sexual relations with women as well as men. Part of this was the narcissistic satisfaction of being preferable in his female identification. That is, he enjoyed the fact that these men who could have been making love with a woman preferred to make love with him. A discussion of this revealed the reverse Oedipus complex. It was as if his father were choosing him in preference to his mother. He again described to me that when he lay supine with his legs around the man, penetrated anally by the man's penis, he felt as if he had really achieved the sexual pleasure of a woman. Although, as previously noted, I thought all this was evidence of the early preoedipal origin of his homosexuality, and that his feminine identification was probably fixed and immutable, but then he began to speak of the "trade" aspects of his lover. It was better to be loved by a bisexual man because he was closer to a real man than one who could only be a homosexual. He felt that his anus as well as his mouth could incorporate the strength of the penis. In his supine sexual position he could alternate in pretending he had no penis to feeling that his erection and the lover's were fused and his penis was becoming stronger by its closeness to his lover's penis.

As a small child Harry had been taken to dancing school with his sister. She dropped out when he was prepubertal but Harry liked dancing and continued. In adolescence he had become interested in classical ballet. Recently his interest had increased and he was spending considerable time in a dancing school which put on performances. He was assigned to a pas-de-deux with a petite ballerina. She was even smaller than he and he enjoyed dancing with her. He sometimes thought of her as the kind of girl he would like to be. They danced very well together. He liked the feel of her waist as he spun her around.

He liked putting his hands on her hips. In the rest periods they stayed together and fooled around, or, as he laughingly put it, "feel around." She got him to put his hands on different parts of her body "to get the best balance," but she laughed when he seemed shy at touching her too close to her breasts or her pelvis. He began to notice that he felt aroused during these periods, especially when she frankly told him what felt sensuous to her. He developed the idea in the analysis that he had gotten so much penis from his lover that he could be more of a man with the ballerina. Sometimes he came home from a dance class feeling sexually excited and needing his lover immediately. All this was going on for many weeks before he brought it up in the analysis. Since he had always seemed so frank and free of shame, I wondered why this material was harder for him to talk about. He then confessed that strangely enough, although he sensed that I wanted him to be a man, he had felt uncomfortable telling me how he enjoyed touching the girl's body. It was crazy but he thought that I would have disapproved of it and might hurt him in some way for doing it. It was the same way he felt when his father came home and caught him in the bedroom with his partly undressed mother. I wondered with him whether his eagerness to be with his lover after a dancing session could be to overcome anxiety he felt when he was with the ballerina. That is, could being with a woman and having sexual feelings for her make him need to act like a woman to get out of the danger but also then have his penis restored by sex with a man?

We spent many sessions on the connections between his identification with his bisexual lover, his shifting self identification between male and female gender, his phallic wishes, the anxiety they caused, and the protective function of retreating to feeling like a woman as well as having his penis restored by incorporation of the penis of the male lover. Harry described how he imitated his lover in so many ways that their friends teased about copycatting him. The function of identification in this case has been previously described (Freedman and Slap, 1960).

Other aspects of Harry's character were changing. He had often told me of what happened at homosexual parties and of the chagrin of the host when he saw what was missing after the guests had gone. Many homosexuals were wont to steal small objects such as silverware, bric-a-brac, small pieces of jewelry, lighters. In the bedroom where they put their coats, they laughed and showed their plunder to close friends. Harry had never stolen himself but he used to join in the fun and the laughs. Now, he was disgusted at such delinquencies. He felt that they were not honest "the way men should be." He recalled the strict honesty of his father in the business as compared to the looser values of his mother. She would not be inclined to correct a cashier's error if it was in her favor. She could readily lie and have him tell social lies to her friends when it was easier than the truth. He never had qualms about answering the phone, learning who was calling, and saying "she's not home" when he knew his mother did not want to talk to a particular woman. He recalled how his mother could manipulate people but his father was always honest with others. He now felt that it was easy and fun to be able to be like his mother but he was developing a sense of justice and honesty like his father that was causing conflict when he didn't follow his conscience. He discovered how this was connected with obsessional thinking. When he wished to do something wrong he ruminated about it, trying to prove to himself that it was right. He no longer absented himself from the business with a phony excuse when he wanted to be with his homosexual friends. His life was becoming more organized. He had regular hours in the business and regular hours for the dancing. The class was preparing for a semiprofessional performance; he was practicing earnestly for one of the leading roles and spending more time with his ballerina.

One Sunday he invited the ballerina home for dinner after informing his parents that he had a girl friend. Both parents seemed very pleased. However, at the dinner table his mother asked many questions and soon found out that the girl had an Irish-Catholic background. She remained pleasant but after dinner she took the girl aside and said, "You're a very nice girl but wouldn't it be better if you found a boy of your own kind." Harry found the girl crying in the kitchen. He was pale and speechless with anger and chagrin but was unable to say anything to his mother. He took the girl home and when he returned he was gratified to find that his parents had been having a quarrel over the incident. The father accused the mother of emasculating Harry his whole life and this proved it. She would prefer Harry to remain homosexual rather than marry a non-Jewish girl.

He continued in the dancing group and they had a creditable performance, but he stopped taking the ballerina out socially. In the analysis it appeared that he had a terrible fear of separating from his mother, even though he was enraged at her behavior with the girl. He recognized that his mother wanted him as a part of herself and did not want him to have an independent existence. We repeatedly took up separation themes in the analysis, concerned not only with his mother but also me. He was thinking of going to college and taking a business course with the aim of eventually running the family business. He felt it would be good for him if he went out of town for college, as this would be a natural way to encourage the break from his mother. Although I would have liked him to stay in analysis until I saw more gains in his sexual problem, I thought that the ability to separate from me was also an advantage. The compulsive–obsessional symptoms were much improved to the point of not being noticeable for weeks at a time. There was considerable character change. He was more appropriately mature for his age (now 23), had a sense of identification with me and his father, a strong masculine superego, and a sense of what he wanted to do in life. Still, I felt that his mother had dealt a fatal blow to his heterosexual strivings when she had quashed the first and only attachment to a female outside the family, and I did not expect him to be heterosexual at the end of the treatment.

Epilogue: About four years later I began to see delivery trucks on the street with the name of his father's company and with Harry's name on the side, but I was totally surprised one night when I was leaving a good restaurant and saw Harry seated at a table with a beautiful young woman. He stood as soon as he saw me, greeted me warmly, and said, "Dr. Freedman, I want you to meet my wife." I have no other follow-up.

I don't know if this was a marriage of convenience or what his sexual function is. But it was evident that in his work and personal relationship he had identified himself as a man.

DISCUSSION: TREATMENT CONSIDERATIONS

Considering the circumstances under which both Mr. B. and Harry came into treatment, we can see that there were both external and internal factors. Mr. B. had developed a phobic reaction after being stressed by an arrest for homosexuality and becoming the object of possible blackmail by the arresting officer. The event stimulated internal conflicts. He could either follow his ideals and insist on a trial which would expose him or submit to the blackmail. The conflict was between submission and fight, or more specifically, between passive submission and active fight. He was also faced with the conflict of trying to get homosexual gratification in the face of the possible repetition of the threatening situation that had just traumatized him. Mr. B., although a practicing homosexual, was conflicted about being penetrated in the anus and derivatives of this conflict were evident in his relationships to other men in general. This conflict appeared early in the transference. A repressed Oedipus complex became evident only in the course of the analysis, but his conflict between activity (masculinity) and passivity (femininity) was evident during the evaluation process.

Harry openly accepted his homosexuality and was indifferent when asked by his parents to be treated for it, but he had a compulsive–obsessive neurosis and was dissatisfied with the lack of goals in his life. He was conflicted by his attachment to his mother and identification with her, which he accepted as part of his sexual preference, in contrast to resentment at being controlled by her. Later it developed that his feminine identification was in conflict with an abortive early phallic relationship to his mother and an Oedipus complex.

The feasibility of bringing the unconscious conflicts to consciousness in each patient made it possible to treat them with psychoanalysis. The social milieu of patients treated in the 1960s was different from that of patients today. It might be argued that the general social disapproval of homosexuality might arouse conflict and make the patient more amenable to treatment. However, this was more true in the case of Mr. B. than in the case of Harry, whose open attitude about his sexual choice was similar to that of many homosexuals today. He did come at the instigation of his parents but, as the analysis showed later, the opposition of his mother to his femininity was a surface attitude. Unconsciously, she needed to have her son as a part of herself and accepted the sacrifice of his masculinity. Bringing him to the analyst seemed to be an attempt to undo this, partly because of her superego conflicts and partly because she needed to disprove her husband's accusation that she wanted to feminize their son.

In each case, the suffering of a psychoneurosis was paramount in causing the patient to accept the treatment. It is up to the analyst during the psychoanalytic evaluation to make the patient aware that he has conflicts and suffers from a form of neurosis. Admittedly, the nearer the conflicts and neurotic suffering are to consciousness the easier it is to get the patient to enter psychoanalytic treatment, but this is generally true, not just in the treatment of homosexuals. In other cases the onset of depression following the loss of a lover might bring a homosexual for treatment, but it is necessary to find conflict in order to begin a psychoanalytic process.

Another patient was a corporate executive who functioned well but led a lonely, desperate life. He had no close friends. His homosexual activity was by casual contact that threatened him with physical harm or mortifying exposure. His opening interview was a tearful recital of his lifelong loneliness and unhappiness and he came for treatment because if it went on he saw no reason for living. His father had gone into the service when the patient was an infant. They lived in a small town where his mother worked in the bank. She took her infant child to work with her in a carriage and he was kept with her all day. He was the object of her loving attention as well as that of the other workers and customers. At age four there was a sudden change when his father returned from the service. He recalled being abruptly put out of his mother's bed and his struggles to return. His father seemed to be a dangerous ogre and he and his father vied for his mother's attention. He won but always feared that his father would destroy him for it. His parents were divorced and he had much more contact with his mother than his father, but as the analysis progressed, he began to see more of his father. He recalled that his mother used to teach him to wrestle when he was a boy. She was strong and wiry and as they struggled on the floor, he felt sexually excited. These feelings were very frightening. He had few boy friends but always tried to play with his sister and her friends when they let him. Sometimes they teased and mocked him. He did not feel like a boy but he hated girls. In adolescence, he was aware that he hated girls and was afraid of them, but did not get along with the boys, and his loneliness grew. Occasionally he found boys who masturbated with him but the word got out that he was "queer" and his loneliness increased. He went away to college where he had casual homosexual contacts.

In the course of his analysis, his problems with identification, his heterosexual awareness, and castration anxiety became conscious. He had long periods of silences in which it developed he was having erotic transference fantasies. He wished that I would stroke his hair or gently rub the nape of his neck, but felt very ashamed if I knew what he was thinking. The fantasies were repetitions of the way his mother soothed him. This patient became more outwardly friendly in the course of the analysis. He developed better relationships in the company where he was employed and was able to have nonsexual relationships with men as well as more meaningful homosexual attachments. He became much friendlier with his father, now retired, and bought a rural property adjacent to where his father lived. He began to speak of his mother humorously and could see himself more separated from her. He became more friendly with his sister and enjoyed being an uncle. He stopped analysis with a fear that if he continued it might interfere with his homosexuality and leave him lonely again. He was happy to settle for the gains he had made and was afraid of jeopardizing them.

I believe that a psychoanalyst must begin the treatment without any bias as to the outcome of the patient's sexual preference. His aim must be to conduct a psychoanalysis, that is, to allow the transference to develop, analyze it, and help the patient to become aware of unconscious conflicts so that they can be analyzed. However, despite the analyst's neutral position it is probable that he has a point of view. It should be noted that if he has an unconscious aim of heterosexuality it will in some manner become evident to the patient and derivatives of the analyst's unconscious will enter the countertransference. Likewise, in a psychoanalyst whose unconscious sexuality has a high homosexual content, derivatives favoring the retention of the patient's homosexuality or reaction formation against it would be countertransference factors that could influence the analysis. It is important to handle problems of countertransference, whatever they are, as in any psychoanalysis, and not let them become confused with extra-analytic phenomena such as political issues.

The developmental histories in both cases support Socarides's (1978) theory about the importance of a preoedipal attachment to a disturbed mother in the etiology of homosexuality and perversions. However, this factor alone might be seen in borderline and narcissistic pathology where obligatory homosexuality or perversion is not necessarily present. In my clinical experience, the factors of identification, specific variations of the nature of castration anxiety and the Oedipus complex, have produced homosexuality and sexual perversions as the outcome in cases where the preoedipally derived psychopathology has increased the susceptibility to disorders of psychosexual development. The psychoanalysis of the phallic and oedipal conflicts in the transference and genetically can produce a redirection of the Oedipus complex and influence sexual orientation toward its original biological path. The preoedipal part of the psychopathology is treated by interpreting the conflict in gender identification, allowing identification with a (male) psychoanalyst, and allowing the growth of autonomy to replace the symbiotic bond with the preoedipal mother. The conflict between the wish to remain attached or to become autonomous must be repeatedly interpreted. With female psychoanalysts I would speculate that the analyst becomes a new oedipal object in the transference and there is a tendency for the patient to revive old masculine identifications and oedipal strivings in pursuit of the new oedipal object. The conflict over attachment versus autonomy might be more easily seen with female analysts in some cases, but it is also ever present with male analysts.

CASTRATION ANXIETY

The hypothesis of increased castration anxiety-provoking events is more readily confirmed in the early history of other perversions than in homosexuality. An excellent example is in the case of a man with an unusual barbershop perversion (Freedman 1978). When feeling overwhelmed by anxiety stimulated by any set of external circumstances, the patient would seek a one-barber shop in a quiet neighborhood where the barber was a heavy set man with pinkish skin and jowls. After being draped, the patient would order a shave. When it was almost done, he would complain that areas on his neck had to be reshaved. As he repeated this order the barber would signify his annoyance by heavier breathing. The patient would then have an ejaculation, get up from the chair, hurriedly pay the barber and leave. In the analysis, it was disclosed that every detail of this ritual was related to castration threats in his childhood which were much greater than an average expected occurrence. His perversion was a defense against and an undoing of this threat when it occurred in later life. An unpublished case of foot fetishism that I presented to the American Psychoanalytic Study Group on the Perversions (1987) had the following early childhood experiences: Born with an umbilical hernia, the patient had corrective surgery at the age of a few months. At age two years he was operated on for inguinal hernia on the other side and also had a correction of his circumcision (note the tendency of families and surgeons to attack the penis directly when there is need for some other surgical intervention as in the case of Harry. Also note the observations of Lipton on the history of tonsillectomy and its relation to the threat of castration [1962]).

At age nine he was operated on for a recurrence of the first inguinal hernia. There were also events related to an absent father who returned from military service when the patient was two, and the patient had spent the first two years of his life sleeping in his mother's bedroom or bed.

There is a hierarchy in the effect of castration anxiety. Waelder believed that there was a genetic factor in susceptibility to it. He cited (personal communication, ca. 1960) a five-year-old boy who was told by his nursemaid that his penis would fall off if he played with it and replied, "No, it can't, it's attached." In the presence of preoedipal pathology, a moderate increase in castration anxiety can produce homosexuality while an unusually large amount can produce a nonphallic perversion. If the castration factor is too high, the penis either cannot be used as the locus of sexual pleasure and is symbolically represented in the perversion, or where the penis is used it is only to deny its loss as in the case of exhibitionism. In homosexuality, it is castration anxiety that prevents the exposure of the penis to the female genital and derails the sexual drive from its normal heterosexual aim. Total denial of the possibility of castration is seen in transsexualism where the fear of loss of the penis is changed into a wish for its loss accompanied by a somatic delusion that the individual is a woman who has a penis in error. That is probably why more cases of transsexualism occur in psychotics or psychotic character disturbances (Lothstein, 1983) than in other perversions. The ability to deny the appropriateness of the penis as a part of the body often cannot occur in the absence of a reality testing disorder. Note that Harry could temporarily fantasize having no penis in the regression of sexual passion but had no delusions about being a female and was never close to becoming a transsexual.

Castration anxiety without severe preoedipal pathology has preoedipal anlage (such as anxiety over loss of the breast, loss of the stool) but normally arises during the oedipal period. It is managed by a variety of defenses, compromise formations, symptoms, and character change, any or all of which can result in normal resolution of the Oedipus complex with or without becoming the foundation of a psychoneurosis or neurotic character structure. Preoedipal psychopathology interferes with the acquisition of ego functions that are needed in this process. The average expected castration anxiety cannot then be managed as well as in the individual who has experienced a more normal maternal–infant dyad. In addition, if the fate of the individual is to suffer more castration threats from the real world (within or outside his own body), the Oedipus complex either cannot be fully developed, is abortive, or cannot be resolved. Homosexual rather than heterosexual object choice can then provide sexual gratification with less castration anxiety. If the castration factors are still higher, the homosexual defense is inadequate and the sexual drive is diverted into a perversion. In some cases, high castration anxiety with homosexual activity has to be managed by accompanying nonphallic perversions. The pleasure of gratification becomes fixed to these behaviors and adds to the need to maintain them. Any obligatory homosexual or pervert has found what is best for him, that is, what gives him the best chance of gratification with the least chance of castration or other loss. Aside from autoerotic activity, he has rarely or never experienced any form of sexual gratification other than his obligatory practice. His autoerotic activity is accompanied by fantasies related to his perversion. It is expected that he will not want to change and will find many rationalizations for his state of being. However, if the necessity of change is not made a part of the treatment contract, he might be capable of undergoing a psychoanalytic process. Then, if the defenses against castration anxiety are analyzed in the transference and in the genetic reconstructions, an opportunity for resumption of the development and resolution of the Oedipus complex is created which can result in a return to the course of heterosexual psychological development.

This course will not be a smooth one. Renewed heterosexual strivings will usually lead to events or fantasies which arouse castration anxiety. Now, however, the conflicts are arising de novo, exposed to the scrutiny of patient and analyst as a rerun of the homosexual defense system is activated. The repetitious reworking of the cycle of phallic drive, castration anxiety, and homosexual defense leads to the same weakening of defenses and strengthening of unconscious drive derivatives that occur in any analysis.

Mr. B. was born to a mother who was physically damaged by his birth. The damage to her body image resulted in narcissistic damage. Her abnormal closeness to the infant was an attempt to restore her own body image by treating the infant as a phallic part of herself. Also, there appears to have been some wish to damage his masculinity in revenge for the damage he caused her at birth. The result was an ambivalent attachment to the son. The closeness was gratifying to the child but conflicts arose during the normal separation phases. As he grew into the oedipal phase, the closeness was stimulating but the physical defect of the mother's damaged leg was added to the fearful image of her genital. The continued closeness of the mother interfered with the late oedipal identification with the father, although the fear of the punishing father was present. Actually, as the analysis disclosed, there was much unconscious identification with the father which was repressed in order to maintain the closeness with the mother.

The analytic transference provided the opportunity for identification with a father figure. The patient expressed openly the wish to be able to behave as the analyst did, especially in the face of symbolic castration experiences. Later in the analysis, as heterosexual wishes occurred, he feared the analyst would be disapproving as a castrating father. When there were failures in heterosexuality due to castration anxiety, there was a demonstrable return to homosexual defenses. One of the most striking series of events in the analysis had to do with the identification with the father's occupation and creativity. The strength of this identification replaced the negative Oedipus complex which was a part of the homosexuality. As the patient felt more masculine with his growing identification and revival of heterosexual interests, there was amelioration of his damaged narcissism. He no longer had to defend against feelings of humiliation as he had been doing in his homosexual practices.

In the beginning, the identification with the analyst was permitted to occur without interpretation. This was important because early interpretation would have been experienced as the mother forcing herself on the child. Gradually it was gently noticed that identification had occurred. The later identification with the creative father hardly had to be interpreted as it was a source of joy for the patient. Derivatives of castration anxiety were interpreted whenever they appeared. It was especially important to remark upon the anxiety he had around his mother and other women. It was also evident that the anxiety around women could be eased by identifying with them and this was especially true with the sister with whom he was close.

The attachments to other women as his heterosexuality was freed tended to occur during the analyst's absences. Interpretation of the Oedipus complex was necessary in order that the return of the analyst not produce so much anxiety that the attachment to the woman would have to be broken.

Mr. B. had come for treatment of a phobia that was interfering with his daily life as well as with his chance of sexual gratification. Although there was nothing said at the beginning about treatment of homosexuality, he became increasingly interested in exploring the roots of his homosexuality as the treatment progressed. It was as if he had used the phobia as an entrance ticket. The phobia disappeared early in the course of treatment, but it was clearly evident that Mr. B. intended to try to change his sexuality. The psychoanalysis allowed him to do this rather than induced him to do it.

The situation precipitating the phobia was the conflict between passive surrender (bribing the officer) and actively fighting charges that would have brought about public exposure of his homosexuality and humiliation. I was reminded of the famous case of Oscar Wilde, who chose to fight the charges and suffered greatly as a consequence. I believe that the resolution of the dilemma was helped by chance when the patient saw me calmly accept a bump in the rear of my automobile. He needed to identify with a man who could accept the passive role when necessary and did not fear symbolic castration. His father and brothers were all "macho" and could only defend against passivity by total denial. Since the patient had so much passivity in his character, the defense of total denial was not successful with him and must have increased the difficulty of identifying with his father. Certainly the master–apprentice relationship had given ample opportunity for ego-syntonic identification, but the patient refused it and looked on his apprenticeship as a submission which must be fought against. But the admiration of the apprentice for the master appeared as identification issues came into the analysis and he had a second chance to use it.

His conflict over passive anal submission appeared directly in the analysis with the symptoms of muscle rigidity and back-ache. It is always fortunate for the progress of analysis when symptoms closely related to the transference occur and can be understood in the present.

In summary, the psychoanalysis of Mr. B. proceeded by permission for identification without loss of autonomy, resolution of the conflicts over passive submission to a man in the transference, interpretation of castration anxiety, and its connection with heterosexual oedipal wishes, and, finally, replacement of fear of the father with a strong identification with him, as occurs in the natural resolution of the oedipal complex.

Harry was born to a mother who was the dominating person in the family. Even before I heard about her from Harry in numerous accounts, I had observed it directly in the opening interview with the parents. She had had considerable struggles with her daughter, Harry's sister, who was difficult to dominate. This might have started early enough so that at Harry's birth, most of her attention and hopes were directed toward the infant son. Their close attachment had existed as long as Harry could remember. He first recalled it as immensely gratifying. Later in the analysis he became aware of the intense rages he had had when he could not do what he wanted. His adaptation was in two directions: he found pleasure in the domination and attachment. The rage was suppressed lest it threaten the attachment. The obsessional symptoms were derived from the conflict over the rage toward his mother.

The struggle became fierce in the anal period and centered not only over excretory behavior but also over motor activity. Passive submission was enforced and rewarded by love. His mother was interested in his masculinity only as if it were a part of herself. She and her husband often argued over his observations that she was feminizing her son. Her defense was angry denial. The denial could not be sustained when her hairdresser informed her of Harry's homosexual associations. She must have been conflicted over what she was doing to his masculinity because she felt intensely guilty and mortified when she learned about it. It seemed obvious that she must have been aware that she was treating him as if he were a daughter and not a son. On the other hand, there was much maternal sexual seduction in her behavior which produced an exaggeration of the oedipal romance and a failure to bring it to a close. Thus her attachment to her son resulted not only in his abnormal preoedipal identification with her but also in an intense, prolonged oedipal sexual striving to possess her. In Harry's case, the identification and resulting character were conscious and ego syntonic. The heterosexual oedipal drives toward the mother were less conscious and became clear only in the analysis.

It is often overlooked that the mother who is preoedipally too close and interferes with the autonomy of her infant son is also physically too close in the oedipal period. The boy is intensely stimulated by his access to her body and his oedipal fantasies are enhanced by it, as well as the castration anxiety and defenses against it.

The work of the analysis therefore had two main components. It had to make clear to him that he could identify with a man and that such identification would not interfere with his autonomy as had his maternal identification. It had to give him awareness of his heterosexual oedipal wishes as well as the castration danger connected with them.

Actually, the move to separate from the mother begins with association with homosexuals who replace her and prevent separation anxiety in the process. The tendency to depression when a homosexual object is lost is a common clinical phenomenon. It is usually taken as evidence of the strong preoedipal maternal attachment. The important intervening step is that the boy has had an autonomous need to separate from the mother but could not do so unassisted, and the homosexual attachments form the means by which separation and autonomy can be achieved. In analysis, the transference provides another step by offering a figure for attachment that not only does not interfere with autonomy but offers the attachment without erotic demands. At first, the patient has erotic fantasies about the analyst. Harry combined the erotic fantasy with his identification with his mother and wished that I would father our child, symbolized by the dachshund puppy.

The erotic fantasies in the transference became a bridge in the recovery of early memories. After conscious experience of oedipal fantasies occurs without the carrying out of the dreaded castration, the patient becomes ready for other heterosexual wishes. In Harry's case, he could not achieve heterosexuality because of the phallic weakness derived both from preoedipal feminine identification and castration anxiety. By identification with a bisexual lover he was able to improve his phallic strength and could see himself bisexual as his lover was. Then he experienced fear of the analyst's disapproval and sexual rivalry. His earlier frankness was replaced by a disinclination to tell the analyst of his sexual interest in his ballerina girl friend. This led to awareness of the oedipal fear of the father and he saw his father not as the milquetoast who was dominated by the mother but now as a man whom he once feared and can now respect and identify with. The result was a renewed interest in the father's business and his working seriously in the business himself.

All these steps toward a mature masculinity seemed to have been smashed by his mother's attack on his romance. However, her action also brought into the open his rage at her for the damages she had inflicted on his masculinity throughout his life. It enabled more analysis of the obsessional symptoms and further identification with the analyst and his father. His decision to return to college and interrupt the analysis presented the analyst with a dilemma. More analytic work could have been done, but insistence on this position would have been too much like the insistence of his dominating mother to do things her way. I felt that it was time to let him finish growing up and separate.

These two patients bore little outward resemblance to one another. Mr. B. was a mature man who was already successful in a career. He did not appear effeminate and kept his homosexuality a guarded secret. He felt that any disclosure of his sexual preference would be intensely humiliating. Harry was a late adolescent, seemingly unashamed and even boastful of his homosexuality. He had obviously effeminate mannerisms. Mr. B. was a cold, rigid person, afraid of feelings and distrustful of others. However, he had one strong attachment to another homosexual toward whom he felt protective. His usual sexually gratifying homosexual activities were without permanence and were accompanied by fantasies by which the act would restore his masculinity. Harry was ebullient, emotional, gushing, and seemed like a very warm person. However, he had no important homosexual object relationships until the analysis.

Nevertheless, these two patients had much psychological commonality. They were both attached to mothers who had strong personal needs for the attachment in order to restore their own injured narcissism. In both cases, there was a firm oedipal situation along with attachment to the mother. The castration factor was stronger with Mr. B. but it was present in both. Both had need of the homosexual activity as a means of separating from the mother and to restore the phallus as well as to prevent further dama' e to it. In both cases the analysis provided a means of shifti .g the identification from a female to a male object while allowing the development of autonomy. The analysis allowed a reconstruction of the repressed Oedipus complex and amelioration of the resultant castration anxiety. In each case the analysis resulted in the discovery of the masculine creativity of the father and identification with him.

It is likely that the analyses were enabled to proceed because of the favorable factors such as the Oedipus complex, which were present in each case. However, these factors were not so readily apparent with superficial descriptive evaluation; they appeared in the course of the analyses. The psychological structures these men had in common were discovered by the analyses and could not be known without analysis. In each case, the analysis was acceptable to the patient because there was a seeming nonsexual condition which he wanted to have treated and that he was able to use as his excuse for accepting the treatment, but it seemed probable that these two outwardly differing men wanted to have their homosexuality treated.

SUMMARY

The psychoanalysis of these two cases causes us to question some myths about the treatment of homosexuality. Masculine-appearing and effeminate-appearing homosexuals are not entirely different species, and the nature of treatment should not be determined by external appearances or circumstances. Radical changes in analytic technique are not required in the treatment of homosexuals. Focus on transference, conflict, and defense functions well in these cases, as in others. Treatment does not depend on the outward expressions of the patient about whether he prefers or does not prefer to be homosexual. That is not a conscious decision any more than other decisions in life. We do not ask a patient what his sexual preference is and we certainly do not impose our wishes upon him. All we ask of the patient is consent and conscious cooperation in the analytic process.

Therefore we heartily disagree with the warning of those who say that homosexuality is a way of life that the analyst must not interfere with. Morganthaler (1988) warns that homosexuality in the character, like narcissism, must not be changed lest the patient suffer irreparable damage. He believes that the balance achieved by homosexuality is necessary to existence. He echoes sentiments expressed by a number of analysts in our country who accuse analysts who treat this condition of being homophobes (Isay, 1986). This point of view is like demanding that the patient's sexual orientation be changed. The psychoanalytic treatment of homosexuality is the psychoanalysis of the homosexual who is given the same respect for his decisions as any other analysand. In the course of the analysis his sexual orientation and behavior may change just as other factors in life can change in the course of psychoanalysis.

CHAPTER 9

The Psychoanalytic Treatment of an Oedipal Male Homosexual

FELIX F. LOEB, Jr., M.D.

INTRODUCTION

Sexual deviations are collections of usually ego-syntonic behaviors that result from a compromise formation. They arise out of unconscious conflict between unacceptable infantile sexual impulses and defenses against them. In all perversion there is a repetitive fixed behavior leading to orgasm. The perversion itself represents an interference by a component drive with the integration of genital sexuality.

In this paper I describe a milder form of oedipal homosexuality (Socarides, 1978) in which disturbances in the Oedipus complex and accompanying castration anxiety undid an integrating genital primacy. Anxiety led to preoedipal infantile sexuality because genital enjoyment had become threatening and therefore impossible. Anxiety also led to a negative oedipal position. The treatment recounted herein was successful without the use of parameters, through the psychoanalysis of the transference, dreams, fantasies, associations, and with the technique of free association. The psychoanalytic process gradually released the patient's isolated affective states, gave him insight into the genetic and psychodynamic origin of his symptoms, and led to the disappearance of homosexual and other symptoms associated with his oedipal conflicts.

191

CLINICAL ILLUSTRATION

Cal, an international sales executive, was a handsome, well-built, casually dressed thirty-eight-year-old, divorced man. He sought therapy because he had difficulty choosing the right words and deciding what to say when he had important things to communicate to significant people. As a consequence, his speech was punctuated by long pauses. This embarrassing problem had begun in his childhood, and was now humiliating him at work.

Although Cal could easily talk to his employees, people younger than himself, and strangers, he became tongue-tied when speaking to superiors, executives, older men, large groups, close friends, or certain women. Cal had no difficulty finding words or deciding what to say when he spoke in any one of five foreign languages, nor did he have difficulty communicating in writing. Cal did not seek therapy for his homosexual behavior. This apparently was ego syntonic and to his mind unalterable.

BACKGROUND

Cal was an only child, born to a fifty-year-old father and a forty-year-old mother. He remembered nothing of his early development. When he was five, his father had a heart attack and remained mostly bedridden. Thereafter, Cal's mother often told him to be "quiet" and "good" or else his father might die. Following father's heart attack, mother began a prolonged affair with father's cardiologist. She confided in Cal about this affair, but insisted that he not tell his father. Cal's father spent little time with Cal and always seemed angry, especially on those rare occasions when he was drunk. When Cal was nineteen, his father died of an acute infection.

Cal described his mother as a "prim and proper housewife" who was always dressed "formally" in silk stockings and high heels. Cal ate dinners with his parents in a formal candlelight setting until his father became ill. Then Cal and his mother continued to eat these formal dinners in the dining room while his father ate alone in bed upstairs. Mother insisted that Cal dress properly for these meals. Cal hated these dinners and always tried to eat alone. Mother never allowed Cal to play with the other children in the neighborhood because she considered them to be "low class." Mother repeatedly attributed her chronic physical complaints to Cal's birth and delivery; and Cal feared that, if he allowed himself to get too close to other women, he might similarly harm them.

When eight, Cal was sent off to a boarding school; thereafter, he spent little time at home. He attended an exclusive prep school and an Ivy League university. His grades were always excellent.

Cal's homosexual activity began soon after he arrived at the boarding school and was his exclusive sexual outlet until his freshman year in college. Then, over a three-month period, he tried dating several girls. He was "never comfortable" with these girls. Following his father's death, Cal abruptly ceased dating and resumed having multiple, brief, homosexual encounters. In these encounters he sought sexual release, never love. His homosexual activity included oral and anal sex, and he alternately played the active and the passive role. Although he preferred the active role, he often fantasied himself to be a woman pleasing a man. Cal had an unusually high sex drive, requiring three to five orgasms per day.

When Cal was thirty his mother became terminally ill. Shortly thereafter, he was pursued by a woman, Jane. Jane was the first woman he dated since early college and the first woman with whom he had sexual intercourse. After a short courtship—just before his mother died—Cal married Jane. Cal was warm and affectionate with her, but he avoided looking at her naked body and never touched her genitals with his hands. He and Jane seldom had intercourse, abstaining for periods of up to two years during their eight-year marriage. During intercourse Cal's fantasies were always homosexual. While married, although Cal did not engage in homosexual activity, he masturbated three to five times a day with homosexual fantasies. Cal eventually became convinced that he preferred homosexuality to heterosexuality and he divorced Jane.

COURSE OF THE ANALYSIS

Shortly thereafter, Cal began psychoanalysis five times a week. The analysis required no parameters and lasted three and three-quarter years. For the first six months of the analysis Cal complained meekly about my passivity and tried to get me to tell him what to do. He compared my inactivity and silence to his father's feebleness and felt that my silence meant that I was critical of him.

On a business trip to Spain, he met Nancy, a "casually dressed," attractive American woman ten years younger than he. He found he could speak in Spanish without difficulty to Nancy. Nancy displayed interest in him; and, at her suggestion, they began a sexual relationship. It was Nancy who always initiated sexual intercourse; and Cal was surprised and pleased that she did so three to four times a day. Cal avoided looking at Nancy's vagina because it disgusted him.

On their return to the United States, when Cal and Nancy began conversing in English, Cal became tongue-tied with her and tried to avoid eating meals with her in a formal setting because it made him anxious. On resuming his analysis, he construed my silence to mean that I was critical of him for having had sexual intercourse with Nancy. He then became increasingly sexually inhibited with Nancy; and he avoided her by compulsively reading detective stories. During this period, homosexual fantasies inundated his thoughts, and he was driven to engage in multiple, brief sexual encounters with men. Eventually, I asked him what had led him to believe that I was critical of him for having had sexual intercourse with Nancy. Unable to summon any evidence to support his belief, Cal realized that he had felt that I was critical because "in the back of his mind" he had a fantasy that I was jealous of his sexual relationship with Nancy. He knew there could be no truth to this fantasy because I had never seen Nancy, knew practically nothing about her, and could not, therefore, desire her sexually.

Several days later, at the end of a session, while deferentially handing me a payment check, Cal haltingly and with long pauses asked me to change an appointment time so that he could spend a weekend away with Nancy. That night, Cal dreamed: "My car would not go up a slippery ramp and I resented having to pay a mechanic to fix it."

The next day Cal admitted that at the end of the previous session he had withheld the following series of thoughts. At first he was pleased that he would be "outdoing" his analyst when he went off for the weekend to have sex with beautiful Nancy. Second, he thought that I would be jealous of him for planning this trip and would, therefore, resent being asked to change the appointment time. He then felt anger at me for apparently not wanting to change the appointment time, and he felt guilty for this anger. He defended against his anger and punished himself by doubting: He began to ruminate obsessively over what to say, how to say it, and when to say it. He defensively isolated this entire series of thoughts from himself and withheld them from the analyst until the next session. Finally, to conceal his anger further, he used reaction formation by presenting his analyst with the payment check in an overly acquiescent and subservient manner.

Upon reviewing this series of associations, Cal understood that the dream of the night before meant that he resented having to defer to (pay) his analyst (the mechanic) to fix his penis (the car) so that he could go away with Nancy and have his penis go up Nancy's slippery vagina (the ramp). This was a consequence of his having projected onto his analyst both his own competitive desire to have sex with Nancy and his own guilty self-critical attitude for having these competitive sexual desires for her. Cal learned that he had defensively projected his own unacceptable, competitively aggressive wish to sexually outdo his analyst onto his analyst, and imagined that his analyst was competitively jealous of his sexual activity.

This pattern of projecting onto his analyst his own competitiveness with him was repeated many times and worked through in the transference. At various times, Cal felt his analyst was competitively jealous and critical of him (1) for having too much sex with Nancy; (2) for going away on trips to work in distant countries; (3) for overeating gourmet food; or (4) for reading entertaining detective stories instead of working. I pointed out to him that the criticism he imagined to be coming from his analyst was similar to the criticism he had directed toward his father. Cal had criticized his father for (1) requiring too much of mother's time; (2) spending too little time with Cal; (3) overeating; and (4) reading entertaining detective stories instead of working. With surprise, Cal acknowledged this correlation.

Cal came to understand that he projected his own early, aggressive–competitive criticisms of his father onto the image of his father which he then transferred onto his analyst. In other words, after Cal transferred his father imago onto his analyst, Cal projected his own aggressive–competitive criticisms toward his father onto this transferred father imago. In this way, once this transference and projection had taken place, Cal felt that the aggressive–competitive criticisms which he had originally felt toward his father were being directed toward him by his analyst.

In support of this interpretation, Cal recalled that during adolescence he felt that his enfeebled father envied his (Cal's) youth and health. Cal now speculated that this could have been a projection of his own jealousy of his father's relationship with his mother onto his father. It then occurred to him that almost all his homosexual fantasies contained the theme of an aggressive man "winning out" against and "demeaning" a passive man. Cal recognized that this fantasy represented his unacceptable competitive–aggressive childhood wish to demean and depose his enfeebled father.

Next, Cal realized that he made both his ill, feeble father and his "passive," "ineffectual" analyst seem less delicate and vulnerable by projecting onto them his own aggressive–competitive feelings toward them. Cal then used these contrived, frighteningly prohibitive representations of his father and his analyst to restrain and control his own feared aggressive–competitive impulses toward them. For example, Cal unrealistically exaggerated his father's anger during the latter's drunken rages to make him seem more formidable.

Cal now understood why male authority figures whom he had initially seen as likeable, but ineffectual and weak, he later saw as autocratic, irascible, and invulnerable: He had unconsciously transferred his feeble-father imago onto these men and seen them as likeable, but powerless; later he unconsciously projected onto them his own aggressive–competitive feelings toward them and saw them as irascible and invulnerable. For example, Cal's belief that the president of the company he worked for was an irascible, dogmatic figure was a fantasy that Cal had created to protect the president from Cal's own competitive wish to be smarter, more competent, and more productive than the president.

Now that Cal was consciously aware of his own competitive aggressiveness, he realized that he had always treated his male employees better than his female employees, not, as he had thought, because he preferred men, but because he had used reaction formation against his hostile competitive feelings toward these men.

After achieving these major new insights, Cal became considerably less inhibited. He was able to express anger directly toward his analyst, his male colleagues, and Nancy; and his dreams became openly aggressive. For example, Cal dreamed that he robbed a bank, and a policeman, who resembled his analyst, severely damaged his getaway car, so he killed the policeman. In another dream, "An older man was recommending that natural gas be socialized." Cal associated that he wished his analyst would recommend that he (the patient) "blow farts" in an aggressive masculine way. This meant that he wished his analyst would "kiss his ass" instead of his having to "kiss his analyst's ass." In a third dream, Cal aggressively pulled down a woman's pants and kissed her genitals.

His presenting symptom of obsessional doubting often appeared during his analytic sessions. For example, when I made an interpretation, instead of responding, he first fell silent; then his speech was interrupted by long pauses; his sentences became vague and confused, and his mannerisms became passive and childish. When I pointed out this behavior to him, he said he was having difficulty finding words and deciding what to say. I encouraged him to verbalize his thoughts. He said that his speech was blocked because he felt that his analyst would become angry if he told him what he was thinking, namely, that the interpretation was incorrect. He knew that the interpretation was made tentatively and that I never displayed anger toward him, but he could never be sure that I would not get angry. He remembered that, when drunk, his usually docile father had flown into rages. After working through many similar episodes, it became obvious to Cal that his obsessional doubting occurred regularly, not, as he first had thought, when he feared his analyst's anger, but when he felt guilty for wanting to aggressively confront and outdo his analyst. He then recalled many past episodes in which he became tongue-tied when he wished to confront or outdo a male authority figure.

As Cal worked on his uncontrollable and disabling speech inhibition he recalled that, when he was a child, his mother often told him that if he did not keep quiet he might disturb and thereby kill his ailing father. After mother told him this, Cal always worried he might harm his father if he spoke to him too loudly or too forcefully. This worry turned out to be an early instance of Cal's obsessional doubting and the origin of his speech inhibition. He now realized that he was unconsciously inhibiting his speech with his analyst because he unconsciously feared that, if he aggressively confronted his usually silent analyst with words, his analyst might become even more "passive" and die.

He began to accept that he had exaggerated his father's and then his analyst's omnipotent invulnerability to protect them, not only from his own unconscious competitive–aggressive feelings toward them, but also from what he felt to be the magical power of his aggressive words, and his speech inhibition gradually began to diminish. On another occasion he realized that he was forgetting the names of prominent visitors to punish himself for having unconscious aggressive–competitive feelings toward them. Now he began to have less trouble remembering names.

Cal lost fifteen pounds and bought new clothes more appropriate to his age and station. Instead of casual clothing, Cal began to wear more formal suits; he replaced his old Volkswagen with a new Porsche. He moved his keys and wallet from his back pocket to his front pocket, saying he was no longer embarrassed about "the bulge in front." After Nancy agreed to move in with him, he made a "fool" of himself at a party. He then dreamed that people jeered at him and avoided him. This "foolish" behavior and self-punitive dream brought home to him that he was guilty, and was punishing himself, for having succeeded with Nancy.

Suddenly it occurred to him that, in his usual homosexual fantasy of an aggressive man "winning out" against and thereby "demeaning" a passive man, there was generally, somewhere in the background, an attractive woman who was intimately, but indirectly, connected with the passive man. Associating to this fantasy, my patient concluded that the aggressive man represented himself, the passive man represented his feeble father, and the attractive woman represented his mother. Having made these discoveries, Cal realized that his usual, manifestly homosexual fantasy had *always* concealed his unconscious heterosexual wish to have sex with the attractive woman (his mother) who was indirectly connected with the humiliated man (his father). Cal learned that in his sexual fantasies he had identified with both of his parents: Although he consciously imagined himself to be the woman (unconsciously his mother) sexually pleasing the man (unconsciously his father), in his unconscious he had been the man (his father) being sexually pleased by the woman (his mother). It became evident to Cal that, beginning with his parents, he had concealed his heterosexual inclination and identification behind his homosexual fantasy and identification. This new insight showed that Cal's identification with his mother constituted a negative oedipal position rather than a preoedipal fixation. He now understood the formerly inexplicable envy he always felt toward the men with whom he had sexual encounters.

At this point Cal dreamed: "A doctor was doing plastic surgery on people to make them all look alike." He concluded that in this dream he was making men and women alike so that there would be no reason for men to compete for women.

In another dream Cal was alternately being treated by two analysts. He told only his romantic thoughts to one, and only his erotic thoughts to the other. Working on dreams such as these and on his memories of his old former wife Jane and his interactions with Nancy, Cal learned that he isolated his erotic feelings from his affectionate feelings because he did not want to know that he had had erotic feelings for his mother. He

realized that he was avoiding eating dinners in a sexually seductive, intimate, formal setting with Nancy because such dinners
threatened to remind him that the candlelight meals he had
once had with his primped-up mother had been not only intellectually stimulating, but also sexually provocative. Cal gradually became able to be simultaneously both romantic and erotic
with Nancy.

Emerging sexual desires led to a dream of performing
fellatio on his analyst. Fellatio would placate his analyst's resentment and jealousy of his new heterosexual fantasies and activities. In a similar vein, he dreamed that he was climbing up a
steep cliff with another man. He felt he could get to the top if
the man could. A dream of "looking for a spicy salad dressing"
led him to state that he wanted to "spice up" his life with heterosexuality.

Just before leaving on a trip, he said he experienced strong
dependent feelings toward his analyst and irrationally felt his
analyst was about to abandon him. He compared these feelings
of frustrated longing to those he had experienced when his
mother "dumped" him into a boarding school when he was
eight. This was the only time during the analysis that Cal reexperienced in the transference, anxiety related to separation
from his mother. Cal quickly worked this through in the transference. He realized that he had avoided getting close to
women, not only because he feared taking them away from
other men and feared having simultaneous erotic and affectionate feelings for them, but also because he feared being abandoned by them as he felt he had been by his mother.

PRIMAL SCENE MATERIAL

Cal had a series of dreams over a period of several months that
contained at least one of the following elements: (1) a man
watching Cal and Nancy having intercourse; (2) two men fighting over an exotic spice shop (a woman); (3) the Mafia trying
to "get" him because he killed the Godfather; (4) coming to his
session, Cal finds his analyst is not there, so Cal climbs into bed
with his analyst's wife; (5) Cal is observing two people having
intercourse (a) through a balcony railing, (b) through a net, or

(c) through a wall; (6) Cal is surprised by a light shining through a window which reveals a crime in progress; (7) Cal is in a wire shopping basket watching "a black kid shoving something up a white kid's ass." To the dream elements "balcony railing" and "wire shopping basket" Cal associated a baby crib. From Cal's associations to these dreams the analyst suggested the following reconstruction: While watching through the railing of his crib, Cal observed his parents having sexual intercourse. This spectacle excited him and led him to make noise which disturbed and angered his parents. This experience frightened Cal and led to his heterosexual inhibition.

Reconstruction of the primal scene (Freud, 1939) was supported and refined by work on two subsequent dreams: (1) Cal was watching a man having intercourse with a woman; Cal could see that she had no penis. (2) While Cal was watching a man have intercourse with a woman, Cal wanted to reach out and touch the woman's genitals, but the man became angry. To these two dreams Cal associated that if he had interrupted his parents while they were having intercourse and had noted that his mother had no penis, he might have fantasied that his father had cut his mother's penis off. Cal could then have further fantasied that his angered father could cut Cal's penis off for interrupting intercourse. Cal might then have fantasied appeasing his angered father by presenting his anus for intercourse. This could explain, in part, the origin of Cal's homosexual predilection.

Following these new insights, Cal dreamed that he was in his analyst's bedroom with his analyst. Nancy walked in, but Cal could not introduce his analyst to Nancy because he could neither speak nor think of his analyst's name. He realized that his inhibition in the dream expressed his hostile wish to keep his analyst away from Nancy. Cal then had other dreams which further convinced him that the origin of both his speech and his heterosexual inhibitions might well lie in his oedipal conflict as he and his analyst reconstructed it. Understanding that he avoided looking at Nancy's genitals because he did not want to see that she lacked a penis and that he could therefore lose his penis, Cal became able to look at Nancy's genitals without disgust. Cal and Nancy were now planning to get married.

As the analysis proceeded, Cal became more productive at work and earned several promotions. Eventually he received an offer to manage another company in a distant city. This job would allow him to do many of the things he had wanted to but had been unable to because of his inhibitions. More work had been achieved in his analysis than he had anticipated.

Cal did not relapse with these successes as he would have in the past. Instead, he had dreams which indicated that he did not want to interrupt the analysis: In one the water ran out of his tub before he finished taking his bath. In another his analyst was a devil whom Cal blamed for not "pulling everything together." In a third, Cal was "gay," which "proved" he was not ready to terminate. In these dreams Cal recognized his dependent wish to remain in analysis, but he also knew that he had overcome his speech and sexual inhibitions and that he was ready and able to be on his own. Relatively undisguised dreams, confirming what Cal had already learned about his unconscious fears, guilts, and needs, were now occurring almost daily.

Over the course of the analysis, as Cal became able to express his anger toward his analyst more openly, he became less inhibited and more comfortable when speaking to superiors, executives, older men, large groups, close friends, and women. He also became more friendly toward both men and women and was able to enjoy the power and prestige that his achievements warranted. His sexual fantasies gradually changed from his observing an aggressive man "winning out" against, and thereby "demeaning" a passive man (who was intimately, but indirectly, connected with an attractive woman), to his having sexual relations with a woman other than Nancy, to his having sex with Nancy. Eventually, Cal ceased having homosexual fantasies entirely and was able, without anxiety, to kiss Nancy, look at her genitals, and talk intellectually, seriously, and tenderly to her about their relationship. Cal came to see that his homosexual fantasies and activities had served to defensively interpose his father between himself and his mother.

DISCUSSION

Cal's pathological, unconscious intrapsychic conflict began when he was five years old, following his father's heart attack and the beginning of his mother's affair with his father's cardiologist. These two traumatic experiences reinforced Cal's presumed earlier traumatic experience of the primal scene. They produced intense castration anxiety and led to the development of the following defense mechanisms against both his aggressive–competitive feelings toward his father and his sexual desires for his mother:

1. *Projection* of his own unacceptable, aggressive–competitive wish to take his father's place with his mother onto his father. He then imagined that his father was competitively jealous of Cal's closeness to his mother. This projection furthermore unconsciously protected his father from Cal's aggression by making his father seem indomitable and invulnerable.
2. After mother told Cal that he might cause his father to die if he spoke too loudly or too aggressively, he unconsciously inhibited his speech by *obsessional doubting*. This was the basis of the symptom for which he initially came for treatment: a difficulty in deciding what to say and how to say it, as well as remembering what to say.
3. *Reaction formation* to conceal his aggressive–competitive feelings toward his father. This made him acquiescent, subservient, passive, and effeminate toward his father and later toward other males.
4. *Isolation* of his erotic feelings from his thoughts of his mother.

In this patient there was a failure of resolution of the Oedipus complex; castration fears led to a negative oedipal position. He suffered from a *structural conflict* (Dorpat, 1976) between major structures of the ego, id, and superego, that is, between his aggressive, sexual, and other wishes and his guilt and ideals. His nuclear conflict consisted of a renunciation of oedipal love for his mother. This is in contrast to preoedipally fixated homosexual patients who suffer from an object relations class of conflict: for example, anxiety and guilt associated with the failure of development in the phase of self–object differentiation (Dorpat, 1976; Socarides, 1978). In the latter case, we would have to deal more with nuclear conflicts which consist of desire for and dread of merging with the mother in order to reinstate the primitive mother–child unity with its associated separation and/or fragmentation anxiety (Socarides, 1978). Fortunately, the status of ego function in my patient, including his object relations, was relatively intact.

Socarides (see Chapter 14) enumerates four specific therapeutic tasks which must be completed to successfully treat sexual deviations. Although these tasks are especially significant in the treatment of preoedipal perversions, they also are useful as guidelines for the treatment of oedipal sexual perversions. They are: (1) separating and disidentifying from the preoedipal mother; (2) decoding or analyzing the symptom to show its unconscious meaning and thereby (3) providing insight into the function of the erotic experience in the perverse acts; and (4) "spoiling" the perverse gratification.

Because Cal's illness was of the oedipal form, little work needed to be done in the analysis to facilitate the process of self–object differentiation and separation and disidentifying from the preoedipal mother. However, anxieties relating to separation from the mother were indeed present. It was separation anxiety, emerging when his mother became terminally ill, that led him to turn immediately to Jane, a substitute heterosexual object for the love and support he knew he was about to lose. Once during the analysis, after he had regressed into the mother transference, Cal experienced similar separation anxiety. Just before leaving on a prolonged business trip, he developed a feeling of frustrated longing and said that he unrealistically feared that his analyst was about to abandon him. Immediately and without difficulty he recognized and worked through that this feeling was similar to the way he felt when his mother had sent him away to boarding school.

Decoding or analyzing the unconscious meaning of the perverse symptom was accomplished through the analysis of Cal's transference to his analyst. The patient noticed himself assuming a passive, effeminate role toward the analyst. He learned that this feeling was a result of his having defensively projected onto his analyst his own unacceptable competitively aggressive wishes to outdo his analyst sexually.

He next recalled that as a child he had hidden his own aggressive–competitive heterosexual inclinations behind passive homosexual fantasies and activities while concurrently projecting the same inclinations onto his father. This was enacted in the transference and interpreted. Cal also observed in the transference that he was using his speech inhibition to protect his analyst from what he felt to be the destructive magical power of his hostile aggressive words. He then remembered that his speech inhibition began when his mother told him to be quiet or his father would die.

The fourth task, which involves the "spoiling" of the perversion—altering the pleasure of the sexually deviant acts—occurred gradually throughout the treatment, spontaneously and without the use of parameters or in any sense prohibition of the sexual acts. Once the meaning of the unconscious fantasy system hidden behind his deviant acts was uncovered (decoded) and made conscious through the process of analysis, Cal began to notice a decrease in his desire and need to arouse himself by fantasies of, or sex with, men.

This paper demonstrates that a patient suffering from the oedipal form of homosexuality is an ideal candidate for successful psychoanalytic treatment of this disorder.

CHAPTER 10

Homosexual Enactments

ROBERT D. STOLOROW, Ph.D.
JEFFREY L. TROP, M.D.

The understanding of and analytic approach to homosexual enactments illustrate a number of general psychological and therapeutic principles developed in earlier works (Atwood and Stolorow, 1984; Stolorow, Brandchaft, and Atwood, 1987). Two basic theoretical tenets are central to our understanding of homosexual enactments. The first postulates, as a supraordinate principle of human motivation, that the need to maintain the organization of experience is a primary motive in the patterning of human action. The second proposes that the essential psychological process that mediates this functional relationship between experience and action is concretization—"the encapsulation of structures of experience by concrete, sensorimotor symbols" (Atwood and Stolorow, 1984, p. 85). The concretization of experience is a ubiquitous and fundamental process in human psychological life, underlying a great variety of psychological activities and products. Concretization can assume a number of forms, depending on what pathways or modes of expression it favors. In dreams and fantasies, for example, perceptual imagery is employed to actualize required configurations of experience. When motor activity predominates in the mode of concretization, then behavioral enactments are relied upon to maintain the organization of experience.

The proposition that the patterning of human conduct serves to maintain the organization of experience can be understood to apply in two senses. On one hand, a pattern of conduct may serve to maintain a *particular* organization of experience, in which specific configurations of self and other, deriving from multiple origins and serving multiple purposes, are materialized. Such configurations, when actualized, may in varying degrees fulfill cherished wishes and urgent desires, provide moral restraint and self-punishment, aid adaptation, and repair or restore damaged or lost self and object images. They may also serve a defensive function in preventing other, subjectively dangerous configurations from emerging in conscious experience. Any or all of these aims can contribute to the formation of a pattern of conduct, and it is essential in psychoanalytic therapy to determine the relative motivational salience or priority of the purposes that a pattern of action serves.

On the other hand, a pattern of conduct may serve not so much to materialize a particular configuration of experience, but rather to maintain psychological organization per se, as when behavioral enactments are required to sustain the structural cohesion and continuity of a fragmenting sense of self or other. It is this most fundamental functional relationship between experience and conduct, whereby concrete courses of action are required to maintain the structural integrity and stability of the subjective world, that we illustrate through a consideration of homosexual enactments.

The question arises: Why can some people actualize their psychological structures primarily in dreams, fantasies, personal myths, social role relationships, and other such systems of symbolization, whereas other people need to perform dramatic, often bizarre behavioral enactments to maintain their psychological organizations? In general, to the extent that severe developmental traumata, voids, and derailments have interfered with the structuralization of the subjective world, vivid concrete enactments tend to be required for restoring or maintaining vulnerable, disintegration-prone structures of experience (Stolorow and Lachmann, 1980). This formulation is crucial to the understanding of and analytic approach to both overt destructiveness and sexual perversion. So-called sexual and aggressive acting out is conceptualized not in terms of a defective "mental apparatus" lacking in "impulse control," but rather in terms of the person's need for behavioral enactments to shore up an imperiled subjective world.

A second question arises: Why do many people use *sexual* enactments for this purpose of restoring or maintaining precarious structures of experience? Some answers to this question can be found by examining the contribution of early psychosexual experiences to the development of the subjective world and to the structuralization of the sense of self in particular, and also by considering a special quality of the experience of sexual pleasure with respect to the affirmation of truth and conviction.

With regard to the role of sensual experiences in articulating the developing child's subjective world, a number of authors (Hoffer, 1950; Mahler, Pine, and Bergman, 1975) have suggested that the delineation of a rudimentary body image is accomplished through the sensual stimulations of the child's body surface resulting from pleasurable contacts within the mother–infant interactions. More specifically, the epigenetic unfolding of psychosexual modes, as described by Erikson (1950), can be shown to serve in critical ways the consolidation of a sense of an individualized self differentiated from primary objects (Stolorow, 1979; Stolorow and Lachmann, 1980).

Experiences and fantasies in the oral-incorporative mode contribute to the process of self–object differentiation by making concrete the subjective distinction between inside and outside, between the self as a container and the nonself that can be taken in. At the same time, the child may employ incorporative fantasies to symbolize the appropriation of valued and admired qualities of others to his own sense of self, contributing further to its structuralization.

Experiences and fantasies in the anal-retentive mode provide concrete symbols for a stubborn affirmation of the boundaries separating self and nonself, a definitive milestone in self–object differentiation. Through anal-eliminative acts and fantasies, the child symbolically ejects undesirable contents from his sense of self, further promoting its individualization and refining its demarcation from the object world.

A decisive step in self-definition occurs with the discovery of genital differences and the unfolding of the intrusive and inclusive genital modes, which begin to distinguish the sensual self-experiences of boys and girls respectively. As with oral-incorporative and anal-aggressive fantasies, phallic imagery too can serve to buttress the vulnerable sense of self of developing children of both sexes. The oedipal saga itself may be viewed as a pivotal phase in the structuralization of the self (Kohut, 1977), which finds its unique form in emerging from the conflictual flux of experiences of phallic grandeur and depletion, rivalrous triumph and defeat, idealizing love and disappointment, threats to genital intactness, and envy of the penis or womb.

Nature, in her evolutionary wisdom, has harnessed the exquisiteness of sensual pleasure to serve the ontogenesis of human subjectivity. The sensual experiences and fantasies that occur in the course of early development may be viewed as psychic organizers that contribute vitally to the structuralization of the subjective world and of the sense of self in particular. Psychosexual experiences provide the child with an array of sensorimotor and anatomical symbols that serve to concretize and solidify developmental steps in the articulation of his subjective universe. When these developments are seriously impeded, leading to structural deficits and weaknesses, the person may as an adult continue to look to psychosexual symbols to maintain the organization of his subjective life. By dramatically enacting these concrete symbolic forms to the accompaniment of orgasm, he gives vividly reified, tangible substance to his efforts to restore a failing sense of self. In such instances of sexual perversion, it is not, contrary to what Freud (1905) maintained, the infantile erotic experience per se that has been fixated and then regressively reanimated. Instead, it is the early *function* of the erotic experience that is retained and regressively relied upon—its function in maintaining the cohesion and stability of a sense of self menaced with disintegration. Analytic exploration of the details of perverse enactments, their origins and functions, should reveal the particular ways in which they both encapsulate the danger to the self and embody a concretizing effort at self-restoration.

A number of analysts have contributed important insights into the function of perverse activity in shoring up precarious structures of experience. Socarides (1978, 1988), for example, has shown how perverse patterns can protect against the danger of self-boundary dissolution. The function of sexual activity in restoring or maintaining a fragile sense of self has been explored in detail by Kohut (1971, 1977) and Goldberg (1975). They found that a wide variety of perverse activities may be viewed as sexualized attempts to compensate for voids and defects in the sense of self and to counteract experiences of inner deadness and self-fragmentation. In the perverse enactment, the person sexualizes a fragment of an archaic self–object configuration in an effort to find an eroticized replacement for needed self–object ties that in his formative years were missing, insufficient, or unreliable (see also Trop [1988]).

In previous work (Stolorow and Lachmann, 1980), an attempt was made to develop some of these ideas further by examining the functions of masochistic perversion. It was suggested that in persons with deficits in psychological structure formation, masochistic experiences can serve to restore or sustain a damaged, menaced, or disintegrating sense of self through the stimulations afforded by pain and skin eroticism, through exhibitionistic displays of suffering, through mergings with omnipotent object images, and by actualizing an archaic grandiose self. Extrapolating from the ideas of Nydes (1950) and Eissler (1958) on the power of sexual pleasure and of orgasm to create and affirm conviction, it was proposed that the experience of orgasm in sadomasochistic perversions serves to revitalize ecstatically the person's sense of conviction about the truth and reality of his having a bounded and cohesive self. The Janus-faced quality of the orgasm, it was further suggested, in both offering the hope of self-articulation and posing the threat of self-dissolution, accounts for the elaborate ritualization often surrounding perverse enactments.

IMPLICATIONS FOR PSYCHOANALYTIC TREATMENT

The therapeutic implications of viewing perverse sexual enactments as concretized symbolic residues of developmental derailments in psychological structure formation are profound.

The patient must be permitted to revive with the therapist the archaic mirroring, idealizing, and other self–object ties on which the early development of his subjective life had foundered and through which this development can be once again resumed. Ordinarily, once the self–object transference relationship becomes reliably established, it tends to absorb the functions previously served by the sexual enactments in maintaining the intactness of the patient's self-experience. Hence the perverse activity tends to recede and even disappear, only to return, intensify, or assume a more primitive form when the self–object transference bond becomes significantly ruptured by misattunements or separations (Kohut, 1971). Sexual enactments —indeed, all products of the concretization process— cannot be comprehended apart from the "intersubjective contexts" (Stolorow, Brandchaft, and Atwood, 1987) in which they arise and recede. Understanding the meaning of perverse enactments, in particular their functions in shoring up an endangered sense of self in the context of a disrupted self–object tie, can be pivotal to the analysis and working through of the transference, and hence to the formation and consolidation of new structures of experience.

We now illustrate these principles with material from an analytic case in which the investigation of the meanings of homosexual enactments played a prominent role.

CLINICAL ILLUSTRATION

History

Alan is a thirty-four-year-old attorney who has been in analysis for seven years. He sought treatment because he felt deeply depressed about himself and was confused about his sexuality. He said he did not know whether he was homosexual or heterosexual, but felt an intense need to resolve this question. His sexual experiences with women were few; he had engaged in heterosexual intercourse five or six times. His primary sexual activities were homosexual, and he described having about fifteen isolated homosexual experiences with different partners.

Alan said that the urgency he felt about his sexuality was precipitated by recent experiences with two women. He met the first woman about three months prior to seeking analysis. She had been working at his law office and had avidly pursued him, expressing much admiration for his legal expertise. As they began seeing each other, he felt a vague sense of sexual confusion and uncertainty, and he disclosed that he had engaged in sexual activities with men. She then became suspicious of him, and he began to feel demoralized and even more confused about his sexuality. On one occasion after sexual intercourse, she remarked that his "rear was flabby" and told him he needed to shape up. He then became intensely depressed, withdrawn, and lethargic, had suicidal thoughts, and, in desperation, decided to leave the country and visit friends. While away he felt vaguely attracted to a second woman, and it was clear to him that she was sexually interested in him. He was unable to approach her and felt even more depressed, and did not contact the first woman upon his return. It was after this trip that he decided to seek analysis, because he had "lived with these problems long enough."

Gradually, Alan described his history. He was an only child, born to older parents. He described his mother as both intrusive and distant. She was very concerned about his school performance, inquired constantly about his schoolwork, and was obsessed with his health and worries that he might injure himself. He also described her as extremely cold and physically distant and said that, when he would kiss her, she would be stiff and turn her head away. His mother was also highly critical and could not tolerate any disagreement with her. Whenever he did disagree with her she would ignore him and not speak to him until he apologized. This was enormously painful and humiliating for him, and on a few occasions she even made him kiss her feet. She would always extract from him a promise "never to do it again." This recurrent pattern of interaction produced an enduring sense of despair in Alan, because he felt he had no choice but to surrender and apologize if he was to get along with his mother.

The patient described his father as a hard-working man who was absorbed in his business and had little time for his son. His father had not graduated from college and was much invested in Alan's academic achievements, taking great pride in his success. It had seemed clear to Alan since he was a small boy that it was his destiny to become a lawyer, because his father admired lawyers greatly. Although he described his father as warm and affectionate, the father worked late every day and had little energy to devote to Alan. When the patient was twelve his father had a heart attack and became less active. Thereafter, a sense of doom pervaded the family, along with a constant dread that his father would die. He did die suddenly when the patient was twenty-four.

The patient indicated that in high school he had felt very distant from his classmates. While they were becoming interested in dating, he felt strange and withdrawn. At one party when he was fourteen, he was sitting next to a girl and put his arm around her. Then he experienced an uncanny feeling that his mother was actually staring at him through the wall with a disapproving glare. He became acutely disorganized and immediately left the party and went home. Afterwards, he was uninterested in girls and had little awareness of any sexual feelings. Neither of his parents seemed to notice what was becoming an enduring pattern of social isolation.

The Course of Analysis

In the sessions the patient continued to speak of his lifelong feelings of isolation and to describe how he experienced himself with women. He believed that his body was unattractive, that his shoulders and chest were underdeveloped, and that his penis was too small. When with women he felt constantly terrified of being exposed as undesirable. In short, he suffered from a profound sense of being defective as a man. He wanted to be heterosexual, marry, and have children, but felt he ought to consider that he might be fighting a losing battle and that he was truly homosexual. He did not want the analyst to shrink from helping him face this if it proved to be true.

As Alan described these feelings and past experiences, the analyst communicated his understanding of how painful they were for him. The analyst also noted that the patient's mother and father seemed to have been unable to assist him in developing social confidence, often undermining his hopes to be more outgoing by being preoccupied with what *they* needed him to be. The patient gradually became somewhat more at ease at work and began socializing there with both men and women. About eight months after beginning analysis, he reported that there was a woman at work whom he found "interesting looking." He knew, he said, that she would see him as an "undesirable wimp" and that there was no way he could ever ask her out. This, he believed, would be an absolutely humiliating experience, confirming his worst fears. As it turned out, a colleague told the woman of the patient's interest, and she invited him for brunch. With great trepidation, the patient accepted. The analyst acknowledged that this exposed Alan to intense anxiety about being found undesirable, but the analyst's affect communicated his own enthusiasm about the patient's willingness to take the risk.

Initially, the patient felt quite interested in this woman, as she was very responsive and admiring of him. After several dates he had sexual intercourse with her and felt pleased by his capacity to be excited. His experience of her, however, began to change rapidly. He began to feel that she was controlling and selfish, more interested in her own sexual satisfaction than in him, and he felt used by her. He also began to feel depressed and self-critical, believing that his feelings about her were his problem because he was looking for a perfect woman who did not exist. The situation came to a crisis when she asked him about his attitude toward having oral sex with her. He became acutely anxious and told her he had problems doing this. She wanted to discuss it further, making him feel pressured by her. He ended the date early and immediately felt defective and demoralized because of his sexual problems. He saw himself as a sexual cripple and felt devastated because he thought it would be different this time. After he left her, he began to fantasize about having sex with men. He drove around aimlessly in his car, eventually finding himself in the section of town where homosexuals congregated. Several of the men called out to him, and he found this intensely exciting. He desperately wanted to have sexual contact with a man, but knew that going to a prostitute would be dangerous. He drove home and masturbated to a fantasy of holding a man who passionately desired him. That night he dreamed:

> There was a young man going into a room with a woman to have sex. Two people looked into the room. One said, "Oh, no!" and the other screamed while he was looking. A naked woman ran out and said she was disappointed in the people who were looking into the room. She said her husband had been hung, but that there was a chance the noose had not been tied tightly enough and that he was still alive.

Associating to the dream, the patient said that sex with a woman was like having a noose around his neck. He felt depressed and discouraged and believed the dream meant he was a homosexual. The analyst asked if the dream brought anything to mind about the analyst, and the patient replied that he felt angry. With embarrassment he disclosed that he felt the analyst had pressured him into becoming involved with the woman and had set him up for defeat. The patient had perceived that the analyst was eager for him to be with a woman, and he had tried to give the analyst what he thought the analyst wanted.

The analyst inquired further about the emergence of Alan's homosexual fantasies. The patient replied that he had felt an enormous conflict. He experienced the woman's communications as demands that he perform sexually for her, and he urgently wanted to avoid disappointing her. However, it was impossible for him even to consider having oral sex with her. He pictured himself as a minuscule Lilliputian who would fall into her cavernous vagina and be lost forever. His inability to comply with her request led to an intense feeling of danger and a total collapse of his sense of self. He felt he was an inadequate and loathsome person because he could not give her what she wanted. This replicated recurrent childhood scenes with his mother, in which she made him feel defective and selfish when he failed to please her: for example, when he expressed wishes that were at variance with hers. The analyst conveyed to the patient his understanding that the homosexual fantasies and

urges seemed to counteract the intense feelings of endanger-
ment, defectiveness, and self-loathing that were evoked when
the patient felt unable to comply with the woman's wishes. The
homosexual desires, the analyst further interpreted, represented the patient's attempt to restore a sense of himself as
worthy and desirable, which had completely collapsed. The patient felt greatly relieved by this explanation and that the analyst had understood his inner experience.

Alan's dream clearly depicted his anxiety about his sexual
relationship with the woman. Its imagery also alluded to two
sets of transference feelings that were gradually articulated
over the next several sessions. On the one hand, the patient
feared that the analyst would think his feelings about the
woman were wrong, that she was really very nice, and that
he was unable to appreciate her. This reproduced countless
experiences in which his mother relentlessly undermined his
confidence in the validity of his own perceptions of her during
their interactions. At these times Alan experienced his father
as an "onlooker" who allowed his mother to mistreat him and
failed to intervene on his behalf, and the patient expected the
analyst to disappoint him in the same way.

On the other hand, the patient was convinced that the
analyst would regard the sexual problems he was having with
the woman as a terrible setback, and he feared that the analyst
would be disappointed in him and that the therapeutic relationship would thereby be jeopardized. This replicated numerous
experiences in which his father seemed consumed with Alan's
academic success, about which he bragged incessantly, and was
completely oblivious to his son's intense performance anxiety
and painful sense of estrangement from peers. Similarly, the
patient felt required to perform flawlessly and suffer no difficulties in his analysis in order to sustain the analyst's stature
and self-esteem, and he feared the analyst's disappointment
and dejection if he failed to meet this expectation.

As these transference feelings were clarified and interpreted, the patient felt increasingly certain of his feelings toward
the woman and decided that he wanted to break up with her.
This was very difficult, as he had many hopes for the relationship and still believed that his inability to adapt to her needs

reflected a loathsome deficiency in him. At these moments the analyst interpreted the patient's longing in the transference for the analyst unfailingly to support the patient's reliance on his own feelings as the basis for his decision. Gradually, his decision to break up became firm, and he presented it to her assertively.

About two months later the patient went to visit his mother. From the beginning of the visit he felt anxious and depressed. His mother complained that he was inconsiderate because he was staying for only four days and yet had scheduled time with his friends. She told him that none of his friends in their home town really cared about him anyway. She was also upset because his hair was too long, and she wanted to schedule a haircut. When Alan spoke up and tried to defend his right to make his own decisions, she became self-deprecating and despondent, making him feel increasingly guilty and powerless. One evening as he was about to leave the house wearing an old pair of jeans, she insisted that he change them. When he tried to protest, she said he was not her son if he could go out looking like that. He felt himself become confused and begin to crumble, and he changed his pants. It seemed as if all his feelings about himself had been drained away and that he had literally turned himself over to her. He was a robot, completely under her control. He felt empty, depressed, and suicidal. As he was leaving, she insisted on putting hair spray on his hair, and he dutifully complied.

The following night he went to visit an uncle, the only male relative whom he regarded as strong and admirable, and afterwards he felt somewhat better. On the bus back to his house he noticed an attractive man looking at him. The patient felt both anxiety and intense excitement. They began to converse, and eventually the man inquired about his sexuality. The patient replied that he was basically heterosexual, but open to other experiences. The man expressed admiration of Alan and showed interest in his career, and then asked him to come to his apartment. There the man performed fellatio on the patient, who experienced intense excitement and orgasm. In return, the patient masturbated the other man to orgasm, but felt little enthusiasm for this.

The patient was apprehensive about disclosing this event to the analyst, believing that the analyst would be repulsed. The analyst interpreted the patient's fear that the analyst had an agenda of his own for him and would not support his rooted-ness in his own inner experience. The patient felt relieved and said he needed to know that if he were homosexual, the analyst would not abandon him.

Feeling more confident in the analyst's acceptance of him, the patient continued to explore the meanings and functions of his homosexual experiences. His first homosexual encounter occurred when he was eighteen, while staying at a resort with his family. An older, attractive man had approached him and invited him to his room. The man asked him many questions and was very admiring of him, and the patient felt exhilarated by the attention and compliments. Unexpectedly, the man then kissed him on the back and masturbated him to orgasm. The patient then experienced an intense fear that he would be dis-covered by his mother.

The patient described having had approximately fifteen similar homosexual experiences prior to entering analysis. The patient was always alone, it was late at night, and he was not thinking consciously about any sexual activity. In each instance the other man would actively pursue him, and the patient would feel both anxiety and intense excitement about being sought after and admired. He would always allow the other man to perform fellatio or masturbate him to orgasm. He might then masturbate the partner if requested to do so, but this was done only out of obligation and with little enthusiasm. Al-though the other man might want to see him again, the patient would refuse any additional contact. Another feature of these experiences was that the man was seen as attractive, with the patient wishing to be attractive in a similar way.

It seemed apparent that Alan's homosexual experience after leaving his mother's house was an attempt to repair his fragmenting sense of self and to stem his mounting depression. His mother had concretely communicated her perception of him as physically unappealing. More profoundly, he felt she had invaded him and completely obliterated his sense of per-sonal agency, so that he was crumbling into pieces. He had been unable to counter her perception of him as valuable only if he substituted her experience for his own, and thus he had surrendered his sense of himself to hers. The homosexual activity, in which he felt intensely desired and admired, represented an effort to avert the feelings of worthlessness and nonbeing that had resulted from the interactions with his mother and to restore his vanishing sense of aliveness and intactness. When the analyst offered these interpretations to the patient, he once again felt calmed and deeply understood.

The patient had four additional homosexual encounters over the next year. Three occurred while he was out of town and away from the analyst, missing the analyst's self–object functions. The fourth and last took place during a weekend, following a painful interaction with a woman he was seeing. She had made some critical comments about his communication skills and capacity for intimacy. He did not say much in reply, but felt increasingly hopeless and despairing. The next night he sought out a man whom he had met through his law firm, and they went out to dinner. Afterwards, the man invited him to his apartment, avidly pursued him, and then masturbated him to orgasm. The patient said he had thought about calling the analyst prior to the enactment, but felt the analyst would not want to be bothered. He also remarked that during the homosexual experience his teeth had chattered and that he found this curious. The patient then recalled that the first time this had happened was when his father died. When he learned of his father's death, his teeth had begun chattering uncontrollably. The patient mused that maybe his homosexuality was connected to the loss of his father.

The analyst replied that the homosexuality did seem related to Alan's loss of his father, but that, in addition, his father's death served as a metaphor for the patient's sense of never having had a father who could protect him from the invasive and usurping impact of his mother's criticisms. The patient became very sad and subdued and said that his mother had often been depressed while he was growing up. He then recalled seeing a letter his father had written to him on the occasion of his first birthday. It was very important, his father wrote, that both he and Alan "take good care of Mommy." The patient felt sad and angry upon recognizing that his father had consecrated both himself and his son to his wife's well-being. Alan remembered many instances in which his mother was upset and yelling at him, and his father would either withdraw or attempt to comfort his wife. Sometimes, when he approached his father tearfully, his father would caress him affectionately, but still tell him he must be kind to his mother.

The analyst commented that he now understood the patient's longing to have his father, and now the analyst, help him maintain his sense of himself and of his value in the face of his mother's criticisms. In addition, the analyst interpreted that the patient's homosexual activities seemed both to embody and substitute for a developmental need for the confidence-promoting alignment with him that his father had been unable to provide. The homosexual enactments were thus understood as concretely encapsulating the patient's hope of restoring and consolidating his fragile sense of self when it disintegrated in reaction to criticism, intrusion, or rejection by his mother or mother-surrogates. The patient responded very favorably to this series of interpretations and, five years later, he has not engaged in overt homosexual activity since. The function of self-restoration gradually came to be absorbed by the self–object transference bond with the analyst, making the concrete homosexual enactments unnecessary.

The patient's insights into the meaning of his homosexual enactments were consolidated as the analysis progressed. He continued to be apprehensive about pursuing women, but felt that his new awareness that his homosexuality was an attempt to repair himself would help him maintain a sense of perspective. About six months after his relationship with the woman who had criticized his social competence had ended, a friend introduced him to a woman who was a college professor. His initial feelings toward her were very positive, and he felt attracted to her in a way that he had never felt with a woman before. Previously he had found women attractive in an abstract sense, almost as if he were looking at a work of art. With this woman, in contrast, he experienced sexual fantasies in which he pictured holding her and touching her body, and he felt intense excitement, along with a new sense of his own manliness. When they had sexual intercourse, he felt more involved and more connected with his body than ever before. He did, however, have difficulty sleeping when with her, and during the night he became agitated and got up to read. As he discussed this with the analyst, he described feeling overwhelmed by the physical closeness. The analyst commented that he seemed to need the separation and physical space in order to assure himself of his intactness, and the patient agreed.

After about two months the woman invited him to a family reunion that would involve three nights together at a hotel. The patient felt very anxious about this, as it would be the first time he had ever spent such a prolonged period with a woman, but he decided to take the risk. During the second night that they were sleeping together he had become agitated, and the next day she commented on this in an irritated tone. He did not say much in reply, but began to feel like a failure. She asked him what he would like to do that evening. Wishing for a respite from his fear of losing himself, he told her he would like to see a movie. She reacted angrily, telling him she was disappointed that he did not want to be alone with her and talk about their relationship. He felt devastated and experienced an intense feeling of being exposed as someone completely incapable of intimacy. At first he was silent and withdrawn, but as she persisted in her criticism of him, he apologized profusely and berated himself in her presence. That night he had homosexual fantasies, but they were of a different quality than before, in that they involved images of being hugged and comforted by a man. Also, the fantasies felt less urgent and were not accompanied by a desire to enact them. He also thought of the analyst and, when he recalled comments the analyst had made about the meaning of his homosexuality, he felt calmed.

As the patient discussed this episode, the analyst conveyed his understanding that the patient had automatically organized the woman's criticism as an indication of a shameful defect within himself. Alan felt that he was worthless, globally unresponsive, and incapable of intimacy. He had adopted the woman's characterization of him, just as he had found it necessary to accept his mother's criticisms in order to maintain his tie with her. There were, however, some new elements in the patient's experience, manifestations of his deepening bond with the analyst. The homosexual fantasies were less eroticized, reflecting the patient's increased understanding that beneath his homosexuality was a longing for comforting responsiveness from a father-surrogate. Yearnings for a responsive and warm man who could help him maintain his sense of himself in the face of a woman's criticism were less disguised and more directly expressed. The patient's growing trust in the analyst as a comforting figure reliably aligned with him had replaced the need for concrete homosexual enactments. The patient agreed with these formulations and said that he now clearly recognized that his homosexual thoughts were a direct response to being injured by a woman.

The patient continued to see the woman for several months and then decided that he wanted to consider ending the relationship, because he continued to feel she was intrusive. At one point when the patient was articulating his perception that she was an extremely critical person, the analyst commented that it seemed that she did wish to discuss the relationship often and that perhaps the patient felt threatened by this and misinterpreted her wish as criticism. The patient immediately felt crestfallen and depressed and reported a fantasy of jumping out the window. The analyst acknowledged that his remark had not taken into account the patient's repetitive experience of the woman's criticisms and that he needed the analyst's support for using his own experience as a guide for his decision making. The patient left the session visibly shaken. That night he felt agitated and apprehensive and went out to buy some food. There was a salesman at the market who seemed to be very attracted to him, and the patient engaged him in conversation. The man expressed admiration for Alan's profession and education and asked if they could meet. The patient took his phone number and said he would call.

The next day the patient described this episode to the analyst and said he was still feeling upset and confused. He said that the analyst's comments in the previous session had made him feel as if his whole world had been turned upside down and that he felt completely alone. The analyst interpreted that the functions he had been serving for the patient had been abruptly undermined by his comments. These functions included helping the patient articulate his own distinctive affective experiences and trust in the validity of his own perceptions. The analyst had unwittingly allied himself with the woman's perceptions and had thereby severed the sustaining bond between him and the patient. The consequences for the patient were suicidal despair and a reactive mobilization of homosexual desires, in an attempt to replace the lost tie with the analyst. The longings embedded in the homosexual wishes were for an intense mirroring response that would counter the feeling of self-loathing and the sense of invalidity. The patient replied that he could see clearly that the homosexual desires had been directly evoked by the rupture in his relationship with the analyst.

The disruption of the self–object transference bond was worked through over a period of several weeks, and the patient slowly regained his trust in the analyst's alignment with him. Alan did decide to break up with the woman because he felt she was critical and intrusive. This pattern continued repetitively over the next three years. The patient dated a series of women and invariably found something wrong with each of them. The analyst helped him to sort out and identify his affective experiences with these women and to formulate ways of communicating his feelings. The homosexual fantasies receded and eventually disappeared, as the self–object tie to the analyst became firmly consolidated and, concomitantly, the patient acquired confidence in his ability to articulate and trust his own inner experience. Increasingly, he felt able to make his own decisions about the women he was seeing.

During the seventh year of treatment an important shift occurred in the self–object dimension of the transference. Previously the patient had primarily needed the analyst to help him delineate and trust in his own experience, so that he could sustain his sense of himself in the face of criticisms and intrusions by mother-surrogates. Now he wanted the analyst to assist him in examining the underlying fears of losing himself and of being taken over that led him defensively and repetitively to find fault with women and retreat from involvement with them.

At this point the patient was reviving with the analyst his developmental longing for a connection with an idealizable father whose strength and support would help him face the extreme dangers of immersion with women. As this idealizing self–object tie has become established, Alan's involvements with women have deepened, his pattern of avoidance has diminished, and he is confronting his anxieties more directly. Homosexual desires no longer concern him, and he now feels secure in his identity as a heterosexual man.

CHAPTER 11

Homosexual Cruising Compulsion

HARVEY L. RICH, M.D.

INTRODUCTION

Marcel was a man in his twenties, originally from Eastern Europe, working in the U.S. at an international architectural firm. He complained of preoccupations with homosexual thoughts and activities, which occurred in public bathrooms and the like with anonymous men both at home and during his many travels. He was deeply troubled by his obsessive–compulsive cruising and homosexual engagement, which offered him no other joy save momentary orgastic pleasure. A fear of sexually transmitted disease and a true sense of being overwhelmed by his symptoms, which he was incapable of resisting, brought him into analysis.

During the diagnostic consultation, I was impressed by the depth of interpersonal engagement conveyed by Marcel. His marked displeasure over his cruising compulsion followed by a form of anxiety secondary to the compulsion offered me the hope that, while he clearly had formed a homosexual symptom, his personality was organized at a higher, neurotic level rather than at a more fixed narcissistic level as one might expect to encounter. For this reason I agreed to start analysis with Marcel.

What follows is a description of Marcel's analysis from its beginning and including the working through of the cruising compulsion. Currently, Marcel is in the midst of an oedipal

neurosis with powerful competitive libidinal and aggressive instinctual derivatives centered squarely in the transference.

HISTORY

Marcel was born the youngest of two sons, with a half-brother
from his father's first marriage. Marcel's father, a Jewish scientist, had lived in relative affluence with his first wife and their
young son, but with the advent of World War II, the family
was forced to flee from the Gestapo. The wife was caught and
killed, and Marcel's father and the child spent the years of
occupation in hiding. Following the war, Marcel's father met a
Jewish woman, younger than himself, who had also survived
during the Nazi occupation, though she had done so not by
hiding but by assimilation. They were married and established
themselves in another Eastern European country where Marcel's father "could not work as a scientist, but could trade in
scientific instruments."

Marcel was born and grew up in the drabness of postwar
Europe, a Europe which he remembered colored gray and lacking any amenity or joy, although his own circumstances were
reasonably comfortable. Even though he was born after the
war, the image of the concentration camps pervaded his daily
life. When he saw men working on the street, digging a hole
with shovels, he saw mass graves and people being machine-
gunned and buried.

Marcel's family were orthodox Jews who "huddled"
around the synagogue and whose life was very confined by
social fear and religious ritual. He went to a Jewish school and
during his early years associated only with Jews—with one set
of exceptions. The family took many trips, both winter and
summer, to countries all over Eastern and Western Europe.
Often just the mother and boys traveled, while Marcel's father
remained at home working. A summer favorite was Italy, where
Marcel had a memory from age two to three of being left with
the Italian women who ran the boarding house at which they
stayed. He recalled being alone with this woman who, while
changing his diaper or bathing him, sucked his penis and
brought him great excitement and some pleasure. A few years

later (age six to eight), Marcel remembers the man of the house taking him swimming, exposing his penis, and getting Marcel to play" with it in the water. Marcel was tremendously excited by this and sought its repetition a few times. He also remembered how hurt he was to hear the man laugh about him to his friends, for he imagined that the man was denigrating his (Marcel's) own penis.

Raised by an aloof father and an anxious mother, and lacking friends, Marcel saw himself as a nerdy kid walking the streets of his city in awkward clothes which marked him as a Jew, alone and looking for comfort. When Marcel was thirteen, his half-brother, always a shadowy figure in Marcel's life, left the family, and Marcel found the comfort he sought in the local movie theater when a man reached over and masturbated him. The man then headed toward the bathroom, indicating that Marcel should follow him, but Marcel, excited but fearful, made his escape. He returned, however, in subsequent weeks, found the man and maintained the liaison, until fear of his own urges frightened him off.

Marcel came to this country to attend college and graduate school. He grew to be an attractive, intelligent, scholastically and socially successful young man, but his image of himself as nerdy and perverse remained unchanged. He had girl friends, some for quite a long time, but he never consummated these relationships sexually. Marcel needed supportive psychotherapy to accomplish his first sexual intercourse, which took place with a prostitute in Washington when he was a graduate student. Following that, his heterosexual sex life achieved a reasonable norm alongside his obsessive–compulsive homosexual adventures. By the time he entered analysis he had been married for two years to a Jewish Guatemalan woman and had what he described as a "quite fine" marriage. He functioned well at a high-level job, was an extraordinary linguist—he spoke eleven languages fluently and five other languages "good enough to get by"—and was charming, although his charm was used to defend against a certain underhandedness that he could not completely hide. All in all he was a very impressive fellow who strode confidently through life and into my office.

THE ANALYTIC PROCESS

Marcel spent much of the early phase of his analysis speaking of his background. He spoke with poetic and dramatic flair and thoroughly enjoyed this tale, which included the history of his father's and mother's generation and their lives before and during the Nazi occupation. My inquiries or comments were seized upon as opportunities for detailed elaborations and clearly meant a great deal to Marcel. My silences forced him into a skillful meandering in his tales, looking for areas that would "interest" me. Marcel remained unaware of my importance to him as audience to his performance. He showed an idealized regard for me which he meant to be flattering, but instead made me feel that he was managing me.

Sporadically, Marcel would feel compelled to go out to a public bathroom to seek and find a man for mutual masturbation. The stimulus for the compulsion was many things and nothing—his wife spoke sternly, I agitated him with an intepretation, the endless intrigues at work were endangering him. All seemed true; all led to associations of childhood or of the Nazi era and the camps; all carried very little emotional weight. It gradually became clear that cruising was an escape from anything that provoked unconscious anxiety—anything depressing or conveying a sense of desolation. But there was tremendous conscious anxiety afterward about his moral degradation, about the possible disease risk to himself and his wife, and about his having to tell me of these adventures. I pointed out that he obviously believed that he should be punished for his behavior and that punishment seemed quite important to him on these occasions. Marcel, feeling these comments to be true, associated from punishment, to sadistic Nazi guards, to his older brother—who was mercilessly cruel to him—and, on occasion, to his "old, distant uncaring father who did not lend help when needed."

I interpreted that on certain occasions Marcel felt at great risk in the world and did not, at these times, feel that I was being helpful. In response, Marcel was able to finally express, with considerable sadness and trepidation, that he felt he could be "snuffed out" at any time. He used a German word which was used in relation to the Jews during the war, a word which he translated as "rubbed out."

The major work in this early phase of analysis was in the realm of the therapeutic alliance. Marcel had a tendency to present consciously altered versions of whatever events he might be describing—a tendency toward an easily discernable deceitfulness—in order to conceal a deeper deceitfulness toward me or toward his colleagues at work. Marcel in effect invited me to explore this deeper deceitfulness, which had at its root an unconscious identification with his father—one which said to Marcel, "I'm alive." Throughout the war Marcel's father had to be sneaky to survive. Following the war, and until his death, his father continued to be secretive and sneaky about such things as his business success and the amount of his income, which he covered up by hiding different amounts in different Swiss bank accounts. It took continuous and painful work on this element of his character defenses to secure the therapeutic alliance and to bring Marcel to the issues of the middle phase of work in his analysis.

In time, it became evident that the cruising compulsion was linked to this theme of sneaking and covering up. I speak of the compulsion as a cruising compulsion rather than as homosexual behavior because it became increasingly clear through detailed examination of many episodes that all elements of a neurotic compulsion—powerful instinctual aggression and equally powerful superego punishment—were present, mediated by ego mechanisms. Marcel was compelled to cruise in order to escape a sense of "existential death," his version of Nazi extermination, a sense that powers beyond his control were about to snuff him out. The most euphoric moment of the seek-and-find-and-be-found ritual was in the mutual discovery and genital manipulation and fantasies of being "fucked" by the other man (although, he had never, in fact, submitted to anal intercourse). This experience provided him with a fleeting sense of affirmation. Following orgasm, however, Marcel had absolutely no interest in the other person and couldn't escape fast enough.

It was becoming clear that by cruising, Marcel's ego was removing anxiety-provoking conflicts from the transference

and diffusing them outside. As mentioned, the cruising episodes were used to cover up anything that was *unconsciously*
anxiety-provoking, be it from the analysis, home, or work. After
two years of treatment I felt that the alliance was solid enough
to make a tactical decision: Explaining this dynamic to Marcel,
I stated that as a condition for the continuation of treatment,
the cruising must stop. Marcel responded immediately with a
great sense of relief. He felt cared for; and he felt, he said, "a
sudden rush of warmth and holding." In the weeks following,
Marcel would report the moments when cruising was very powerfully needed. We would analyze that moment, but there was
little dramatic insight. Then a new theme—one that had always
been there but not seen—moved to the forefront. I noticed that
as soon as Marcel announced plans for a work-related trip, his
cruising compulsion would disappear. He would then have no
compulsion to cruise until he returned from that trip, when
again we would hear about it. Marcel was doing a great deal of
traveling, however, and he recognized that it intruded upon
his analysis. He tried mightily to convince me to place the same
restrictions on his traveling that I had placed on his cruising,
even though he also assured me that traveling restrictions
would wreck his career.

    Sitting tight was hard for me. Marcel kept increasing the
number of his business trips, causing weeks of dead time in the
analysis around each trip. At the same time there was now
increasing anxiety attached to his travels. But I could not yet
see the need for the travel restriction he demanded, nor could
I fully understand the demand. What was clearer, however, was
Marcel's reaction to *my absences,* expressed in his free associations. As soon as he heard my travel plans, he instantly started
planning his own trips. He rationalized that he was simply coordinating his travels with mine, to avoid missing analytic hours,
but this rationalization soon fell to the interpretation that he
was really dealing with his anxiety over my leaving. Marcel was
amazed to recognize that he could feel anything about my trips.
It was *his* trips that were important, and departures were never
a problem. On trips in his youth, he had his mother, and they
traveled first-class everywhere they went. Leaving his father

behind, he "husbanded" his mother by handling travel schedules and errands on her behalf. Marcel remembered that as a child he spent hours poring over train schedules to plan their trips together. He also remembered the train station where he would recognize the old Jews who would just watch trains come and go, reliving their own wartime horrors. I could see the condensation of early preoedipal dread of annihilation and maternal loss onto this oedipal configuration.

Marcel began to link his urge to cruise to specific anxiety-provoking situations, such as fleeting, denigrating thoughts about overpowering his wife sexually or outwitting me, and to the unconscious conflicts associated with them. He then discovered a greater tolerance for his anxiety, and the compulsion to cruise waned. He also, without my forbidding it, significantly reduced his professional travel.

One day Marcel reported a strong urge to cruise: "No, to be *able* to cruise." He "would give anything to me to be allowed to cruise just once." I interpreted that he had been constantly calling me his "Nazi guard," who had control over his behavior, and deriving satisfaction from this arrangement. Now, I said, he seemed to want to take back that control from me, not necessarily in order to cruise but in order to be the one who decided whether to cruise. Following this interpretation, old images gave way to the deeper images below. Mother, with whom the patient traveled so much as a child, was remembered as often disappearing, when they stayed at that Italian boarding house, with the man whose wife had sucked his penis, the man whose penis Marcel had played with, too. Oh, mother! She chose so many men before Marcel. She liked Marcel's capacity to arrange things and to be the little man, but the one she loved, passionately, was his older half-brother, her other son by Marcel's father, although he was wild and unruly and very mean to her—like a Nazi guard. Marcel noted that his mother "had two modes: Mimi from *Boheme* and Mata Hari." Mimi was sickly and needed care. Mimi was taken in during the war and cared for by Christian families who risked their lives for her. Mata Hari could take care of herself as mother clearly did throughout the war. She was, after all, no frail young waif at the time; rather she was a voluptuous woman in her mid- to late thirties, he

reminded himself. Later, mother cheated on her old-man husband, but seemed to remain a virgin (a part of her he identified
with in his compulsive cruising). Her interest in Marcel was not
his manhood, but his power. Mother was the perfect victim who
grew powerful on the cruelty of the abusing man (brother/Nazi
guard). As a child, Marcel enjoyed fantasies of being sexually
submissive to a Nazi guard and in so doing saving everyone
with the power he would gain over the guard's cruelty.

Marcel described father as a "silly old man," devalued by
mother as stingy and overly religious. Marcel, too, devalued
his father to me endlessly, in subtle and obvious ways. Father
couldn't give expensive flowers; he bought "cheap flowers."
"Cheap flowers," I repeated. "That was mother's expression,"
Marcel exclaimed. Yet when I spoke of how hard it was for
Marcel to proclaim his love for his father, he sobbed for the first
time since his father's death. This moment marked a significant
change in Marcel, namely, his capacity to mourn his father.
Father had indeed survived in hiding with a small child. Father
had picked up the pieces of his life and started again. Marcel
wanted to remember the many warm and wonderful times in
the synagogue with his father, memories which he had repressed. It became clear that within his wish to be homosexually
discovered and submissive was a wish to find his father and be
saved by him rather than being the potent son admired by his
father for his phallic narcissism. Saved from what? His associations led to an unconscious fantasy of his own annihilation,
learned in the arms of a survivor mother who also lived on the
brink of annihilation, who had seen her own parents taken
away.

A major watershed in Marcel's recent analytic work was his
own self-criticism over his being a "little prick" at his job. When
I interpreted that I thought it was more like a clitoris, he joined
in with "and slimy too!" (I was referring to his coy, indirect
manipulativeness, which was also his mother's style.) Marcel
recovered his feelings of risk in the gloomy early days of his
life. He returned to his next hour with a dream of feeding rats
from a basket of fruit which he held in front of himself. His
associations were to the "fruit of his loins," which he fed to his
mother as she grew and grew and as he tried not to disappear.

He ended his hour wishing to "cling to my leg for love and security." The allusion to touching my penis was not missed by him either, demonstrating the growth of his observing ego.

About thirty months into the analysis, a son was born to Marcel and his wife. Marcel greeted his arrival with very appropriate phallic–narcissistic pride and some vague fear that he could damage the child. As the child grew and the months passed, Marcel immensely enjoyed his son's growth and developmental milestones. I noticed, however, that he always said "the sweetie" after referring to his son and interpreted that this semantic ritual was covering some other thoughts he was having about his child. In yet another example of the generational continuity of psychological injury, Marcel realized he was having a constant whispering of hurtful and damaging thoughts regarding his son and was mortified. He reported the following dream: "I was with a woman with a child who never grew much and was quiet. She showed me a toothbrush with a speck on it which, on closer examination, was an embryo! I thought, 'Jesus this is trouble . . . shouldn't it be bigger?' " He associated that he had showed his son how to brush his teeth. He remembered a story where the soul of a child was contained in the child's tear. He had felt so small and skinny as a child—like a miscarriage, which is what his brother had called him. Marcel began to realize how damaged he felt at the hands of his mother, who worried about his survival, but never made him feel cared for. He was handled, manipulated, controlled by her, and yet he remained unsafe, and very alone. He recalled a terrible fight he had with her, during which he had called her a word he translated as "child-killer"—a word reserved for the Nazis who threw children to their death.

In the following weeks, Marcel began to feel far less constricted at work and with his wife. His personal and professional life were rapidly improving. Marcel was given a tremendous promotion and came in quite excited about it, but he quickly began to discuss, then lovingly dwell upon, the "chess game" —the convoluted politics of his new position. He would be used by the higher-up men in their machinations with each other, in their quest for power, and he would be, he felt, well suited to such usage. He asked if I understood what he was saying, inviting me, in effect, to concur in his assessment of himself as the valued pawn of powerful men. I replied by saying, "I understand that you are excited about being used by these men to fight for power, but in doing so you put aside acknowledging your own achievement and power in this new job."

I could actually hear a gasp as Marcel received the interpretation, finally saying, after a long silence, "Each word is like crystal." He went on to talk about World War II, the Holocaust, and the issue of survival, particularly in his own family. He had tried so hard to find his place in this family story of survival. Father had survived by hiding, mother by assimilation, his half-brother by being hidden, his other brother by becoming controlling and mean—a Nazi guard. What powers of survival were left for Marcel? He recognized that he had identified with his mother's indirect manipulative power and his father's stealth, and that this makeshift combination had given him his place in the family story. But he also now realized that along with this "feminine" power was a more masculine phallic power, the power that won him his job. He was thrilled with my interpretation because it led him to recognize not only his place in the family story but the kind of power he was exercising in the world.

DISCUSSION

Marcel was born to parents who had lived through hell and who had surrendered to the idea of their mortality in a way that few of us must face. The sense of risk and need for self-preservation they must have conveyed to their offspring (the other sons are doctors) could not be avoided. Marcel's first affect image of himself is captured in the bleak, cold, gray, bombed-out atmosphere he describes himself wandering through during his childhood. When asked to freely associate to this image, he came to the story his mother told him about her visit to the deportation center. There she approached the barbed-wire periphery of the camp to bid farewell to her parents, who had been taken away before her eyes, and who now pleaded with her to get away and save herself. Such images of desolation, displacement, helplessness, and mortal danger became part of Marcel's self concept and were naturally incorporated into his developing gender identity (Loewald, 1978).

We saw how at that most crucial time of gender identity development—the practicing and rapprochement subphases of early separation from the maternal symbiosis (Mahler, Pine, and Bergman, 1975)—Marcel was the passive recipient of fellatio, with its bewildering excitement, from the Italian boardinghouse keeper. Thus, instead of using his penis as a pleasurable transitional object around which he could organize a sense of himself first in mother's presence and then confidently away from her (Galenson and Roiphe, 1980), he found his penis appropriated to another's purposes. As this phase led into the phase of phallic bravado, Marcel was also aware that his mother was taking day trips with the Italian host. His phallic exhibitionism was already showing signs of disturbance. During this period, he recalled, he shunned rough play with his brother and other children for fear of being hurt. Instead, he enjoyed going to the beach by himself in the hopes that by looking forlorn and needy and playing a small ukulele, he would be discovered by a beautiful young couple and win their love. Already, Marcel was developing a sense of his power as a passive seducer-survivor, like his mother.

Father could not help Marcel develop a sense of male power. He was busy putting his own life back together. Furthermore his own propensity, as witnessed by friends from his youth, was to be a bachelor—he had married and had children as a religious duty. Marcel's father was devalued by his wife and he often wasn't there (Tyson, 1982). Regrettably, the man who was there (the Italian boardinghouse keeper) had interested himself both in Marcel's mother and in Marcel, who, in addition, he had shared with his wife. This was most exciting to Marcel, who cemented one more reason for seeing himself in the gender role of a male/female with a penis. Close examination of Marcel's adolescence showed that he never abdicated a so-called normal male adolescent interest in women, although he did fear sex a bit more than the average male. Such longings existed alongside Marcel's compulsion to affirm his existence with homosexual rituals.

By his scheming, provocative behavior, Marcel seemed to invite castration anxiety—the threat of father's retaliation for incestuous desire, the threat which is supposed to give pause to all children—throughout his young life. Marcel did indeed suffer from castration anxiety, but it was a fear of the power of the female to appropriate and rule his penis. Marcel, missing a male model whom he had permission to emulate and fearing his own aggression against his father, chose instead to identify with the mysterious power of women and with the mystery of female genitality. This is why the analysis of his transference to me, the mere man who could be managed by him, the wily female, led to the emergence of his true phallic longings to be with his father, to emulate his father's strength, and, importantly, to observe and acknowledge his own powers. Not surprisingly, the emergence of phallic longings coincided with the capacity to mourn his father which had previously been frozen in overpowering ambivalence toward his father and the enormity of the Holocaust which his father had come to represent (Volkan, unpublished).

Marcel's growth in his capacity to embrace me as a transference object and to feel and tolerate loss was illustrated when I took a recent trip. In anticipation of my departure, Marcel first "enjoyed the fantasy of telling you [me] that the need to cruise bathrooms is strong and I cannot promise I will not do it while you're away." I said that he just wanted one last fuck from me before I left him. He sighed and agreed, but then said that it was inconsiderate of me not to tell him of my summer vacation plans. My not telling him would prevent his coordinating his vacation with mine, which I would then later criticize. I said, "Yet another try." This remark had a subduing effect; it brought Marcel in touch with the sadness he defended against by action.

Marcel came in for his last session before my leaving with the following dream: "I was at school, in a crowd, being accused that something of cosmic proportions had occurred which I should have done something about. I yelled that if I had known about it, I would have. There was something about Jews. I then dreamt that I was in a clean place with a man, naked, and we simply touched hands and penises." His associations were of

World War II and Auschwitz and how the anxieties of that situation were relieved by the second dream. He went on to discuss a movie about the Nazi occupation of his country but caught himself, saying he was wallowing in the "death cast of post World War II." He then observed, "If I don't [wallow], I will betray a memory . . . it's my cosmic bathroom." I interpreted that it was his mother's memory, her history, which he was born to preserve. His responses were confirmatory memories of how differently his mother treated his brother and himself and of how her treatment of him encouraged him to take on the identity of the sad wandering survivor.

CHAPTER 12

The Course of Treatment of a Case of Photoexhibitionism in a Homosexual Male

WAYNE A. MYERS, M.D.

INTRODUCTION

I will delineate some of the psychodynamic underpinnings of an unusual exhibitionistic phenomenon seen in a male homosexual patient. Specifically, the patient believed that when his penis was erect, its size was large enough to enable him to "get" almost any man he wished to have. When his penis was in the flaccid state, however, he felt that the discrepancy in its length, as compared to the erect state, was so enormous that he was frequently unable to "get" the men he desired to have.

After many years of suffering inner turmoil about this problem, and in the setting of losing his third analyst just prior to beginning the treatment with me, he evolved a new strategem to deal with his anxiety: rather than having to always actually be in the erect state when he was in the presence of "desirable men," he decided to carry a photograph of himself in a "presentable" condition to show to men he wished to have when he was unable to attain an immediate erection. When he informed me of this phenomenon, he spoke of the photograph as "my American Express card . . . I never leave home without it."

While exhibitionistic phenomena are not at all uncommon in male homosexual patients, I have not been able to find another example of this particular mode of exhibiting described in the psychoanalytic literature. In the body of the paper to follow, I will describe some of the patient's history and treatment with me. In the discussion after, I will limit my remarks to ones dealing with the intense increment of aggression present in this man's photoexhibitionistic acts.

CLINICAL MATERIAL

Mr. A. was thirty-three years old when he entered treatment with me. He had been in three previous psychoanalytic treatments over the preceding dozen years or so, each of which had had unfortunate endings. The first two analysts had died and the third had decided to leave New York City, which resulted in the patient being referred to me.

Without going into enormous detail about his early history, let me simply mention that the patient's perception of his early family life was seen as paralleling his prior treatment history. Specifically, Mr. A. noted that his mother had gotten "rid of" his biological father when the patient was about a year old, and then had proceeded to get rid of one stepfather and emasculate another over the next decade and a half. The family patriarch, Mr. A.'s wealthy maternal grandfather, served as a father surrogate both during and in between the mother's marriages.

Several salient themes stand out from the patient's childhood. The first was Mr. A.'s overriding feeling that his mother was never even remotely attuned to his needs. It was as if she were incapable of having empathic responses where he was concerned, or was somehow totally indifferent to the very fact of his existence. In addition, she never seemed satisfied with anything he did. His perception was that he never quite "measured up" to her requirements of what the ideal boy child should be like. This idea was accompanied by the fear that she would replace him with a "more perfect boy."

A second important organizing tenet of Mr. A.'s childhood centered around his perception that his first stepfather had a very large penis. In his comparison of their two organs as a child, Mr. A. felt his own penis to be small and inconsequential. The discrepancy between their two phalluses tormented him and he felt a great deal of envy toward the older man's organ. He dealt with this envy by treating the stepfather with the same sort of indifference and scorn which he felt he had received at the hands of his mother.

The final issue of significance in the patient's early life dealt with his feeling that both his mother and grandfather conveyed the message that if you wanted something or someone, you should go out and get it or them. It was hardly any surprise, then, that this manifesto should be acted out so dramatically by the patient in his adult sexual life. To wit, whenever he saw a man whom he wanted, he went after him, frequently regardless of the potential cost in terms of physical danger or emotional rejection.

From his early twenties until he entered treatment with me, the patient spent a good part of each day in the gay theaters and bathhouses of New York and San Francisco. He had at least one sexual contact (and frequently more) each day for all of these years. The "idyllic" aura of this life was frequently shattered, however, when he found himself unable to produce an erection (e.g., when he had just finished having sex with one man) to exhibit to a new man he encountered. The thought of "losing" a desirable man was almost intolerable for him and he suffered the agonies of the damned in such situations.

While this material was alluded to in the sessions with the first two analysts, it began to come to the forefront of the treatment in the work with the third analyst. Unfortunately, the third man elected to move his practice, and the patient was once more "abandoned" by the doctor, though he steadfastly refused to acknowledge to me that any of the previous therapists had meant much to him emotionally at all.

Over the first few years of the treatment with me, attempts on my part to connect any of his frequent upsurges of anxiety to feelings of being abandoned by me on weekends or during vacation separations were met with rage or derision. In essence, I was treated with the same scornful indifference which he had meted out to the first stepfather, in an identification with the aggressor mother.

During these years, the patient spoke of numerous instances in which he flashed the photograph at men in order to
"neutralize" their importance to him when he was unable to
produce an instantaneous erection in a particular setting. Such
interactions seemed more like power struggles than mere sexual encounters. What was most imperative as far as the patient
was concerned, was that the other men acknowledge the power
and attractiveness of his phallus. As a result of uncertainties
aroused in specific instances, Mr. A. frequently wanted me to
reassure him that the men had seen the photograph and had
been impressed with the size of his erect phallus, especially in
instances when the desired individuals had turned away or had
seemed offended by the photoexhibitionism. In our understanding of my function in his quests for reassurance from me,
we came to see that I was being asked to serve as a more benign
superego figure than either the mother or grandfather. More
precisely, I was cast in the role of the benevolent grandmother
or of the family maidservant, who seemed to accept him regardless of what he did.

In the fifth year of the treatment, following a session in
which he once more raged at me for my "insisting" on connect-
ing his recent increase in anxiety with my forthcoming vacation
separation, he exhibited the photo to my next patient in the
waiting room. The patient in question was a man of approximately my age.

When I brought up his action to him in the following session, the patient again denied that it had anything to do with
my impending vacation. When I questioned him about the fact
that the man whom he had showed the picture to was approximately my age, Mr. A. laughed derisively and informed me that
I was not his "type." In other words, I was not attractive enough
to warrant his having to show the photo to me. No, my patient
was attractive in his eyes, but I was not.

He did acknowledge, however, that he had been angry with
me in the prior session for my insisting on bringing in "the
transference." When we delved further into his feelings about
my "insistence on the transference," he spoke of his perception
that in my doing this to him, I was oblivious to his own needs,
much in the manner that his mother and grandfather had been

in the past. When I acknowledged to him that I could understand how this might have appeared this way to him, though it
had not been my conscious intention, he seemed pleased by my
"concession."

Following this interaction, the therapeutic alliance, though
still fragile, seemed steadier than it had been before. As a result,
the patient began to speak about the photograph in a different
way. He had previously extolled the virtue of this method of
"neutralizing" men he was unable to actually "get" physically.
He had also spoken of how clever it had been of him to have
come up with this method of dealing with the "bevy of beauties"
who constantly "besieged" him.

Now he revealed how trying this whole approach to life
really was for him. He constantly felt under pressure to exhibit
to everyone whom he considered attractive. As such, he was
living out the injunction from his mother and grandfather to
"get" everyone he desired. It was incredibly taxing for him and
he hated the procedure, but he felt powerless to desist from it.

In revealing this issue to me, he had placed himself in the
"flaccid" state vis-à-vis me, and it was a sign of his increasing
trust in me that he was able to do this to such a degree. When
I empathized with the immense sense of pressure that the photograph and the injunction to "get" every man he desired posed
for him, he was quite touched by my comments.

At this time we spoke of attempting to give up carrying the
photograph with him in order to interdict the compulsion to
photoexhibit. The patient tried this for a day or two, but when
he ran into a situation where he was unable to produce an
instant erection for a desirable male and did not have the photo
with him, he felt a sense of panic and depression and was almost
inconsolable for several days. Needless to say, following this
debacle, he resumed carrying the photograph with him at all
times.

In a number of discussions over the next couple of years,
it gradually became clear to us that the patient had seen his
first stepfather's erect phallus on a number of occasions and
had been in awe of its large size. The anxiety and sexual arousal
which he had experienced in those early encounters had been

reversed in his own exhibitionism both of his erect phallus and of the photograph in later years.

He further came to feel that he had operated under the precept that his mother had been indifferent to him as a child because of the inconsequentiality of his "tiny" phallus. Thus the possibility of reexperiencing the childhood rejection by the mother was rearoused every time he was in the flaccid state in his adult life. The rage aroused by such a possibility was profound, hence the need for the aggressively exhibitionistic acts either with the erect phallus or with the photograph. His thinking went that other men must be made to feel the awe which he had once experienced with the stepfather as a child. They too must become aroused and be made to feel anxiety as he had once felt. Only then would he actively master the once passively experienced traumata.

In his relationship with me, my "insistence" on "doing the transference" was seen as being tantamount to my forcing my photograph down his throat, with all of the myriad possibilities contained in that statement. Only when I desisted from making anything but occasional transference interpretations was the patient able to acknowledge his dependence on me.

On one occasion he noticed a book I had written on my desk, and wanted to see it. He informed me that the photograph of me on the cover was not very flattering, but he would like to read the book anyway. He managed to obtain a copy of the book and did read it, and his critique of the case material and of my writing style was quite excellent. In this context, he brought up the idea of his beginning to write again. I was supportive of this "sublimatory act," in that I thought some modicum of success in this area might obviate the necessity to compulsively exhibit the photograph.

By this time the patient had passed his fortieth birthday and his own writing style had matured. His stories in the past had been little more than exhibitionistic attempts to have his verbal phallus admired. Now he was able to describe some of the heartbreaking and humorous encounters he had had in his cruising forays. With the editing help of a friend, he quickly had several of his stories published and was thrilled beyond belief.

At this juncture, now some ten years into the treatment, he has realized that he must soon give up exhibiting the photograph. He has also recognized that despite his good looks, he is no longer a young man and is unlikely to "get" most of the men he desires to have. With these realizations, he is seriously considering giving up the compulsive cruising which has sustained him for the past two decades or more and turning his full attention to his newfound literary career. While we are far from finished with his treatment, both Mr. A. and I realize that it has come a long way from the point at which we started some ten years ago.

DISCUSSION

Stoller (1975b) notes how exhibitionists frequently carry out their acts following current-day humiliations which mimic humiliations experienced in their early lives. In the case of Mr. A., the current day's "humiliations" involved were most often potential rather than actual ones. Not to impress an attractive male exposed him to feeling that he had failed to live up to the maternal grandparental injunction to "get" anyone he desires.

Furthermore, if Mr. A. fails to produce an erection that is comparable to the one produced by the first stepfather, he once more must perceive himself as being "tiny and inconsequential" in the potentially rejecting desirable man's eyes, as he felt as a child in the rejecting mother's eyes. This self-perception is an intolerable one and is accompanied by an enormous increment of anxiety and rage. In order to avoid this, he must exhibit the photograph and "neutralize" the potentially rejecting man. If the man acknowledges his phallic supremacy, then he feels neither humiliated nor castrated. Even when the men turn away, if he is able to believe that they do so because the sight of his phallus has offended them, he feels triumphant, knowing that he is powerful and has "impacted" on them.

If we turn once more to Stoller's work (1975b), we find that he enunciates a half-dozen criteria which define a perverse act for him. While Mr. A. does not always feel conscious erotic excitement in exhibiting the photograph to desirable men, he does feel it on certain occasions. The desire to harm the object, which Stoller speaks of, is usually not consciously present in Mr. A.'s mind at the time of the act, though it clearly becomes conscious when the man disregards him.

In addition, he does not feel a conscious degree of triumph over the early traumatogenic objects (mother, grandfather, and first stepfather) when he exhibits the photo; but that this motivation is operant in his acts has become clear to him through his treatment. In addition, he is quite conversant with the idea that his photoexhibitionistic acts contain a fantasied reenactment of the historical factors subsumed in the genesis of the present-day need to exhibit.

What is also clear in Mr. A.'s photoexhibitionistic acts is the presence of a degree of sexually arousing risk and the need to vengefully dehumanize the object. Thus in all spheres, Mr. A.'s photoexhibitionistic acts can be seen as perverse ones.

It is important here to underscore the intense amount of rage present in my patient's acts. His flashing of the photo is tantamount to a physical assault on the men he intercepts, and can be seen as a belated attempt to master the feelings of "awe" and "assault" which he felt when witnessing the first stepfather's penis as a child.

The need to assault the chosen object assures him that he has had an impact upon it, and ameliorates the rage generated by the original object (the indifferent mother), whom he felt that he never had an impact upon. In the assault he masters large increments of both castration and annihilation anxiety. He also makes the present-day surrogate object experience some of the pain and trauma that he experienced as a child, thus achieving a belated quid pro quo and a modicum of triumph over the originally traumatogenic object(s).

The vengeful dehumanization of the object (Stoller, 1975b) is also a reversal of the dehumanizing treatment that he felt that he received at the hands of his indifferent mother in childhood. In this sense, the acts represent enactments of repressed oedipal wishes toward the mother as well as preoedipal ones.

It was only when I was able to desist from making "forced" transference interpretations that I was able to be differentiated by the patient from the original objects. In this setting, and with the recognition that his age concretely precluded him from "getting" all of the men whom he desired to "get," the patient was able to achieve the sublimated exhibitionistic gratification involved in having his stories published. Our hope is that soon he will be able to give up the need to compulsively exhibit the photograph and will turn his attention to full-time writing.

CHAPTER 13

The Unconscious Wish to Develop AIDS: A Case Report

IRA BRENNER, M.D.

INTRODUCTION

The AIDS epidemic has become one of the major health problems in history. Because this disease was first associated with the homosexual community in the United States, the venereal nature of its transmission has taken on an even greater moral valence than some of its ancestral counterparts, such as syphilis. And, because of the lethal nature of AIDS, preventive measures are essential in dealing with its management. Consequently, the psychological aspects of prevention of this illness are even more crucial. Unfortunately, however, we seem to know more about how to help people cope with their illnesses once they have already been contracted, and then how to support them through the terminal stages of such conditions. Under these circumstances, it is necessary to further our understanding of the motivation of people who, consciously and unconsciously, jeopardize their lives by continuing to follow life-styles that put them at high risk of contracting AIDS. While such a sociological perspective rarely has a place in psychoanalytically oriented therapy with an individual, my work with a patient over the last five years has implications which, I feel, extend far beyond the patient in question.

251

This man, whom I shall call Jimmy, is an obligatory homo-sexual (Socarides, 1978), who did not become sexually active until his fifth decade of life. And when he did, his partners were all high-risk candidates for AIDS. Despite his knowledge of the disease, his cravings were such that he ignored the risk. He had quite disturbed object relations (Volkan, 1976) in that he was unable to develop any ongoing sexual relationship ex-cept with young male prostitutes or "hustlers." In addition, he was profoundly masochistic and suffered from an almost delusional sense of wrongdoing and worthlessness which re-quired that he be punished regularly. In this context, his uncon-scious wish to contract AIDS might be easily understood. Given the principle of multiple function (Waelder, 1936), however, our in-depth work has begun to reveal the complex and overde-termined nature of this wish, which includes seeking revenge, "coming out," being taken care of, and uniting with his dead father. It is with the purpose of demonstrating this aspect of the case that I have prepared this report, and have intentionally disguised and skewed some of the clinical data.

The reader, therefore, is cautioned against concluding that this wish is the only major theme of the case. Furthermore, the technical challenges in working with this patient include, but are not limited to, tolerating the countertransference issues around working with someone who could contract a fatal illness at literally any moment. With this proviso in mind, I shall pro-ceed to describe my work with Jimmy, the prototypical victim.

CASE REPORT

Background History

Jimmy is a fifty-year-old man, in his fifth year of treatment, which has evolved from inpatient psychiatric treatment into psychoanalytic therapy. He was referred to me by an internist who believed that a twenty-pound weight loss was due to a serious depression of six months' duration. A high-ranking em-ployee in the family business of a dear boyhood friend, he had developed a deep feeling of love for this friend which he kept

a closely held secret. During his depression, his former therapist had urged him to "come out" to his mother, but he was
unable to do so. As Jimmy became more dysfunctional, his
mother and therapist became angry, each blaming the other
for Jimmy's regression. Each accused the other of incompe-
tence and neglect, though both were overinvolved and compet-
ing for the lead role in Jimmy's life. In fact, he had spent several
nights at his therapist's house, at which point the latter finally
realized that the boundaries had been overstepped. The therapist felt trapped, scared, and essentially held hostage to Jimmy's
desperate clinging, relentless demands, and suicide threats. It
was at this point that the two of them went to the internist's
office where they were subsequently referred to me on an emergency basis.

In the admission office at the hospital, I met them both;
the therapist was tense and desperate, while Jimmy was stubborn and negativistic. He was ambivalent over signing himself
into the hospital and procrastinated for almost two hours. My
initial transactions with Jimmy clearly foreshadowed a major
part of our work together, as his petulance and defiance were
his only means of self-assertion. He repeatedly mispronounced
my name, and when I corrected it I said, "It's not Brennan, but
Brenner. You know, like the comedian David Brenner, only
I'm not quite as funny." I somewhat surprised myself with this
statement, intending to lighten the mood and facilitate his signing in, as we all were becoming exasperated with his avowed
wish for help but refusal to accept it.

Likening myself to this popular, local comedian, I discovered much later in his therapy, did enable him to sign in, but
for a very different reason. He had received my statement as a
stern threat that he must sign in or he would be severely punished. He decided I was a very mean taskmaster who had no
sense of humor at all and could not be manipulated the way
his therapist had been. In other words, he appeared to develop
an instant paranoid transference psychosis which continued for
many months. He became convinced that I was not only poison-
ing his food, but was also secretly adding medicine to his meals
in order to control him.

This fear was so great, in fact, that he rarely ventured out of his room and spoke in a most guarded and terse way. It took weeks to get a cogent history from him, as he passively complied with the minimum hospital regulations so he would be left alone. In addition, his depression and underlying concreteness made psychotherapy in these first three months almost impossible. He could not tolerate visits longer than ten to fifteen minutes; he was literally frightened of his own shadow and took everything "as a criticism." His basic physical welfare, support, and the prescribing of medication were necessary first steps with Jimmy. Though run down, he was essentially healthy, despite having had a melanoma removed from his thigh several years before. He benefited from several weeks of low doses of Mellaril and responded to Norpramin in high doses for his depression. He was so hypersensitive to any of my comments and self-conscious to paranoid proportions that I waited about six weeks until I commented on the fact that he rarely changed his clothes. As empathic as I could be, he nevertheless reacted with intense shame, humiliation, and embarrassment. He confessed that he did not know where the washing machine was and needed help, but was too afraid to ask. Needless to say, his extreme fragility at this time made it almost impossible to discuss any substantive issues, least of all his homosexuality, which was not acknowledged until shortly before his discharge.

While still hospitalized, he secretly picked up young "hustlers" when he was allowed out on therapeutic passes. Jimmy did not reveal this pattern of behavior and sexual activity until about a year and a half into treatment, after he was severely beaten up. Then he finally had to acknowledge the life-threatening danger associated with his sexuality. I will go into more detail later about how this event crystallized his commitment to therapy. Before that, however, it would be perhaps more useful to describe Jimmy's background and life history, which was slowly revealed over many months.

Jimmy was the younger of two children whose sister was about three years older. Born into a family where social standing was paramount, he was reared in a cold, sterile environment. He was repeatedly told by his mother that she vomited at the symphony just before going into labor with him. At age two, his mother had helplessly witnessed the drowning death of her own mother, and his father's mother had died in child-birth with him. Jimmy, who grew up feeling very unwanted and unloved, had a very revealing early memory of playing in his fenced-in backyard by himself, as he had been locked out of the house by his mother so he could get some fresh air. He felt rejected by his mother, who said it was for his own good. His father, a military man, was overseas during Jimmy's child-hood and essentially absent when Jimmy was between five and eight. When the father returned, depressed and affected by the war, he busied himself in his career, further absenting himself from Jimmy's life. Jimmy blamed his mother's demanding, con-trolling personality for driving father away. This was epito-mized by a memory from when he was nine years old. He vividly recalled a bitter argument between his parents over buying a new car, resulting in father crying and leaving his bedroom to spend the night in bed with Jimmy. He reported feeling overwhelming compassion, sadness, and helplessness for his father, yet relished this very special moment of closeness and commiseration with him. Though he felt abandoned by father and secretly angry at him for his inability to stand up to his own wife, Jimmy could more than understand his father's plight. And being his namesake, he felt a strong bond despite this limited contact. His identification with his crying, helpless father, looking for comfort from a younger man, became more evident as the history unfolded.

Jimmy grew up as a shy, maladjusted child, never living up to his intellectual potential, and avoiding challenges of any sort. Nicknamed "Niagara Falls" by his classmates, he was self-conscious and hypersensitive and cried easily and was subject to perpetual narcissistic injury. He described a regular scenario at school, where he would get picked on by the other boys, start crying profusely, and then run away to hide behind a large rock on the playground. This well-known hiding place gave him both a refuge and an easily discoverable hiding place, where, huddling and crying, he awaited someone to find and comfort him. His shame over behaving like a "sissy" or a "mamma's boy" was very palpable as he first related this memory, which had enormous transference implications. Feeling awkward, ugly, unliked, and unhappy, he was taken to a number of psychiatrists throughout his childhood and teenage years. Surprisingly, he had easy access to various reports and eagerly offered them to me as some evidence of his long-standing and intractable condition. It seemed to me at the time that he did not want to be questioned further about his childhood, but needed to prove to me that he should be believed. I accepted the reports as he dutifully tried to convey to me his willingness to participate in his own recovery. All the while, however, he was entrenched in his stubborn conviction that he did not deserve to live, let alone feel better, because he was so bad. I wondered how his resistance to recovery would present itself in therapy.

Be that as it may, he continued to inform me about his early life, with sparse memories characterizing his sadness, rejection, pain, alienation, and withdrawal. He had few friends, though two remained throughout his life, one of whom was his current boss. He felt distant from his sister, who he felt was favored and endowed with everything he lacked. Consequently, he felt very jealous, angry, and fearful of retaliation from her for his "bad" thoughts. His only warm memories of growing up were associated with the family maid, Lilly, who essentially raised him. As mentioned, his mother's mother died in a drowning accident when she was very young, leaving her quite desperate, vulnerable to loss, and defensively unapproachable. As a result, Jimmy's mother was chronically depressed, bitter, and quite ambivalent about being a mother herself. Lilly, therefore, provided the nurturing, company, and limit-setting that his mother was unable to do. Jimmy's secret pleasure was getting punished by Lilly, who required him to drop his pants, bend over the dining room table, and get beaten with a belt. It took great effort on his part to disclose this information to me, as he was filled with enormous shame and embarrassment over how sexually aroused he would become during these beatings. He reported this "discipline" occurring until at least age twelve, and seemed dimly aware that this relationship might have implications for his masochistic behavior in later life (Freud, 1919).

At any rate, Jimmy's alienation from others continued throughout his growing up, and intensified around heterosexual relations. He felt greatly inhibited and full of dread,

avoiding young women as though they were extremely dangerous. He never had intercourse and could not even verbalize the
parts of a woman's anatomy. He reported dating one young
woman, who was "approved" by his mother, but felt traumatized by her forwardness. As he described it, after going out
with her for several months, one night she took his hand and
forced him to touch her. He became panic stricken and was
unable to be with her anymore, as he was full of terror and
embarrassment. Though he insisted that he had several female
friends, he was clearly more comfortable with boys and young
men. He enjoyed physical contact with them, but denied actual
sexual behavior. Nevertheless, he was most comfortable by himself, a shy, timid loner who was quite maladjusted and schizoidal.

Jimmy graduated from high school in the bottom of his
class, which further reinforced his sense of failure and worthlessness. He flunked out of college after a year of being on his
own. He then returned home and went to a local college. His
constricted, lonely life was tragically disrupted at age twenty-
one when his father suddenly died of a massive stroke. This
event occurred at home, and Jimmy remembered being asked
by the paramedics to help carry his father out in a chair, but
was unable to. Again, he condemned himself for being too
fragile and weak to help out even during father's dying moments. Like his mother, he watched helplessly while a parent
died in front of him. Though he grieved for his father, it was
incomplete, and his unwanted oedipal victory further terrified
him. By this time, his sister was married and out of the house,
so Jimmy and his mother settled in for the next twenty years. A
formalized, hostile dependent and sadomasochistic relatedness
existed between the two in that they had a standing dinner date
on Saturday night—though they might not speak to each other
for several days prior to it. Furthermore, Jimmy's inability to
support himself required his mother to provide for him financially. With the exception of her own three-month hospitalization for depression when he was thirty, mother and Jimmy were
mutually clinging and inseparable.

Bitter, and complaining that she was always having to go into the "principal" of her rather large trust fund, she begrudgingly doled out money to Jimmy. Beset by an anguishing mixture of shame, despair, helplessness, and entitlement, he ambivalently demanded more and more from her. He would threaten not to speak to her if she didn't pay him, and she in turn would belittle him for being inadequate and weak. This sadomasochistic equilibrium persisted until he decided he was ready to move out of the house at age forty.

He reported that seeing ads in the newspaper about gay movies initially encouraged him to go out. He subsequently mustered up the courage to attend these movies, and ultimately decided to get his own apartment to have more freedom and privacy for his "friendships." Further reasons for his readiness to move out at this point in his life are still unclear, but are perhaps related to life cycle issues and involutional concerns, along with his mother's advancing age. Another possible factor could have been a shift in economic factors within his personality, a change which has been described in schizoidal characters resulting in more object relatedness (Akhtar, 1987). Ultimately it seemed as though he were taking a third chance at separation and individualization during midlife.

Jimmy was essentially asexual until that time, masturbating occasionally, and then being plagued by self-condemnation and self-hatred afterward. He gradually became acquainted with the gay community through the local organization and even became active on the AIDS hotline. He frequented bars but initially walked out alone, feeling rejected and too old before he even got started. His narcissistic vulnerability was so great that he would withdraw for days at a time if no one showed any interest or spoke to him. Eventually, he found his way back to the gay movies, where, feeling safer under the cover of darkness, he "looked for company." Even there, however, he never took the initiative, waiting for someone to approach him and touch his thigh first. His waiting passively for a man to come to him is reminiscent of his memory of waiting for his father to enter his bedroom after the argument with his mother. Then, if contact were made, he engaged in mutual masturbation or fellatio, after which he promptly got up and left. He was usually filled with contempt and self-loathing over his actions, but for that moment of pleasure he felt wanted and loved. He preferred to remain anonymous, so the darkness of the theater was an ideal setting, given his inhibition and fears of involvement. He could not clearly see the faces of his contacts which kept his shame at a manageable level, but inevitably he felt like a failure because of his rapid ejaculation.

Over time, Jimmy became bolder, allowing himself to be picked up by young men, many of whom were homeless, drug addicted, and desperate. His loneliness and wish for "a friend" were so great that he helplessly allowed himself to be regularly exploited. He would pretend that he was their friend, only to discover repeatedly that money, valuable family heirlooms, and many other possessions were regularly being stolen. A vicious cycle of despair, self-hatred, and shame then ensued so that he withdrew, which only magnified his alienation and loneliness. When the latter feelings reached an intolerable level, he then relented and began to "look for company" again. The addictive, obligatory nature of his sexuality was so shameful and private to him that he did not reveal it for more than two years into treatment. He also noted that he became obsessed with "hustlers" immediately after his regular dinner date with his mother. As more material emerged in the transference, which I will further discuss, the multidetermined nature of this behavior became clearer to me.

Several years prior to his admission, Jimmy had a malignant melanoma removed from his right thigh, which after considerable follow-up was determined to have been a complete cure. When initially discussing this crucial medical history, he was bland and blasé, especially as he described the inguinal lymph node resection, which he understood might affect his "immune response." I immediately was struck by the unconscious reference to AIDS, of which he made no mention at the time. I decided not to pursue the issue, given how deeply repressed the connection appeared to be. Within six months after his psychiatric discharge, he contracted a serious cellulitis of that same leg which was diagnosed as erysipelas, a generalized strep infection, and required hospitalization for treatment with I.V. antibiotics. He was clearly shaken up by this illness, which intensified his depression and feelings of worthlessness, but he still was not ready to recognize that this unusual infection was suggestive to him of an AIDS symptom. He was treated by a gay internist who, in addition to providing the needed medical care, spoke frankly to him about safe sex. Jimmy, however, denied any sexual activity, so he also denied the need for precautions, such as condoms, at that time. After many months of follow-up visits and check-ups, he eventually left this doctor, whose caring, warmth, friendliness, and openness so stimulated his longings that he could not tolerate being examined by him.

THE COURSE OF THERAPY

At this point, Jimmy was on psychiatric disability, seeing me regularly twice a week as an outpatient, but constantly deliberating over whether he would return to the hospital. A typical session at this time consisted of his arriving at the waiting room slovenly dressed and smoking heavily, with an overstuffed portfolio full of newspapers and magazines. When greeted for the session, he made no initial facial or behavioral acknowledgment of my presence, but began assembling himself to enter my office. I got the sense of somebody sitting on the toilet having a bowel movement, then getting up without wiping, and moving on. When he arrived in my office, he would turn his back to me and bend over, prominently displaying his back side, and place his belongings carefully around his chair. He would then sit down, take several tissues and loudly blow his nose, often taking a minute or two to wipe his face meticulously of his mucus. When finished, he would stare at me blankly, expectantly waiting for me to tell him what to do (e.g., tell him to wash his hands). Then, there would often be long silences punctuated by a question, usually about his medication, his disability, or what he thought was expected of him in the sessions. He was very constricted in his affect, as his sadness, guardedness, and intellectualization usually prevailed.

As I sat with him, I sensed his desperate longing for contact, yet every intervention was met with denial, perceived criticism, further silence, and phobic avoidance. His stubbornness and withholding, which reflected a major anal contribution to his character, early on tempted me to engage in a power struggle with him over who could keep silent the longest. Fortunately, I recognized this countertransference pitfall, and continued in as empathic a mode as was possible under the circumstances. He at times did not take his medication, as I discovered after the fact, and masochistically deprived himself of needed help, storing up pills for a fatal overdose. As he tested my commitment to work with him, we constantly compared and contrasted my style to that of his previous therapist. Though Jimmy regularly complained about my "toughness," he begrudgingly reminded me how manipulative he could be with the previous therapist, replicating his relationship with his mother. It soon became evident that the stage was set for an intense maternal transference which unfolded during this time.

His hypersensitivity to criticism was so great that my interventions wounded him regularly. He sulked, withdrew, and pouted for sessions on end, until he would at last confess shyly that he was upset over my tone of voice, for example. He then began to talk more extensively about his mother, how unloved he felt, how controlled by her money he felt, and how suffocated he felt by her presence. His need to push her and others away in perceived self-defense reflected his underlying fears of dependency and engulfment by her. He had walked away from work one day and literally disappeared without notice, explanation, or forewarning when he was hospitalized. His walking away from life, a symbolic suicide as it were, had a fuguelike quality to it (Akhtar and Brenner, 1979). His boss and coworkers knew absolutely nothing of his whereabouts for over six weeks, until he finally made contact with them. Though he negativistically refused to inform them, he nevertheless became indignant that his boss, who was worried sick over him, ultimately became very angry at Jimmy's thoughtlessness and disregard for him. Needless to say, he was not rehired, which Jimmy regarded as a major injustice and proof that no one could be trusted or depended on. I was impressed with a genuine lack of awareness and empathy for others as Jimmy bemoaned his fate, crying and blaming his friend and his mother for his current state of misery and helplessness. My attempts to point out to him that he had made a contribution to his getting fired were met with disbelief, blankness, and a sense of futility. His blaming of others and his profound sense of entitlement were so great that not only his mother, but everyone else who came into his life needed to make reparations to him for his feelings of deprivation. I nevertheless persisted when the opportunity arose, by gently pointing out to him that he had a lack of awareness of other people's feelings, and anticipated along with him that he might develop similar feelings about me.

What Jimmy manifested intially, however, was an obsequious gratitude for my acceptance of him as an outpatient, and an overly accommodating attitude about schedule changes. But when patterns of prompt payment developed into late payment, and ultimately nonpayment, I pointed out to him that he was feeling something other than deep appreciation for me. His fears of abandonment were so great that he warded off consciousness of his anger toward me for over two years, when he finally acknowledged that he was angry that I charged so much, and that he felt rejected if I were even a minute late, despite his blank exterior which I described earlier.

The emergence of conscious homosexual fantasies in the transference was heralded by a dream: He was in a gay bar and was sitting on a chair waiting to get picked up. In walked a tall thin man, who was a psychiatrist on his inpatient unit. The doctor greeted him in a friendly way and tapped him on the shoulder.

Jimmy was mortified to report this dream, which was stimulated by running into this psychiatrist earlier in the day on the way to a session. In addition, his current hustler was also a tall thin man. Though it appeared to me that Jimmy had made the connection in his mind between the psychiatrist and me, he said nothing, looked quite ashamed and guilt ridden, and sat blankly for most of the session.

Several months later he reported another dream where he was riding backwards on a rocket ship which I was on, when a penis emerged, ejaculating semen in an explosive way. Again, though the content was even more explicit, he tried to avoid recognizing that his erotic interests had included me. His feelings of loss and abandonment were, however, more on the

surface and more tolerable for him. Again, his own contribution to feeling abandoned was not recognized on yet another
occasion when he feared doing harm to himself, and called the
hospital late one Friday night. Interestingly, he did not call my
office directly and desperately waited by the phone for hours.
When no call was forthcoming, he assumed I was punishing
him for being weak and became enraged. That he was able to
tolerate his affects, however, gave him confidence in himself,
and this was no small consolation. Nevertheless it was difficult
for him to see how waiting until late evening and not calling
my office directly increased the chances of my not receiving the
message. In addition, not being able to reach me at the hospital
revived his longings for his mother during her hospitalization,
a connection he was able to appreciate.

As his feelings of attachment increased in intensity, he began to open up more about the nature of his sexuality. As after
Saturday night "dates" with his mother, he often left my office
in a highly stimulated state and went "looking for a friend."
Though he did not reveal this sequence until much later, he
did bring up material about how seductive he felt his mother
was. He agonized in psychic pain as he described her tucking
him in one night when she was intoxicated and wearing a sheer
nightgown. He could see her breasts through the flimsy fabric
and actually felt them on his chest. He abreacted his sense of
fright during the hour, and his conscious sense of disgust and
revulsion made him shudder. In a sense, then, he realized that
his picking up young men after an evening with her undid his
feelings for her, while at the same time he did something
naughty, which he knew would displease her.

Several months after this revelation, his current lover, who
was particularly punishing and abusive to Jimmy, came home
one evening in a drugged stupor and became disgusted with
Jimmy's passivity. Though he desperately craved anal sex,
Jimmy was terrified of it and refused it; a fight ensued. He was
beaten unconscious, and awoke in a pool of blood, his face
grotesquely disfigured by swollen and bloodshot eyes. I hardly
recognized him in his subsequent hour, since his face was mas-
sively bruised and misshapen. As he took off his sunglasses and
looked at me he burst into tears, sobbing uncontrollably for the

duration of the hour. I felt sorrow and pity for this man, who seemed to be headed inexorably toward a violent death, uncontrollably motivated by his profound loneliness and wish for punishment. Until this time, the dangerousness of his behavior was discussed in more detached terms such as riding in a taxi through bad neighborhoods with the doors unlocked. And despite this vicious assault, Jimmy was unable to let his attacker leave. It became evident to us that he needed both pain and punishment in order to allow himself sexual pleasure. His current boyfriend provided both the pain and the pleasure and it seemed impossible for Jimmy to give these up.

I felt in a dilemma at this time in that I did not think I could sit back and remain neutral in the face of his obviously self-destructive direction. On the other hand, he was unable to stop himself and did not want to come into the hospital because his insurance had lapsed, so that he would have had to go to a state facility. He feared I would abandon him because he was a bad patient, further adding to his sense of helplessness and worthlessness. Furthermore, he had not "come out" to his mother and sister, who seemingly had no idea why he was still seeing a psychiatrist, especially since he was less depressed, doing volunteer work in his own field of expertise, and seemed to be recovering. He seemed to have little support at this time, and was at great risk for regression. I felt that some active intervention was necessary in order to save his life. And, if I were to continue treating him, I felt I even might be subject to litigation by the family were he to die under these circumstances with my knowledge of the dangerousness of his behavior. I shared my concerns with him, and though he promised to try harder to "behave," he was unable to. I pointed out his own wish for punishment by me, alluding to Lilly's eroticized spanking. Jimmy was not amenable to interpretive intervention at this time, so I suggested an alternative. I asked him to write me a letter that I could give to his mother, should he get killed, which would explain to her what his problem was and why he did not want her to know. (She was subsidizing his therapy and periodically demanded a status report from him regarding the frequency of visits and estimated duration of treatment.) He readily agreed to this project, but avoided the issue for several

weeks. When I reminded him of his procrastination, he sheepishly acknowledged how unable he was to write because he
became flooded with sadness and grief each time he tried.

My purpose in introducing this "parameter" was to help
the patient stop his involvement with dangerous hustlers who
threatened his life. I had hoped to increase his self-awareness
and in the short run set an external limit on his behavior. By
mobilizing his shame and sense of wrongdoing in his mother's
eyes, he felt inhibited. Furthermore, by putting himself in his
mother's situation, he was able to surmount his egocentricity at
least temporarily. His newly acquired empathy, and his realization of his love for her, was a maturing experience for him
which enabled him to develop more impulse control. The internalization of an active, protective, and demanding transference
figure who was needed in order to make him behave, seemed
to be required at this time. I intended to deal with this departure from neutrality at a later time, but as soon as possible, given
the implications for my supplementing his ego functioning; that
is, regression to a more passive and dependent state.

At any rate, the memories of "Niagara Falls" reemerged
this time, as his intense ambivalence toward his mother became
evident to him. He realized that he both hated and loved his
mother, and could not bear the thought of her enduring another loss, especially at her age. He recalled his father's death,
acknowledging its profound importance to him, but flatly refusing to deal with it. I nevertheless sensed an important shift in
his resolve to take care of himself, and he became convinced
that he could kick this explosive hustler out of his life, which
he eventually did. Ultimately, he did produce a letter for his
mother, as I had asked, which by the time it was written had
already served its purpose.

Jimmy was terrified of dying and his newfound ego
strength, bolstered by the letter activity, persisted with regard
to avoiding violent hustlers. But he continued to "look for company" in bars, the movie theaters, and in a well-known park.
His doorman served as an auxiliary superego, helping him to
say no to the steadily growing number of young men who took
his money after a quick hug and fellatio. Then, in fairly rapid
succession, a number of friends, acquaintances, and lovers of

his lovers began dying of AIDS. At this fresh challenge to his denial, he began to grieve and became more thoughtful about his own behavior. He reconsulted his internist, got a clean bill of health, another lecture on safe sex, and returned to my office with his version of the "latest" information on AIDS, that fellatio did not transmit AIDS; essentially, he was saying that semen was not poisonous and thus safe to swallow. His insistence that stomach acid killed the AIDS virus allowed him to lose sight of the prevailing wisdom that any contact with mucous membranes was dangerous. I asked him about the source of this information, and he vaguely recalled his work on the AIDS hotline. Though he initially denied being at risk for AIDS, and therefore not afraid, I nevertheless pointed out his wish for punishment for his sexual "sins." A slow dawning of awareness then seemed to come over him, but he did not volunteer any more thoughts on the matter.

While waiting for a session during this time, he arrived early, eagerly licking an ice cream cone. I surprised him as I emerged from my office for a break, as I had a cancellation that day. He jumped off his seat and tried to hide the ice cream cone, and when I returned to start the session he entered sheepishly and began with a series of random thoughts, hoping to avoid discussing what had happened. Given his propensity for obtuseness, about halfway into the hour I pointed out to him that he had said nothing about his ice cream cone. An embarrassed silence was followed by his halting confession of wanting to hide his pleasure from me and his being afraid that I would interpret his wish for fellatio with me. By now he was fully conscious of his sexual wish for me in the transference, which humiliated him because again he had to pay for what he wanted, and not have reciprocity out of love. He also associated to a memory at age nine of being chastised by his mother for eagerly slurping an ice cream cone in public, at which he became embarrassed and was condemned as being a bad boy for licking. He then spoke more openly about his enjoyment over taking the penis in his mouth, sucking on it until ejaculation, and eagerly swallowing the semen. He felt his own penis was defective in that it was too small and that his orgasms happened almost immediately. He was not yet aware of any link between the penis and breast, despite his specific emphasis on sucking.

At any rate, he unconvincingly insisted that stomach acid killed the AIDS virus, so that he was not at risk, despite his practices with the highest risk group of sexual partners. It was quite a devastating blow when candidiasis on his feet, rectum, and mouth was diagnosed. Even with this almost presumptive evidence of AIDS Related Complex (ARC), Jimmy avoided telling me about this development for several weeks. Again, as when he was beaten up, his feelings of helplessness, resignation, and sadness were profound. He grieved for himself, his dead friends, and his father, whom he yearned for in an anguished way. And in consideration of inevitable death, his multiply determined wish for AIDS became clearer to us:

1. He could announce to his mother and the world that he was indeed homosexual.
2. He could come out as a member of the gay community.
3. It served as a capital punishment for his sexual "sins."
4. His untimely death would also represent a wish for reunion with his dead father.
5. His becoming progressively sicker would legitimize his dependency while evoking pity and sympathy.
6. He could get revenge against his mother by humiliating her with his inglorious cause of death.

Jimmy then decided to finally confront the issue of his susceptibility to AIDS, allowing himself to undergo a full workup with HIV antibody testing, which was negative. He agreed to treatment for candidiasis which was successful, giving him a feeling that he had a new lease on life. Riding the crest of his optimism, he decided that he wanted to openly and actively inform his family about his sexuality. Upon his request I agreed to facilitate such a meeting. His mother did not appear shocked by his revelation and talked about him in glowing, idealized terms, while she condemned and described "those other men" with whom he associated. This tendency toward denial, idealization, and devaluation demonstrated his mother's narcissistic proclivity. His sister, on the other hand, was superficially supportive, but was frightened for her children and barred him from visiting her. Nevertheless, his self-esteem increased as he felt more true to himself and more willing to accept responsibility for himself. In the sessions that followed he expressed curiosity about more in-depth therapy, like psychoanalysis, and I offered him a copy of the handbook published by the American Psychoanalytic Association, *About Psychoanalysis*, which he read with little hesitation. His interest was encouraging in that it reflected his newly emerging belief that even he might deserve to live and to feel better about himself.

While it might appear that facilitating and participating in a family meeting would be at cross-purposes if one were considering a patient for analysis, it was clear to me that this was an unusual circumstance. I felt that I needed to be ready to work with this patient at whatever level he was capable. Though he tested HIV negative, he remained at great risk of becoming ill at any time, and agreed to retesting every six months (the result has remained negative up to the time of this writing). Furthermore, his capacity for regression was such that he might have required psychiatric hospitalization again. And, finally, should he indeed continue to move toward an analytic process, it would be long and difficult. He simply did not have the resources on his own to undertake this venture and needed family support. He needed their endorsement to temporarily neutralize his savage superego in order to feel permitted to get the help he needed.

He recognized that his ingrained character traits of passivity, stubbornness, narcissistic vulnerability, masochism, and dependency were maladaptive. Furthermore, he now knew that his very life was at stake. His desire to develop a long-term loving relationship came to the fore as a goal, as he openly wept about his loneliness, alienation, and feelings of unlovability. His fears that I might reject his wish for analysis had kept him from broaching the subject earlier, but now he felt ready to confront the issue. I pointed out, in lay terms, that people are often referred for analysis to another analyst after they have been in psychotherapy for several years, because of limitations in the development of optimal conditions for resolution of the transference. He seemed to understand and dutifully agree with everything I said, until the next hour, when he protested quite openly. Again, his assertiveness and wish to take some control over his life were a significant departure from his usual passive stance. I consulted a colleague about the case, who pointed out that despite its curious complexities and the limitations in being able to apply a classical technical approach, the patient already was internalizing an analytic process, enabling him to work through some "parameters." His hospitalization, the medication, the writing of the letter, and the meeting with mother and sister exemplified some of the special features in his management. The consultant also pointed out, which we both knew, that if anything could help, an analytic experience would be most likely. I also carefully explored my countertransference and whatever hesitations I might have, either in letting him go or making a commitment to more intensive work at a possibly reduced fee with someone who might have an interminable analysis or die of AIDS during the process. I also recognized that the seriousness of his psychopathology and the nature of his sexuality rarely, in my experience, lent itself to in-depth work; so an element of entering relatively uncharted territory with the analytic lens, so to speak, was alluring. It was agreed that Jimmy's visits would increase to four times per week as he entered his third year of treatment.

In the first two months, he avoided looking at the couch, let alone using it. His resistance to "complying" with the standard expectations of lying down on the couch was eventually understood and worked through. We discovered that he did not want to lose eye contact with me because of his fears that I would disappear on him and because he was used to looking for perceived signs of approval or disapproval from my facial expression while he was sitting up. He also did not know whether to lie on his back or his stomach; both positions brought anxiety. Lying on his back exposed his genitals, which frightened him and left him feeling vulnerable to attack; being on his stomach made him feel vulnerable to anal assault. Instead, he procrastinated, and passively waited to be ordered to lie down. When it became clear to me that he also understood how much easier it would be for him to deal with some of this material while lying down on the couch, I pointed out his continuing efforts to undermine himself in his therapy. What he thought was self-protection was actually slowing down his progress and therefore self-destructive. He then confessed that every morning before his appointment he went through an obsessional ritual of trying to decide if he would use the couch that day or not. He talked more openly about his fears of getting better and ultimately having to leave. When he arrived for the next session, he promptly lay down on his back and felt quite triumphant. Much to his relief and pleasure, he found the couch liberating and comfortable. His fear of uncontrollably crying, "Niagara Falls," reemerged as he discovered that it was okay for him to just let go. He had been using the couch for almost a year, with an intensification of and elaboration of the maternal transference, when his next crisis occurred.

For several months he had become involved with a man about his own age and was feeling coerced into making a choice. This new lover insisted that Jimmy move in with him and that they get married. Though this relationship was physically safer than his previous ones, the attempt at something that resembled a mutual relationship with a contemporary proved to be an emotional disaster. Jimmy did trust this man enough to permit anal intercourse as he acted out his transference wish with this partner. He was quite reticent in his associations about the relationship, since it deflected much of the heat of the intense transference. Jimmy was aware, though, that the mental cruelty inflicted upon each other in this homosexual relationship was very similar to how he felt with his mother, in that the struggle to control one another through witholding, and frank meanness in a childish way, were typical of their interactions. Jimmy was also ashamed to be in public with this man, whose noticeable physical features reportably drew attention to them both. When I pointed out to Jimmy how this relationship seemed to answer some of his prayers, yet got him involved and overwhelmed in such a way that he was avoiding analysis, he helplessly agreed. He felt desperately engulfed and terrified of this man's love for him, and proceeded to extricate himself from his lover only to reexperience an upsurge of his longings in the transference.

Then, in order to defuse the intensity of these feelings for me, he temporarily extricated himself from treatment by getting fired from his job. His newfound pride and confidence prevented him from running to his mother for financial rescue, so he became convinced that a hiatus in analysis was the mature step until he could get another job to clear up his backlog of debts. Despite my interventions and his own awareness of flight from me, he discontinued treatment. About three months later, just prior to my vacation, he contacted me in a panic, requesting hospitalization. In the interim, he had regressed considerably and began experimenting with drugs. His new "friends" were a variant of the violent hustlers from before, but instead of being beaten up, he was now becoming addicted to I.V. cocaine. He shared needles with high-risk homosexual drug users, letting himself be injected by them in exchange for sex and providing them with shelter. He also began experimenting with different sexual behaviors, including being urinated upon and using foul-smelling underwear for fetishistic purposes.

His self-hatred and wish to die were agonizingly painful, evoking great pity in me. His awareness of the way in which he was playing Russian roulette regarding contracting AIDS was simply yet profoundly communicated to me by his pathetic, mute stare in which his eyes pleaded for help. His bill remained overdue; this had been very much on his mind during his decline, but he needed to get into an emergency situation in order to ask for help again. I facilitated a brief rehospitalization which coincided with my break, during which he detoxified and spoke quite openly about not only his homosexuality but also his profound attachment to me. His sociability and frankness were in marked contrast to his first hospitalization; despite his behavioral regression, his increased self-awareness and insight gave him the appearance of being healthier than before and he made progress in his therapy.

This contrast, in my view, supported the notion that he was indeed fleeing from the transference. But was this degree of acting out and intolerance of affects in the analytic situation too risky to resume treatment? I posed this dilemma to Jimmy, who sheepishly acknowledged more openly than ever that his wishes to be lovingly held by me sometimes and to be painfully anally penetrated by me at other times absolutely terrified him. He felt he had no choice but to run and hide behind his proverbial rock, but this time the rocks were chunks of cocaine. He was then able to openly cry about his loneliness, his sadness, and his father. He described in detail his male ancestors who were both gifted and flawed. His paternal great-grandfather typified this profile; a Civil War hero who ended up dying as a disgraced morphine addict. Jimmy feared for his own life, once again, and quickly rededicated himself to therapy. At the time of this writing, we are still discussing this dilemma. He has stopped using drugs, has remained HIV negative, and fears that I will punish him for his "bad" behavior by refusing to continue to work with him.

DISCUSSION

Much of Jimmy's pathology appears to center around oral and anal fixations along with conflicts over separation and abandonment. Such preoedipal and early dyadic problems argue against his being a suitable candidate for analysis. His propensity for acting out, his hospitalizations, the need for medication, and the active interventions on my part are certainly departures from the optimum situation for an analysis to take place. In addition, the severity of his character pathology, with schizoidal, sadomasochistic, narcissistic, and obsessive features, requires a long, arduous commitment to character analysis, with uncertain results at best. His unresolved grief for his father was another crucial issue to be considered. The risk of depressive regression, along with self-destructive behavior, and a negative therapeutic reaction would seem to make working with this patient all the more untenable. Certainly one might wonder about the analyst's own masochism and grandiosity in working intensively with such a seemingly hopeless case. Yet, not only has Jimmy stayed in treatment, but he has shown signs of improvement and made a deeper commitment to therapy. As illustrated, though his ego strength has increased in that he has better impulse control, tolerance of anxiety, and has been able to work again, his regression in the transference is of concern.

His superego remains savage and unforgiving, but he is beginning to internalize the analyst who does not punish him like his mothers or lovers. The end point of his progress is not clear at all, however, in that his analytic journey has really just begun, but one should continue to expect major ups and downs.

What is clear is how difficult it is to work with such cases, and how the need for flexibility and modifications may be necessary in order to further the process. A turning point in his case occurred when he finally confronted and affectively experienced the life-threatening nature of his behavior and his death wish through AIDS. When he was faced with the seeming inevitability of his death, I feel that a psychic reorganization took place which called forth his narcissism in the service of survival (Kestenberg and Brenner, 1987). He essentially got a new lease on life, which, rather than reinforcing his denial and underlying death wish, strengthened his will to live. His emerging capacity for internalization of a benign object in the transference was a determining factor, I feel, in this crucial shift. The life-threatening behavior was then repeated as a flight from the transference, but was more quickly contained.

Heretofore, his intrapsychic world had been populated by cruel, exploitative, primitive, overcontrolling, and rejecting internalized objects. The profound sadomasochistic essence of his character, which originated in his early relationship with his mother, has become the cornerstone of his sexuality. The erotically stimulating spanking on his bare behind by the maid, Lilly, was both reward and punishment, and was reenacted in his homosexual encounters. His intense shame with feelings of badness, inadequacy, and passivity with regard to his mother appears to be his predominant affect. He was unable to differentiate from her, and his inadequate and unavailable father failed to provide the leverage necessary to promote his separation and individuation. His wish to find a friend in a man may also reflect a very intense negative oedipal striving. However, his partial identification with the father, who himself felt rejected by the mother and unable to confront her, further complicated the situation. Then, with the father's traumatic and untimely death, Jimmy's dreaded oedipal victory and unresolved grief resulted in a massive regression to his earlier fixation points. His delayed emergence from his state of solitary sexuality into the homosexual world, was, in a sense, a prolonged latencylike phase in adulthood. His search for his mother's love in men was determined by his incomplete differentiation from mother and a passive, masochistic feminine identification. In addition, he longed for reunion with his loving but inadequate father who was driven away by his cruel, rejecting, and sadistic mother. The theme of "paying for love" became a predominant issue as he began to recognize that he himself controlled his mother by withholding and treating her cruelly until she paid him. The role of how paying his hustlers became a sadomasochistic reenactment for his own sadism to mother, and how his fantasies of being beaten and anally penetrated get reenacted in the transference, were in their early stage of exploration at this time. His giving to and nurturing of his hustler friends which, although increasing his victimization, was his only pleasure in life, had been guarded from any scrutiny in therapy.

The primitive rage directed toward his mother, against her introject, and against himself continues to be the challenge for him to overcome in therapy. As the transference deepens and evolves, his tendency to provoke his analyst and others to mistreat him through reenacting the projective identifications with his mother poses potential countertransference pitfalls. Another countertransference issue mentioned earlier presented a perennial challenge because of the dangerousness of his behavior: feeling and behaving like a protective mother. Indeed, his states of regression became so profound at times that action seemed necessary. When he was able to, though, we tried as best as possible to analyze his passivity and need for help, which over time, may occur less and less. Over time we have seen the emergence of his very dry sense of humor, and a facile mind. My own unapppreciated sense of humor in the admission office has not been forgotten and continued to be a significant medium of communication even during his regressions.

In conclusion, this patient's unconscious wish for AIDS was an overdetermined phenomenon, with contributions from multiple sources. This wish incorporated not only his sexual and aggressive drives, but also included unresolved grief for his father. Through the ongoing therapeutic process, he began to understand how he was unwittingly contributing to his premature death. He then experienced a life-threatening attack that ultimately resulted in a strengthening of his will to live. He then reexperienced, in the transference, a self-destructive regression which, when managed, furthered his understanding about his wish for AIDS. Though he continues to be at risk to develop AIDS, his increased ego strength and somewhat improved capacity for object relatedness have provided him with a fighting chance.

The extent to which others at risk of developing AIDS struggle with similar conflicts needs to be ascertained, because in Jimmy's case, mere information or even a "psychoeducational" approach was useless. The degree of his negativism and his self-destructive propensity precluded his being able to benefit from the knowledge he had acquired about AIDS. While long-term analytic work is not practical with large numbers of people, I hope that some of what we can learn from the in-depth study of cases like this one will have broader applicability.

CHAPTER 14

The Specific Tasks in the Psychoanalytic Treatment of Well-Structured Sexual Deviations

CHARLES W. SOCARIDES, M.D.

I offer here a psychoanalytic approach to several clear and explicit therapeutic tasks crucial to the psychoanalytic treatment of deviant patients. This therapeutic technique can be used with patients with well-structured sexual deviations[1] arising from a common core disturbance in the preoedipal phase of development. These disturbances include failure to traverse separation–individuation phases with resultant preoedipal fixations producing a persistence of the original primary feminine identification with the mother, with consequent disturbance in gender defined self-identity, deficiencies in ego functions including pathological internalized object relations, and an object relations class of conflict (Dorpat, 1976); that is, anxiety and guilt in association with insufficient self–object differentiation (Socarides 1978, 1979, 1988). It may be that there are other cases of sexual deviation that do not originate within the etiological framework described. And it goes without saying that

---

[1]These are the cases in which sexually deviant development is clear and definite. Because the sexually deviant acts are usually the only avenue for the attainment of sexual gratification and are obligatory for the alleviation of intense anxieties, and because the intensity of the need for this gratification is relatively pronounced, I refer to such cases as "well-structured sexual deviations."

preoedipal conflict may also be responsible for clinical states other than sexual deviation.

My clinical experience with adult sexually deviant patients has led me to conclude that oedipal-phase conflict in certain deviant patients is superimposed on a deeper basic preoedipal nuclear conflict (Socarides, 1968a, 1978). I have classified clinical forms of deviancy into oedipal, preoedipal (type I and type II, depending on the degree of pathology of internalized object relations), and schizoperversion (the coexistence of sexual deviancy and schizophrenia) (Socarides, 1979). Kernberg (1975) first suggested that male homosexuality may be classified along the continuum that differentiates the degree of severity of pathology of object relations. The patient's ego structure and the preoedipal origin of these conditions (A. Freud, 1954; Eissler, 1958) require deviations from standard technique; for example, positive recognition in dealing with the patient's effective level of performance, promoting maturation of ego functions, and providing empathic understanding of primitive arrested self and object representations. Issues revolving around the analysis of defenses and resistances, and my interpretive stance as regards the analysis of transference, transference neurosis, extratransference interpretations, and the therapeutic alliance in these patients are not dealt with here but may be found in my book (Socarides, 1988).

Having defined the level of ego-developmental arrest, my overall strategy is to discover the location of the fixation point, whether rapprochement, practicing, differentiation, or symbiosis, and define ego deficits and the type of object relationss dominating the patient's life. I make it possible for the patient to retrace his steps to that part of development which was distorted by infantile or childhood traumata, conflicts, and deficiencies due to unmet needs and tensions. I eliminate compensatory, reparative moves in the maladaptive process that have distorted and inhibited functioning, and remove self-perpetuating defenses. With their removal, I encounter head-on preoedipal conflicts, especially reenactments of rapprochement subphase conflict, separation and fragmentation anxieties, disturbances in self cohesion, and castration anxiety of both oedipal and preoedipal origin. No matter the form of the sexual deviation, I routinely find anxieties relating to separation from the mother, which are then relived and abreacted to in the course of therapy. In all patients, my aim is the elucidation of the three great anxieties of the rapprochement subphase (Mahler, Pine, and Bergman, 1975); fear of the loss of the object, fear of the loss of the object's love, and the undue sensitivity to approval and/or disapproval by the parents.

The aim of the analysis is the resolution of preoedipal conflicts in order to promote a process of developmental unfolding, in Spitz's words, "free from the anxieties, perils, threats of the original situation" and through the "transference relationship enable the patient to re-establish his own object relations or form new object relations at the level at which his development was deficient" (1959, pp. 100–101). The removal of these conflicts and obstacles makes it possible for the patient to progress along the road to heterosexual functioning as the need for deviant gratification becomes less obligatory. In time, it becomes neither tension relieving, fear reducing, nor a compensatory mechanism, and must then compete with newly established heterosexual functioning for pleasure and self-esteem. Thus the treatment of all sexually deviant patients is the treatment of the preoedipal developmental arrest, which is the *fons et origo* from which the sexual deviation emerged.

In what follows I describe the strategies and techniques and their rationale which I employ in order to fulfill four *specific* major tasks crucial for the successful psychoanalytic treatment of sexually deviant patients: (1) separating and disidentifying from the preoedipal mother; (2) decoding the manifest perversion; (3) providing insight into the function of erotic experiences in sexually deviant acts; and (4) "spoiling" the perverse gratification. Specific tasks, no matter their importance, are of course always supplementary to the "practical tasks" as envisaged by Freud (1940) fundamental to the technique of psychoanalysis, for example, making the unconscious conscious, the rule of free association, the analysis of transference and resistance. These tasks, of course, in no way minimize the importance of other tasks, either implicit within them or related to them; for example, promoting differentiation and integration of self and object representations, and resolving castration anxieties of both preoedipal and oedipal phases.

SEPARATING FROM THE PREOEDIPAL MOTHER

A central task in the treatment of all male sexual deviants is to disclose and define and provide insight to the patient as to his primary feminine identification with the mother, his conscious and/or unconscious feelings of femininity or deficient sense of masculinity. The ultimate purpose of this interpretation is to effect disidentifying from her (Greenson, 1968), promote intrapsychic separation from her, so that a developmental step, previously blocked, can take place and a counteridentification with the father may occur (Socarides, 1982). The consistently helpful and hopeful attitude of the analyst toward the patient facilitates identification with him and a reopening of masculine identity in a new object relationship provided by the analytic context.

The identification with the all-powerful, all-mighty preoedipal mother has permeated almost every aspect of the sexual deviant's life: he feels he cannot survive without her. From an early age, efforts to make the intrapsychic separation have resulted in separation anxiety, and the anxiety is repetitively revived and affectively relived with insight into its meaning. Castration anxiety, when present, is the result of superimposed oedipal conflict and may be mistaken often for anxieties of the preoedipal phase involving separation and threats to self cohesion rather than castration.

While the patient is symbiotically attached to the mother and experiences wishes/dreads of fusing with her (as elicited in dreams, fantasies, and in actual interaction with her), he is also intensely ambivalent toward her. A severe degree of masochistic vulnerability is manifest, especially in relation to the mother, to whose attitudes and behavior he is unduly sensitive. Threats of early object loss and actual object loss leave their imprint. These include deficits in body-ego boundaries accompanied by fears of bodily disintegration (sensations of a change in organization and sense of unity in the body-ego, its size and configuration), and in an unusual sensitivity to threats of bodily damage by external objects, explainable only in part as a manifestation of castration anxiety.

Sexually deviant practices preserve identification with the mother, albeit in a disguised form. Their major function is to relieve anxiety, tension, depression, and paranoidal feelings. They make the patient feel secure by reinstating a previously disturbed optimal distance from and/or closeness to the mother (Socarides, 1968a), a psychological state in which the patient feels secure against both the loss of the mother and the preoedipal needs she supplies, and his own wish–dread of reengulfment. Flights from and desires for merger with the mother lead to a seemingly endless, obsessive repetition of sexually deviant acts in order to relieve the individual of intolerable anxieties, often made worse during early and middle periods of analytic therapy. The homosexual, for example, is rushing to a man in order to seek salvation from the engulfing mother. Orgastic experience provides affirmation of his own individual existence (Eissler, 1958; Lichtenstein, 1977; Socarides, 1978; Stolorow and Lachmann, 1980).

During analytic work, these patients do not suffer irreversible loss or destruction of object relations or other functions as they attempt to separate. Although they may regress to earlier phases in which there was a threat of loss of ego boundaries between two physically separate individuals, the mother and the patient, they remain in contact with the analyst and are gradually desensitized to such experiences. Such critical events should not be responded to with undue alarm on the part of the analyst that the patient will suffer a break from reality, for these patients are able to maintain the transference relationship despite vivid reenactments of oral and anal fantasies and fears of engulfment.

CLINICAL ILLUSTRATION

Campbell was unable to pass through the development phase in which he could separate his identity from that of his mother and achieve object constancy. Out of the inability to separate and the need to identify with his mother came a threat of merging with her. He was a highly intelligent, attractive, and cultured man who experienced periods of confusion, depression, and anxiety which could be alleviated only by having a homosexual experience. When weakened and defenseless, he underwent regressive experiences with sensations of being engulfed and losing himself in the mother: agonizing episodes of overwhelming anxiety, rolling on the floor, various psychosomatic complaints, overwhelming depression and withdrawal, fears of being physically attacked, fears of losing parts of his body. These attacks of "confusion" began with extremely severe tension headaches, occasionally one-sided and migrainous in nature. At these times he felt he might "crack up" or fragment into a "million pieces." "It's sort of a terrible fright, then a compulsion to homosexual activity." In the third year of his analysis I received a call from Campbell on a Sunday, asking for an immediate appointment. When he arrived at my office he was distraught, flushed, severely agitated, and complained of an excruciating headache. He was nearly screaming and alternated between crying and a bitter, childlike half laughter. Tears streamed down his face. He was unkempt, complained that he felt "paralyzed," and did indeed fall from the couch to the floor. He had, in effect, lost a characteristic behavioral concomitant of the rapprochement phase: the mastery of upright locomotion. Regressive material appeared when the patient, aided by the positive transference, attempted a premature separation from his mother, openly defying her.

The reenactment and analysis of these regressive experiences, wishes, and dreads in almost all instances results in a strengthening of the patient's ego. The strength of isolated affective states which have continually threatened to erupt into consciousness in derivative forms is decreased. These affective states include hypochondriacal attacks representing on a physical level the psychological fear of the loss of self-cohesion and psychic disintegration; masochistic wishes and dreads aimed at solidifying body integrity through enforced sensory stimulation even of a painful nature; pathological perceptions (and externalization of conflicts so that they can be dealt with), and body-ego disturbances experienced as feelings of disappearing into a black void, dreams of elevators accelerating into space, and so on.

To summarize what has already been stated: maturational achievements are unconsciously perceived and equated with intrapsychic separation and reacted to with anxiety and guilt of various degrees, which is then analyzed in a manner similar to neurotic conflict. These anxieties relate to actual or fantasied threats, intimidations by the mother, and are placed in a genetic restructuring of the patient's childhood. Archaic conflicts and rapprochement crises then ultimately lose their strength and disappear.

DECODING THE MANIFEST PERVERSION[2]

The sexual deviation is an ego-syntonic formation, the end result of unconscious defense mechanisms accomplished through the Sachs mechanism (Sachs, 1923; Socarides, 1968a, 1978). This is a solution by division whereby one piece of infantile sexuality enters the service of repression, is helpful in promoting repression through displacement, substitution, and other defense mechanisms, and so carries over pregenital pleasure into the ego while the rest undergoes repression. The repression of the wish to penetrate the mother's body or the wish to suck and appropriate the mother's breast, for example, undergoes repression in homosexuality; instead of the mother's body it is the male body which is penetrated, and through substitution, instead of the mother's breast it is the penis which is sought after. This basic mechanism in the production of homosexuality in both males and females is revealed to the patient through the decoding of the manifest content into its unconscious, more frightening meaning in a manner similar to that of dream interpretation (Joseph, 1965; Socarides, 1978, 1980).

That the manifest perversion is a heavy disguise for "something else" is vividly depicted in my analysis of a spanking perversion, the "Lady Gainsborough woman" (Socarides, 1985a). The woman spanking the patient was revealed to be a substitute for the father and the spanking itself a substitute for anal penetration by the paternal phallus. The manifest deviant content as a disguise for latent content is strikingly evident in those

---

[2]The earlier view that perversion was simply the "negative of neurosis" (Freud, 1905) and that the sexual deviant accepted impulses which the neurotic tried to repress, led to the general belief that the analyst had nothing to uncover or decipher as it regards the hidden meaning of the sexually deviant act itself.

sexual deviations, often with sadomasochistic content, which take an unusual if not bizarre form. For example, a patient could only experience orgasm after he placed a bug on the shoulder of an unsuspecting female, who then brushed it off and crushed it beneath her heel. Fantasies of the crushing of the bug during later masturbation produced orgasm in a case described by Stolorow and Grand (1973).

The object choice in sexual deviations is further determined by certain need-satisfactions (narcissistic needs) to be met through one's sensoriperceptive apparatus[3] These need-satisfactions simultaneously gratify an archaic form of identification with the mother and represent an underground version of a union with narcissistically invested lost objects (Greenacre, 1969).

Through decoding, the patient can experience and perceive his disorder in its original form: the archaic longings and dreads, the primitive needs and fears which arose from his struggle to make a progression from mother–child unity to individuation. He seeks to rediscover in his object choice and aims the primary reality of narcissistic relations with different images of the mother and later with the father. For example, he becomes a woman through transvestitism and transsexualism; keeps the mother close through a symbolic substitute (the fetish). The fetishist realizes that his need for a covering for his body (an underwear fetish, for example) represents a fear of bodily disintegration secondary to identification with the mother, a wish to have babies like her (Van der Leeuw, 1958; Socarides, 1960).

CLINICAL ILLUSTRATION

Calvin was an artistic, intelligent man in his late twenties who suffered from a male underwear fetish whose derivatives went back to the age of three or four. He suffered from intense fears of separation from his mother, clinging to her and intensely

---

[3]The role played by the sensoriperceptive apparatus is strikingly apparent in cases of voyeurism, sexual masochism, and perverse telephoning (Socarides, 1986).

resenting anyone who attracted her interest. His only avenue for sexual orgastic release was procuring the male underwear and masturbating while viewing it without touching his penis. As the analysis progressed, it became clear that the fetish did not simply represent the imagined penis of the mother, but also the breast, the swollen, pregnant abdomen, and other parts of her body from which he did not wish to be separated. It represented himself in the impregnated state and also enclosed in his mother's womb. The patient recalled that between eight and ten years of age the fetish actually consisted of a *man* becoming pregnant: "I would take men with strong bodies and then I would somehow reverse the whole inside process within them and do over the insides of their bodies. I wanted them to become pregnant. I'd have them at the doctor's in these fantasies and they were diagnosed and notified that they would become fat. Where were the babies to come out? They would have to be cut open. It was the most exciting fantasy and a major source of sexual excitement to me. It was too perverse and unreal, however, so I never used it this way for long. A man getting fat is the same thing. It was the man's nonplussed humiliation at finding out that he was going to swell up like a woman that thrilled me, a doctor examining him or a group of men together, all having it happen at once to them. This has to do with the fetish, as the only clothing that they could continue to wear would be the underwear with an elastic band on it as they got fatter and fatter."

Historically, therefore, the pregnancy wish preceded the use of the fetish alone. The underwear fetish or the fantasy of the changing, pregnant, phallic woman, eventually substituted for his own wish to be impregnated.

The homosexual perceives that his fear of engulfment (due to a lack of separation from the mother and his wish and/or dread of fusing with her) forces him to seek salvation from her by running toward men. Ironically, he does not seek femininity in approaching men but is attempting to regain lost masculinity (A. Freud, 1954) denied him in the earliest years of childhood. The voyeur perceives that he must "keep looking" because of his fear of engulfment by the female body (Socarides, 1974) and his fear of object loss (Almansi, 1979). Through visual reassurance he is reassured that he is not female, nor is he merging with the mother. Through distancing he temporarily overcomes his fear of closeness in the destructive maternal body. The homosexual pedophile, in embracing and sexually possessing the body of a prepubertal boy, is capturing through substitution the long lost and wished for symbiosis with the pure, nonmalevolent maternal breast of the hated and depriving mother (Socarides, 1959).

PROVIDING INSIGHT INTO THE FUNCTION OF EROTIC EXPERIENCE

As the analysis progresses, it becomes increasingly evident that it is not the fixated erotic experience per se, the instinct-derivative (its polymorphous perverse derivative) that is regressively reanimated in his sexual deviation, but rather it is the *early function* of the erotic experience that has been retained and regressively relied upon (Stolorow and Lachmann, 1980; Socarides, 1980). In this way, through erotization, the patient attempts to maintain his structural cohesion, and implement the stability of threatened self and object representations.

Analysis of the patient's erotic experiences reveals that they serve functions which can be categorized under two headings: (1) a warding-off function to forestall the dangers of castration, fragmentation, separation anxieties, and other threats; and (2) a compensatory function, for example, intrapsychic activities which help maintain and decrease threats to the self representation and object representations.[4] Through erotization, anxiety and depressive affects are also eliminated. Depression is turned into its opposite through a "manic defense," a flight to antidepressant activities, including sexuality (Socarides, 1985b).

SPOILING THE PERVERSE GRATIFICATION

Sexually deviant patients, unlike neurotic individuals, suffer from a widespread cessation or disturbances of both libidinal

---

[4]The "stabilizing" effect, according to Khan (1965), is effected by displacing and projecting the inner need and tension onto another person or object. It is an attempt to master a traumatic internal problem by controlling the actual external object by concocting "active ego-directed, experimental play-action object relations" (p. 409) in which the "technique of intimacy" plays a major role.

and ego development throughout the major phases prior to the oedipal period. Neurotics, in contrast, show points of fixation in the various psychosexual stages of development without an interruption of the broader development of character structure or a major cessation of ego development. There is a relative absence of *internal conflict* (as regards the enactment of their sexual deviation) in sexually deviant patients, resulting in character structure characteristic of a phase chronologically earlier than the individual's age and always short of oedipal development. Furthermore, most preoedipal developmental arrests, as noted by Kolansky and Eisner (1974), are complicated by an additional factor which we find in sexual deviations: "an unconscious compliance between patient and parent, reinforcing each other's wishes for a continuation of direct instinctual gratification . . ." (p. 24). These patients experience anxiety in the early phases of treatment mostly secondary to *external conflicts,* that is, when gratifications or frustrations are interfered with by the environment.

As a consequence, we are confronted at the outset with a seemingly insurmountable major task: stimulating sufficient neurotic conflict which can then be analyzed. My intention is to bring about this conflictual situation. To this end, I have adopted Kolansky and Eisner's (1974) phrase, "spoiling the gratification of a preoedipal developmental arrest followed by analysis" to connote therapeutic activity which, although leading to discomfort and anxiety in relation to previously held ego-syntonic areas of *immaturity,* results in the conversion of the sexual deviation into a condition similar to a neurosis. "Spoiling" is accomplished through the analytic interpretation of the defined psychopathology resulting from the failure to make the intrapsychic separation from the mother; educating the patient as to the nature of his specific vulnerabilities; and uncovering and decoding the hidden meaning and content of his sexually deviant acts and underlying fantasy system. It is accomplished with tact, without injury to pride, as traumata to these individuals are so early and severe that narcissistic defenses are held onto tenaciously. It would be a narcissistic manifestation on the therapist's part to fail to acknowledge the difficulty or perhaps the impossibility in some instances of the patient ever giving up a specific need. On the other hand, one must keep in mind the *relativity of the need* for perverse gratifications. Such needs are determined by other needs, are not absolute or independent. They are dependent for their existence, intensity, and significance upon the total functioning of the individual. Kolansky and Eisner (1974), referring to such needs in impulse disorders and addictions, point out the differences and distinctions between the phrases "cannot do" and "will not do" or "do not want to," and note that the analyst questions the "cannot" before the "do not want to." The same can be said for the phrase "need for immediate gratification." "Is it a 'need' like breathing is a need or is it a 'wish' for gratification such as a wish for candy?" There is a back-and-forth movement as to the relative strength of "need for gratifications" at various points in treatment.

"Spoiling" perverse gratifications in order to stimulate neurotic conflict which can then be analyzed does not mean that a sexually deviant patient remains without sexual pleasure during the analysis. Prohibitions against sexually deviant activity should not be engaged in, as indicated by the rule of non prohibere. This rule, however, should not be misconstrued by the patient (and the analyst) as representing passive permission to persist in patterns of self-destructive, antisocial, sexually deviant behavior, or an inadvertent permissiveness which may precipitate acting out of sexually deviant impulses. It is not a policy of indifference on the part of the therapist which would tend, according to Arlow (Panel Report, 1954), to perpetuate already established patterns of overt sexually deviant behavior. Working through and reconstruction often leads the analyst to expect improvement and gradual diminution of sexually deviant practices. Increased sexually deviant activity at this point may then lead the analyst to feel that his integrity is threatened by the patient's enactments. An exacerbation of sexually deviant enactments, however, may well be a sign of progress since the need for sexually deviant acts to sustain threatened self representations and ward off fears of engulfment is typically increased as ties to the mother are loosened and heterosexual impulses with their attendant dangers begin to emerge.

Modification of sexually deviant practices should be first suggested by the patient, analyzed fully before they are attempted, and undertaken only when a full knowledge of the underlying structure of the symptom is known and understood by both patient and analyst. Similar ideas have been set forth by Anna Freud (1954), Lorand (1956), and Panel Report (1960). The analysis of successful, short-lived attempts followed by exacerbation of sexually deviant symptomatology yields especially valuable insights into the warding off and compensatory functions of sexually deviant acts.

In making sexually deviant acts no longer pleasurable, we are converting the act from an ego-syntonic one to an ego-alien or ego-dystonic one. Analysis of ego-syntonic sexually deviant acts (whether these be homosexual, pedophiliac, fetishistic, etc.) once again affirms Freud's (1923b) assertion that ego-syntonic formations are *already* the end-result of unconscious defense mechanisms in which the ego plays a decisive part (p. 246).

THE PROBLEM OF AIDS

In a recent editorial in the *New England Journal of Medicine,* Quinn C. Zackaraias (1989) stated that "on the basis of the best available data and with use of mathematical models that incorporate the prolonged incubation period of AIDS, it is possible to estimate that 2.5 million people in the Americas have been infected with HIV-1 to date, and that 500,000 persons will have a confirmed diagnosis of AIDS by 1992" (p. 1005).

The latest statistics released by the Center for Disease Control (CDC) predict that by 1991, "15 million Americans will be infected with the human immuno-deficiency virus (HIV)" (*Psychiatric Times,* April 1988, p. 1). Zacharaias (1989) says

[I]n North America . . . where AIDS is well established, the number of new cases of AIDS increased by 40% between 1986 and 1987. . . . In the United States, for example, the relative efficiency of homosexual transmission and the degree of promiscuous activity were responsible for the rapid spread of HIV-1 and the current prevalence of infection among gay men of 20–70%. . . . Early in the epidemic, many bisexual men became infected, and such men now account for 15–25% of all patients with AIDS in the Americas. . . . Because of the high rate of infection among bisexuals and heterosexual intravenous drug users, increasing numbers of women are infected with HIV-1 by heterosexual transmission. . . . With increasing rates of infection due to these human retroviruses, the necessity of effective control becomes even more compelling. . . . The various forms of sexual transmission—homosexual transmission, bisexual transmission, and heterosexual transmission among prostitutes and their clients—each require different educational approaches and interventions. . . . We know intuitively that what we do or do not do now will have important consequences for the spread of the epidemic in the next ten to twenty years. . . . However, the rate of increase will be influenced markedly by our degree of success in preventing the sexual, parenteral, and perinatal transmission of HIV. . . . Without such immediate action [prevention and control, plans of action, funds and resources committed to fight], the spread of HIV and related retroviruses is likely to escalate throughout our hemisphere and to have a profound impact on the medical, cultural, economic, and political structure in the Americas for at least the next decade [pp. 1006–1007].

In addition to the threat of death for those infected, there are psychiatric organic syndromes which occur in AIDS patients who are not in psychoanalysis. These all deserve the careful attention of the psychiatrist and psychoanalyst.

The homosexual, as well as the intravenous drug user, did not *create* the virus of AIDS, and therefore cannot be held responsible for its occurrence. There is no doubt, however, that the virus will spread in those groups having a higher rate of partner exchange. Homosexuals should not be perceived as guilty and therefore less deserving of our resources and care for their illness. AIDS itself might be transmissible to the heterosexual population by routine close sexual contact. Certainly in sexual intercourse the exchange of bodily fluids or contact with mucous membranes or direct penetration of the virus into the bloodstream through injection are the major modes of transmission.

Among the multiple techniques available in the psychoanalytic treatment of homosexuals is the basic rule that there should be no "mucous membrane contacts" between our homosexual patients. Despite the dangers involved, we hear of many instances in which the imperativeness of need for homosexual encounter overwhelms the fear of dread or illness and dying. Throughout the course of psychoanalytic treatment, we attempt to dissuade the patients from homosexual contacts, relying upon their use of pornographic material, verbal arousal, and nonmucous membrane contacts in sexual intercourse, if it cannot be avoided. This official parameter in the psychoanalytic treatment of homosexuals is an absolute necessity in an era of dreadful plague.

SUMMARY

The psychoanalytic approach defined above is linked to the theoretical proposition that well-structured sexual deviations constitute a disturbance in psychosexual development, and are a form of preoedipal developmental arrest (partial or complete) secondary to preoedipal conflict and fixation. It is my belief that when sexually deviant patients are treated with the method I describe, unconscious anxieties of the preoedipal period (as well as those anxieties of the oedipal period) become manifest and can be dealt with psychoanalytically.

REFERENCES

Abse, D. W. (1980), Transsexuals: A different understanding. In: *Marital and Sexual Counseling in Medical Practice*, ed. D. W. Abse, E. Nash, & E. Louden. New York: Harper & Row, pp. 387–393.

Akhtar, S. (1987), Schizoid personality disorder: A synthesis of developmental, dynamic, and descriptive features. *Amer. J. Psychother.*, 41:499–518.

——— Brenner, I. (1979), Differential diagnosis of fugue-like states. *J. Clin. Psychiat.*, 40:381–385.

Almansi, R. J. (1979), Scopophilia and object loss. *Psychoanal. Quart.*, 47:601–609.

American Psychiatric Association (1980), *Diagnostic and Statistical Manual of Mental Disorders (DSM-III)*, 3rd ed. Washington, DC: American Psychiatric Press.

——— (1987), *Diagnostic and Statistical Manual of Mental Disorders (DSM III-R)*, 3rd ed. rev. Washington, DC: American Psychiatric Press.

Apprey, M. (1985), The primacy of aggression in the analysis of depressed childbearing women. In: *Depressive States and Their Treatment*, ed. V. D. Volkan. New York: Jason Aronson, 1985, pp. 159–167.

Arieti, S., & Bemporad, J. (1974), Rare unclassified and collective psychiatric conditions. Psychose passionelle of Clerambault. In: *American Handbook of Psychiatry*, 2nd ed., ed. S. Arieti. New York: Basic Books, pp. 710–722.

Arlow, J. A. (1978), Pyromania and the primal scene: A psychoanalytic commentary on the work of Yukio Mishima. *Psychoanal. Quart.*, 47:24–51.

Atkin, S. (1975), Ego synthesis and cognition in a borderline case. *Psychoanal. Quart.*, 44:29–61.

Atwood, H., & Stolorow, R. (1984), *Structures of Subjectivity: Explorations in Psychoanalytic Phenomenology*. Hillsdale, NJ: Analytic Press.

Bak, R. C. (1971), Object relationships in schizophrenia and perversions. *Internat. J. Psycho-Anal.*, 52:235–242.

Bell, A. P., & Weinberg, M. S. (1978), *Homosexualities: A Study of Diversity Among Men and Women*. Bloomington: Indiana University Press.

Bellak, L., & Sharp, V. (1978), Ego function assessment and the psychoanalytic process. *Psychoanal. Quart.*, 47:52–72.

Bemporad, J. R. (1970), New views on the psychodynamics of the depressive character. In: *The World Biennial of Psychiatry and Psychotherapy*, Vol. 1, ed. S. Arieti. New York: Basic Books, pp. 219–243.

Bleuler, E. (1908), *Dementia Praecox or the Group of Schizophrenias*, trans. J. Zinkin. New York: International Universities Press.

Blos, P. (1957), Preoedipal factors in the etiology of female delinquency. In: *The Adolescent Passage: Developmental Issues*. New York: International Universities Press, 1979, pp. 221–253.

—— (1963), The concept of acting out in relation to the adolescent process. In: *The Adolescent Passage: Developmental Issues*. New York: International Universities Press, 1979, pp. 254–277.

—— (1969), Adolescent concretization. In: *The Adolescent Passage: Developmental Issues*. New York: International Universities Press, 1979, p. 228.

—— (1979), Character formation in adolescence. In: *The Adolescent Passage: Developmental Issues*. New York: International Universities Press, 1979, pp. 171–191.

Boyer, L. B.(1983), *The Regressed Patient*. New York: Jason Aronson.

Bradley, M. (1983), *The Mists of Avalon*. New York: Alfred A. Knopf.

Brenner, C. (1975), Affects and psychic conflict. *Psychoanal. Quart.*, 44:3–28.

Brierley, M. (1932), Some problems of integration in women. *Internat. J. Psycho-Anal.*, 13:433–488.

—— (1935), Specific determinants in feminine development. *Internat. J. Psycho-Anal.*, 17:163–180.

Burnham, D., Gladstone, A. I., & Gibson, R. W. (1969), *Schizophrenia and the Need-Fear Dilemma*. New York: International Universities Press.

Carroll, L. (1865), Alice's Adventures in Wonderland: Through the Looking Glass. In: *Essays and Criticism*, ed. P. J. Gray. New York: W. W. Norton, 1947.

Cauldwell, D. O. (1949), Psychopathic transsexualism. *Sexology*, 16:274–280.

Coen, S. (1981), Sexualization as a predominant mode of defense. *J. Amer. Psychoanal. Assn.*, 29:893–920.

Coppolillo, H. P. (1967), Maturational aspects of the transitional phenomenon. *Internat. J. Psycho-Anal.*, 48:237–246.

Corwin, H. (1974), The narcissistic alliance and progressive transference neurosis in serious regressive states. *Internat. J. Psychoanal. Psychother.*, 3:299–216.

de Saussure, R. (1929), Homosexual fixations in neurotic women. In: *Homosexuality*, ed. C. W. Socarides. New York: Jason Aronson, 1978, pp. 547–601.

Deutsch, H. (1932a), Female sexuality. *Internat. J. Psycho-Anal.*, 14:34–56.

—— (1932b), On female homosexuality. *Psychoanal. Quart.*, 1:484–510.

Dickes, R. (1967), Severe regressive disruptions of the therapeutic alliance. *J. Amer. Psychoanal. Assn.*, 15:508–533.

—— (1971), Factors in the development of male homosexuality. In: *The Unconscious Today*, ed. M. Kanzer. New York: International Universities Press, 1971, pp. 258–273.

—— (1975), Technical considerations of the therapeutic and working alliances. *Internat. J. Psychoanal. Psychother.*, 4:1–25.

—— (1981), Distinctions between the therapeutic and working alliances. In: *Clinical Psychoanalysis*, Vol. 3, ed. S. Orgel & B. Pine. New York: Jason Aronson.

Doerner, G. (1976), *Hormones and Brain Differentiation*. New York: Elsevier-North.

Dorpat, T. L. (1974), Internalization of the patient–analyst relationships in patients with narcissistic disorders. *Internat. J. Psycho-Anal.*, 55:183–188.

—— (1976), Structural conflict and object relations conflict. *J. Amer. Psychoanal. Assn.*, 24:855–875.

Edgcumbe, R., & Burgner, M. (1975), The phallic narcissistic phase: The differentiation between preoedipal and oedipal aspects of development.

The Psychoanalytic Study of the Child, 30:161–180. New Haven, CT: Yale University Press.

Ehrhardt, A. A., & Meyer-Bahlberg, H. F. L. (1981), Effects of prenatal sex hormones on gender related behavior. *Science*, 211:1312–1318.

Eissler, K. R. (1958), Notes on problems of technique in the psychoanalytic treatment of adolescents; With some remarks on perversions. *The Psychoanalytic Study of the Child*, 13:223–254. New York: International Universities Press.

Erikson, E. H. (1950), *Childhood and Society*. New York: W. W. Norton.

Fast, I. (1984), *Gender Identity: A Differentiation Model*. Hillsdale, NJ: Lawrence Erlbaum.

Ferenczi, S. (1911), Stimulation of the anal erotogenic zone as a precipitating factor in paranoia. In: *Final Contributions to the Methods and Problems of Psychoanalysis*. New York: Basic Books, 1955, pp. 295–298.

——— (1912), On the part played by homosexuality in the pathogenesis of paranoia. In: *Sex in Psychoanalysis*. Boston: Badger, 1916, pp. 154–184.

Fintzy, R. T. (1952), Vicissitudes of the transitional object in a borderline child. *Internat. J. Psycho-Anal.*, 52:107–114.

——— (1971), Vicissitudes of the transitional object in a borderline child. *Internat. J. Psycho-Anal.*, 52:107–114.

Freedman, A. (1970), The effect of a change in the analyst's visage upon transference. *Bull. Phila. Assn. Psychoanal.*, 2:127–130.

——— (1978), A psychoanalytic study of an unusual perversion. *J. Amer. Psychoanal. Assn.*, 26:749–776.

——— (1987), A case of foot fetishism. Paper presented to the American Psychoanalytic Study Group.

——— Slap, J. (1960), A functional classification of identification. *Bull. Phila. Assn. Psychoanal.*, 10:37–49.

Freud, A. (1952), Studies in passivity. In: *The Writings of Anna Freud*, Vol. 4. New York: International Universities Press, 1968, pp. 245–259.

——— (1954), Problems of technique in adult analysis. In: *The Writings of Anna Freud*, Vol. 4. New York: International Universities Press, 1968, pp. 377–406.

——— Burlingham, D. T. (1943), *War and Children*. New York: International Universities Press.

Freud, S. (1896a), Further remarks on the neuropsychoses of defense. *Standard Edition*, 3:158–188. London: Hogarth Press, 1962.

——— (1896b), *The Complete Letters of Sigmund Freud to Wilhelm Fliess, 1887–1905*, ed. J. M. Masson. Cambridge, MA: The Belknap Press.

——— (1900), The Interpretation of Dreams. *Standard Edition*, 4. London: Hogarth Press, 1953.

——— (1905), Three essays on the theory of sexuality. *Standard Edition*, 7:125–214. London: Hogarth Press, 1953.

——— (1910), Leonardo da Vinci and a memory of his childhood. *Standard Edition*, 9:227–234. London: Hogarth Press, 1959.

——— (1911), Psycho-analytic notes on an autobiographical account of a case of paranoia (dementia paranoides). *Standard Edition*, 12:3–90. London: Hogarth Press, 1958.

——— (1914), On narcissism: An introduction. *Standard Edition*, 14:67–105. London: Hogarth Press, 1957.

—— (1915), A case of paranoia running counter to the psychoanalytic theory of the disease. *Standard Edition*, 14:261–272. London: Hogarth Press, 1957.

—— (1919), A child is being beaten. *Standard Edition*, 17:175–204. London: Hogarth Press, 1955.

—— (1920), The psychogenesis of a case of homosexuality in a woman. *Standard Edition*, 18:145–172. London: Hogarth Press, 1955.

—— (1922), Some neurotic mechanisms in jealousy, paranoia, and homosexuality. *Standard Edition*, 18:221–232. London: Hogarth Press, 1955.

—— (1923a), The ego and the id. *Standard Edition*, 19:3–69. London: Hogarth Press, 1961.

—— (1923b), Two encyclopedia articles. *Standard Edition*, 18:235–253. London: Hogarth Press, 1955.

—— (1924), The dissolution of the Oedipus complex. *Standard Edition*, 19:173–179. London: Hogarth Press, 1961.

—— (1926), Inhibition, symptoms and anxiety. *Standard Edition*, 20:87–175. London: Hogarth Press, 1959.

—— (1928), Dostoevsksy and patricide. *Standard Edition*, 21:171–194. London: Hogarth Press, 1961.

—— (1937), Analyses terminable and interminable. *Standard Edition*, 23:216–253. London: Hogarth Press, 1964.

—— (1939), Moses and monotheism: Three essays. *Standard Edition*, 23:3–141. London: Hogarth Press, 1964.

—— (1940), An outline of psychoanalysis. *Standard Edition*, 23:144–207. London: Hogarth Press, 1964.

Friedman, R. C. (1986), Toward a further understanding of homosexual men. *J. Amer. Psychoanal. Assn.*, 34:193–206.

—— (1988), *Male Homosexuality: A Contemporary Psychoanalytic Perspective.* New Haven/London: Yale University Press.

Frosch, J. (1966), A note on reality constancy. In: *Psychoanalysis—A General Psychology*, ed. R. Loewenstein. New York: International Universities Press.

—— (1967), Delusional fixity, sense of conviction, and the psychotic conflict. *Internat. J. Psycho-Anal.*, 48:475–495.

—— (1970), Psychoanalytic considerations of the psychotic character. *J. Amer. Psychoanal. Assn.*, 18:24–50.

—— (1981), The role of unconscious homosexuality in the paranoid constellation. *Psychoanal. Quart.*, 50:587–613.

—— (1983a), *The Psychotic Process.* New York: International Universities Press.

—— (1983b), A note on sociosyntonic psychopathology. *Amer. J. Psychiat.*, 140:947.

Galenson, E. (1976), Psychology of women: (1) Infancy and early childhood, (2) Latency and adolescence. *J. Amer. Psychoanal. Assn.*, 24:141–160.

—— Roiphe, H. (1980), The preoedipal development of the boy. *J. Amer. Psychoanal. Assn.*, 28:805–828.

Gillespie, W. H. (1956), The general theory of sexual perversion. *Internat. J. Psycho-Anal.*, 37:396–403.

—— (1964), Symposium on homosexuality. *Internat. J. Psycho-Anal.*, 45:203–209.

Glover, E. (1955), *Technique of Psychoanalysis*. New York: International Universities Press.

Goldberg, A. (1975), A fresh look at perverse behavior. *Internat. J. Psycho-Anal.*, 56:335–342.

Goldstein, J., Freud, A., & Solnit, A. J. (1973), *Beyond the Best Interests of the Child*. New York: Free Press.

Gould Medical Dictionary (1972), ed. A. Osol. New York: McGraw-Hill.

Greenacre, P. (1950), The prepuberty trauma in girls. *Psychoanal. Quart.*, 19:298–317.

—— (1952), Pregenital patterning. *Internat. J. Psycho-Anal.*, 33:410–415.

—— (1958), Early physical determinants in the development of the sense of identity. In: *Emotional Growth: Psychoanalytic Studies of the Gifted and a Great Variety of Other Individuals*, Vol. 1. New York: International Universities Press, 1971, pp. 113–127.

—— (1967), The influence of infantile trauma on genetic patterns. In: *Emotional Growth: Psychoanalytic Studies of the Gifted and a Great Variety of Other Individuals*, Vol. 1. New York: International Universities Press, 1971, pp. 260–299.

—— (1969), The fetish and the transitional object. In: *Emotional Growth: Psychoanalytic Studies of the Gifted and a Great Variety of Other Individuals*, Vol. 1. New York: International Universities Press, 1971, pp. 315–334.

Greenson, R. R. (1968), Dis-identifying from the mother: Its special importance for the boy. In: *Explorations in Psychoanalysis*. New York: International Universities Press, 1978, pp. 305–312.

Harlow, H. (1975), Ethology. In: *Comprehensive Textbook of Psychiatry*, Vol. 1, eds. A. Freedman, H. Kaplan, & B. Sadock. Baltimore: Williams & Wilkins, pp. 317–336.

Hartmann, H. (1939), *Ego Psychology and the Problem of Adaptation*. New York: International Universities Press, 1958.

—— (1950), Comments on the psychoanalytic theory of the ego. *The Psychoanalytic Study of the Child*, 5:7–17. New York: International Universities Press, 1974.

—— (1955), Notes on the theory of sublimation. In: *Essays on Ego Psychology*. New York: International Universities Press, 1964, pp. 215–240.

—— Kris, E., & Loewenstein, R. (1949), Notes on the theory of aggression. *The Psychoanalytic Study of the Child*, 3:9–36. New York: International Universities Press, 1970.

Hinsie, L. E., & Campbell, R. J. (1975), *Psychiatric Dictionary*, 4th ed. New York: Oxford University Press.

Hoch, P., & Polatin, P. (1949), Pseudoneurotic forms of schizophrenia. *Psychiat. Quart.*, 23:248–276.

Hoffer, W. (1950), Development of the body ego. *The Psychoanalytic Study of the Child*, 5:18–23. New York: International Universities Press.

Isay, R. A. (1986), The development of sexual identity in homosexual men. *The Psychoanalytic Study of the Child*, 41:467–489. New York: International Universities Press.

Jacobson, E. (1964), *The Self and the Object World*. New York: International Universities Press.

Jones, E. (1927a), Early development of female homosexuality. *Internat. J. Psycho-Anal.*, 8:459–472.

———— (1927b), The phallic phase. *Internat. J. Psycho-Anal.*, 14:1–33.

Joseph, E. D., reporter (1965), Beating fantasies: Regressive ego phenomena in psychoanalysis. *The Kris Study Group of New York Psychoanalytic Institute,* Monograph 1. New York: International Universities Press, pp. 68–103.

Kafka, J. S. (1969), The body as transitional object: A psychoanalytic study of a self-mutilating patient. *Brit. J. Med. Psychol.*, 43:207–212.

Kahne, N. (1967), On the persistence of transitional phenomena into adult life. *Internat. J. Psycho-Anal.*, 48:247–258.

Katan, M. (1950), Structural aspects of a case of schizophrenia. *The Psychoanalytic Study of the Child,* 5:115–211. New York: International Universities Press.

Kavanaugh, J. C., & Volkan, V. D. (1978–1979), Transsexualism and a new type of psychosurgery. *Internat. J. Psychoanal. Psychother.*, 7:366–372.

Kernberg, O. F. (1975), *Borderline Conditions and Pathological Narcissism.* New York: Jason Aronson.

Kestenberg, J. (1956), Vicissitudes of early female sexuality. *J. Amer. Psychoanal. Assn.*, 4:453–476.

———— (1968), Outside, inside, male, female. *J. Amer. Psychoanal. Assn.*, 16:457–520.

———— (1982), The inner genital phase—Prephallic and preoedipal. In: *Early Female Development,* ed. D. J. Mandell. New York: S. P. Medical & Scientific Books, pp. 81–125.

———— Brenner, I. (1987), Narcissism in the service of survival. Paper presented at Annual Meeting of American Psychoanalytic Association, Chicago, May 7.

Khan, M. M. R. (1965), Intimacy, complicity and mutuality in perversions. In: *Alienation in Perversions.* New York: International Universities Press, 1979, pp. 18–30.

———— (1979), *Alienation in Perversions.* New York: International Universities Press.

Kinsey, A. C., Pomeroy, W. B., & Martin, C. E. (1948), *Sexual Behavior in the Human Male.* Philadelphia: W. B. Saunders.

Kleeman, J. A. (1976), Freud's view on early female sexuality in the light of direct child observation. *J. Amer. Psychoanal. Assn.*, 24:3–27.

Klein, M. (1946), Notes on some schizoid mechanisms. *Internat. J. Psycho-Anal.*, 27:99–110.

Kohut, H. (1968), The psychoanalytic treatment of narcissistic personality disorders. Outline of a systematic approach. *The Psychoanalytic Study of the Child,* 23:86–113. New York: International Universities Press.

———— (1971), *The Analysis of the Self: A Systematic Approach to the Psychoanalytic Treatment of Narcissistic Personality Disorders.* New York: International Universities Press.

———— (1977), *The Restoration of the Self.* New York: International Universities Press.

Kolansky, H., & Eisner, H. (1974), The psychoanalytic concept of the preoedipal developmental arrest. Paper presented at the American Psychoanalytic Association, December.

Kris, E. (1956), The recovery of childhood memories in psychoanalysis. *The Psychoanalytic Study of the Child,* 11:54–88. New York: International Universities Press.

Leavy, S. A. (1986), Toward a further understanding of homosexual men. *Internat. J. Psychoanal. Psychother.*, 11:155–181.

Lehman, H. (1975), Schizophrenia: Clinical features. In: *Comprehensive Textbook of Psychiatry*, Vol. 1, ed. A. Freedman, H. Kaplan, & B. Sadock. Baltimore: Williams & Wilkins, p. 892.

Lerner, H. (1976), Parental mislabeling of female genitals as a determinant of penis envy and learning inhibitions in women. *J. Amer. Psychoanal. Assn.*, 24:269–284.

Levine, H. (1979), The sustaining object relationship. *The Annual of Psychoanalysis*, 7:203–231. New York: International Universities Press.

Lichtenstein, H. (1977), *The Dilemma of Human Identity*. New York: Jason Aronson.

Lipton, S. (1962), On the psychology of childhood tonsillectomy. *The Psychoanalytic Study of the Child*, 17:363–417. New York: International Universities Press.

Loewald, H. (1978), *Psychoanalysis and the History of the Individual*. New Haven/London: Yale University Press.

Lorand, S. (1956), The therapy of perversions. In: *Perversions: Psychodynamics and Therapy*, ed. S. Lorand & M. Balint. New York: Random House, pp. 290–307.

Lothstein, L. N. (1983), *Female to Male Transsexualism*. Routledge & Kegan Paul.

Mahler, M. S. (1975), Discussion of "Healthy parental influences on the earliest development of masculinity in baby boys" by R. J. Stoller. Margaret S. Mahler Symposium, Philadelphia. *Psychoanal. Forum*, 5:244–247.

——— Furer, M. (1968), *On Human Symbiosis and the Vicissitudes of Individuation*, Vol. 1. New York: International Universities Press.

——— Pine, F., & Bergman, A. (1975), *The Psychological Birth of the Human Infant*. New York: Basic Books.

Mann, J. (1973), *Time Limited Psychotherapy*. Cambridge, MA: Harvard University Press.

Marmor, J., ed. (1980), *Homosexual Behavior: A Modern Reappraisal*. New York: Basic Books.

Masters, W. H., & Johnson, V. E. (1979), *Homosexuality in Perspective*. Boston: Little, Brown.

Meiss, M. (1952), The oedipal problem of a fatherless child. *The Psychoanalytic Study of the Child*, 7:216–229. New York: International Universities Press.

Modell, A. H. (1976), "The holding environment" and the therapeutic action of psychoanalysis. *J. Amer. Psychoanal. Assn.*, 24:285–308.

Money, J. (1986), *Venuses, Penises*. Buffalo: Prometheus Books.

——— Ehrhardt, A. A. (1972), *Man and Woman, Boy and Girl*. Baltimore: Johns Hopkins University Press.

Morganthaler, F. (1988), *Homosexuality Heterosexuality Perversion*. Hillsdale, NJ: Analytic Press.

Nydes, J. (1950), The magical experience of the masturbation fantasy. *Amer. J. Psychother.*, 4:303–310.

Olinick, S. L. (1980), *The Psychotherapeutic Instrument*. New York: Jason Aronson.

Ovesey, L. (1969), *Homosexuality and Pseudohomosexuality*. New York: Science House.

Panel (1954), Perversions: Theoretical and clinical aspects. J. A. Arlow, reporter. *J. Amer. Psychoanal. Assn.*, 2:336–345.
———— (1960), Theoretical and clinical aspects of overt male homosexuality. C. W. Socarides, reporter. *J. Amer. Psychoanal. Assn.*, 8:552–556.
Pauly, I. B. (1974), Female transsexualism: Part I and part II. *Arch. Sex. Behav.*, 3:487–526.
Psychiatric Times (1988), April, p. 1.
Rado, S. (1949), An adaptational view of sexual behavior. In: *Psychoanalysis and Behavior: The Collected Papers of Sandor Rado*, Vol. 1, rev. ed. New York: Grune & Stratton, 1956, pp. 186–213.
Rangell, L. (1991). Castration. *J. Amer. Psychoanal. Assn.*, 39:3–23.
Rees, K. (1987), "I want to be a daddy!": Meanings of masculine identification in girls. *Psychoanal. Quart.*, 56:497–522.
Roiphe, H., & Galenson, E. (1981), *Infantile Origins of Sexual Identity*. New York: International Universities Press.
Rosenfeld, H. A. (1949), Remarks on the relation of male homosexuality to paranoia, paranoid anxiety and narcissism. *Internat. J. Psycho-Anal.*, 30:36–47.
Roth, S. (1988), A woman's homosexual transference with a male analyst. *Psychoanal. Quart.*, 57:28–55.
Sachs, H. (1923), On the genesis of sexual perversion. In: *Homosexuality*, ed. C. W. Socarides. New York: Jason Aronson, 1978, pp. 531–546.
Saghir, M. T., & Robbins, E. (1973), *Male and Female Homosexuality. A Comprehensive Investigation*. Baltimore: Williams & Wilkins.
Sandler, J., & Rosenblatt, B. (1962), The concept of the representational world. *The Psychoanalytic Study of the Child*, 17:128–145. New York: International Universities Press.
Sarnoff, C. A. (1976), Sexual development during the latency phase. In: *Latency*. New York: Jason Aronson.
Schwartz, M. R., & Masters, W. H. (1984), The Masters and Johnson Treatment Program for dissatisfied homosexual men. *Amer. J. Psychiat.*, 141:173–181.
Shengold, L. (1988), *Halo in the Sky: Observations on Anality and Defense*. New York: The Guilford Press.
Siegel, E. V. (1984), Severe body image distortions in some female homosexuals. *Dynamic Psychother.*, 2:18–28.
———— (1986), The connection between playing and adult love: Reconstructions from the analysis of some heterosexual women. *Dynamic Psychother.*, 4:53–64.
———— (1988), *Female Homosexuality: Choice Without Volition*. Hillsdale, NJ: Lawrence Erlbaum.
Socarides, C. W. (1959), Meaning and content of a pedophiliac perversion. *J. Amer. Psychoanal. Assn.*, 7:84–94.
———— (1960), The development of a fetishistic perversion: The contribution of preoedipal phase conflict. *J. Amer. Psychoanal. Assn.*, 8:552–556.
———— (1968a), *The Overt Homosexual*. New York: Jason Aronson.
———— (1968b), A provisional theory of etiology in male homosexuality: A case of pre-oedipal origin. *Internat. J. Psycho-Anal.*, 49:27–37.
———— (1970), A psychoanalytic study of the desire for sexual transformation ("transsexualism"): The plaster-of-Paris man. *Internat. J. Psycho-Anal.*, 51:341–349.

———— (1974), The demonified mother: A study of voyeurism and sexual sadism. *Internat. Rev. Psychoanal.*, 1:187–195.

———— (1975), *Beyond Sexual Freedom.* New York: Quadrangle/New York Times Books.

———— (1978), *Homosexuality.* New York: Jason Aronson.

———— (1979), A unitary theory of sexual perversion. In: *On Sexuality: Psychoanalytic Observations,* ed. T. B. Karasu & C. W. Socarides. New York: International Universities Press, pp. 161–168.

———— (1980), Perverse symptoms and the manifest dream of perversion. In: *The Dream in Clinical Practice,* ed. J. M. Natterson. New York: Jason Aronson, pp. 237–259.

———— (1982), Abdicating fathers, homosexual sons. Psychoanalytic observations on the contribution of the father to the development of male homosexuality. In: *Father and Child: Developmental and Clinical Perspectives,* ed. S. H. Cath. Boston: Little, Brown.

———— (1985a), The psychoanalysis of a masochistic (spanking) perversion: The case of Dr. X. In: *The Preoedipal Origin and Psychoanalytic Therapy of Sexual Perversions.* Madison, CT: International Universities Press, 1988, pp. 393–416.

———— (1985b), Depression in perversion with special reference to the function of erotic experience in sexual perversion. In: *Depressive States and Their Treatment,* ed. V. D. Volkan. New York: Jason Aronson, 1985, pp. 317–334.

———— (1986), The telephone perversion: Meaning, content, and function. In: *The Preoedipal Origin and Psychoanalytic Therapy of Sexual Perversions.* Madison, CT: International Universities Press, 1988, pp. 321–334.

———— (1988), *The Preoedipal Origin and Psychoanalytic Therapy of Sexual Perversions.* Madison, CT: International Universities Press.

———— Volkan, V. D. (eds.) (1991), *The Homosexualities: Reality, Fantasy, and the Arts.* Madison, CT: International Universities Press.

Spitz, R. A. (1946), Anaclitic depression: An inquiry into the genesis of psychiatric conditions in early childhood. *The Psychoanalytic Study of the Child,* 2:313–342. New York: International Universities Press.

———— (1959), *A Genetic Field Theory of Ego Formation.* New York: International Universities Press.

———— (1965), *The First Year of Life. A Psychoanalytic Study of Normal and Deviant Development and Object Relations.* New York: International Universities Press.

Stoller, R. J. (1964), A contribution to the study of gender identity. *Internat. J. Psycho-Anal.,* 45:220–226.

———— (1968), *Sex and Gender,* Vol. 1. New York: Science House.

———— (1975a), *Sex and Gender,* Vol. 2. New York: Science House.

———— (1975b), *Perversion: The Erotic Form of Hatred.* New York: Pantheon Books.

———— (1985), *Presentations of Gender.* New Haven, CT: Yale University Press.

———— Herdt, G. H. (1982), The development of masculinity: A cross-cultural contribution. *J. Amer. Psychoanal. Assn.,* 30:29–59.

Stolorow, R. D. (1979), Psychosexuality and the representational world. *Internat. J. Psycho-Anal.,* 60:39–45.

———— Brandschaft, B., & Atwood, G. (1987), *Psychoanalytic Treatment: An Intersubjective Approach.* Hillsdale, NJ: Analytic Press.

———— Grand, H. T. (1973), A partial analysis of a perversion involving bugs. *Internat. J. Psycho-Anal.*, 54:349–350.

———— Lachmann, F. M. (1978), The developmental prestages of defenses: Diagnostic and therapeutic implications. *Psychoanal. Quart.*, 47:73–102.

———— ———— (1980), *Psychoanalysis of Developmental Arrests: Theory and Treatment.* New York: International Universities Press.

Trop, J. (1988), Erotic and eroticized transference—A self psychology perspective. *Psychoanal. Psychol.*, 5:269–284.

Tyson, P. (1982), A developmental line of gender identity, gender role, and choice of love object. *J. Amer. Psychoanal. Assn.*, 30:61–85.

Van der Leeuw, P. J. (1958), The preoedipal phase of the male. *The Psychoanalytic Study of the Child*, 13:352–374. New York: International Universities Press.

Volkan, V. D. (1973), Transitional fantasies in the analysis of a narcissistic personality. *J. Amer. Psychoanal. Assn.*, 21:351–376.

———— (1974), A cautionary psychiatric insight: A clinical report. In: *Marital and Sexual Counselling in Medical Practice*, ed. D. W. Abse, E. Nash, & E. Lauden. New York: Harper & Row, 1980, pp. 393–404.

———— (1976), *Primitive Internalized Object Relations. A Clinical Study of Schizophrenic, Borderline and Narcissistic Patients.* New York: International Universities Press.

———— (1980), Transsexualism: As examined from the viewpoint of internalized objects relations. In: *On Sexuality: Psychoanalytic Observations*, ed. T. B. Karasu & C. W. Socarides. New York: International Universities Press, pp. 189–222.

———— (1987), *Six Steps in the Treatment of Borderline Personality Organization.* Northvale, NJ: Jason Aronson.

———— (in press), What the Holocaust means to a non-Jewish psychoanalyst without Nazi experience. In: *Meaning of the Holocaust*, ed. R. Moses. Madison, CT: International Universities Press.

———— Berent, S. (1976), Psychiatric aspects of surgical treatment for problems of sexual identification (transsexualism). In: *Modern Perspectives in the Psychiatric Aspects of Surgery*, ed. J. G. Howells. New York: Brunner/Mazel, pp. 447–467.

———— Bhatti, T. H. (1973), Dreams of transsexuals awaiting surgery. *Comprehen. Psychiat.*, 14:269–279.

———— Masri, A. (1989), The development of female transsexualism. *Amer. J. Psychother.*, 43:92–107.

Waelder, R. (1936), The principle of multiple function. Observations on overdetermination. *Psychoanal. Quart.*, 5:45–62.

Zackaraias, Q. C. (1989), A public health crisis posed by acquired immunodeficiency syndrome (AIDS). *New Engl. J. Med.*, 320(15): 1005–1007 (Editorial).

Zetzel, E. (1958), Therapeutic alliance in the analysis of hysteria. In: *The Capacity for Emotional Growth.* New York: International Universities Press, 1970, pp. 182–196.

Name Index

Subject Index

need to achieve cohesive sense of, 3
structuralization of, 6
Self-definition, discovery of genital difference in, 210
Self-destructive behavior, 252–275
Self-dissolution anxiety, defense against, 155–156
Self-esteem
  ego functions used to regulate, 101–102
  homosexual fantasy and behavior and, 104–105
Self fragmentation, homosexual enactment as defense against, 219–220, 221
Self-object differentiation
  analysis to facilitate process of, 203–204
  and incorporative fantasies, 209
Self-object fusions, in female transsexuals, 85–86
Self-object transference relationship, 212
  working through of, 224–225
Sensual experience/fantasies, purpose of, 210
Separation–individuation phase, failure of, 277
Sexual deviation, 191
  insight into function of erotic experiences in, 279
  object choice in, 284
  preoedipal origin of, 1–2
  psychoanalytic treatment tasks of well-structures, 277–291
  therapeutic tasks in treatment of, 204
Sexual enactments, 6
  psychologic purposes of, 208–209
Sexuality, factors affecting development of, 145
Sexualization, as defense, 152
Sexual orientation
  change of with psychoanalysis,

189–190
  and gender identity, 19–21
  problems of changing, 101
  treatment to change, 13–14
Splitting, 3, 41
  in female transsexuals, 86
Structural conflict, 3, 203–204
Survival, need for powers of, 236
Symptom alleviation, 12

Therapeutic alliance, 17–19
  failure of, 98
  maintenance of, 3
  in treatment of male homosexual, 97–108
  work on, 231
Therapeutic tasks, 204
Therapist. *See* Analyst
Transference
  dual aspects of, 18
  homosexuality as defense against, 69–71
  issues of, 22–26
  in latent homosexuality, 109–141
  oedipal, 22
  preoedipal, 22–23
Transference fantasies, erotic, 187–188
Transference neurosis, steps in treatment to reach, 54–55
Transference psychosis, 3
  paranoid, 253–254
Transitional fantasies, 139
Transsexual
  definition of, 75–76
  female, 76–96
  preoedipal fixation in, 76
Transsexualism
  homosexual and preoedipal issues in psychoanalytic psychotherapy of, 75–96
  and homosexuality, 88–89
Trauma
  and development of homosexuality, 136–137